RED STATE RISING

TRIUMPH OF THE REPUBLICAN PARTY IN GEORGIA

TOMMY HILLS

SℲL

Stroud & Hall Publishers
P.O. Box 27210
Macon, Ga 31221
www.stroudhall.com

The paper used in this publication meets the minimum requirements
of American National Standard for Information Sciences—
Permanence of Paper for Printed Library Materials.
ANSI Z39.48–1984. (alk. paper)

Library of Congress Cataloging-in-Publication Data

Hills, Tommy.
Red state rising : triumph of the Republican Party in Georgia / by Tommy Hills.
p. cm.
Includes bibliographical references and index.
ISBN 978-0-9796462-4-9 (hardback : alk. paper)
1. Republican Party (Ga.)
2. Georgia—Politics and government—1951-
I. Title.

JK2358.G4 2009
324.2758'04—dc22

2009036513

Back cover photo credit: Georgia House Photographer/Elizabeth Erikson.

Advance Praise for Red State Rising

Triumph of the Republican Party in Georgia

As a Georgia state senator, governor and U.S. senator, I was witness to a true evolution. As liberalism outpaced the Democratic Party on a national level, the Republican Party in Georgia stepped up and became the people's party, gaining control of our state for the first time since just after the Civil War. A hearty congratulations to Tommy Hills for providing us a candid and engaging record of this rebirth. *Red State Rising* deserves a prominent place on the bookshelves of anyone interested in Georgia history and politics.

—Zell Miller
Former Georgia Governor and U.S. Senator

As either a candidate or elected Republican in Georgia since 1974—back in the days when our party was vastly outnumbered—I have worked tirelessly to help elect other Republicans across our state. Tommy Hills' book, *Red State Rising*, is a detailed and well-written review of the people and circumstances involved in building a Republican majority in Georgia. This book is a must-read for anyone interested in the rich history of Georgia government and politics."

—Johnny Isakson
U.S. Senator

What I look for in my governor is integrity, intelligence, vision, and perserverance. Governor Perdue has furnished this to me in spades! Thanks, Sonny, for the performance. And thanks, Tommy Hills, for putting it down for posterity.

—Larry Walker
Former Democratic Majority Leader
Georgia House of Representatives

Congratulations on a book that covers a significant series of events that have helped to bring about a watershed change in Georgia's political history. In 1964 Georgia had no viable Republican Party. There had not been a single Republican Congressman or even a single Republican candidate for any statewide office since Reconstruction, almost a hundred years. At that time, Georgia was the only state in the country that had never voted for a Republican president. Today Republicans control the Governor's office, both houses of the General Assembly, both U.S. senators, a majority of the members of Congress and a great many local offices in the cities and counties of Georgia. It could be said that Georgia has gone from the most Democratic state in the union to the most Republican in a relatively short time.

A large part of this change began with the elections of 1964 and 1966. For many people, that was the first time that most Georgians realized that the Republican Party could be a viable and electable force in the state. Tommy Hills has performed a service, not only to the political junkies, but also to historians and those who are interested in the development of our State by providing a comprehensive history of the Republican Party in Georgia during this time.

—Bo Callaway
Callaway Gardens
1966 Republican Nominee for Georgia Governor
11th U.S. Secretary of the Army

Tommy Hills has presented an excellent portrayal of the Republican rise in Georgia. I found his book both interesting and accurate, although he may have been too kind to me! Reconnecting with all those who helped along the way was a real joy.

—Guy W. Millner
Chairman and CEO
AssuranceAmerica Corporation

Acknowledgments

I especially appreciate and acknowledge the support given to me by Georgia's first Republican governor since Reconstruction, Sonny Perdue, who invited me to participate in his administration and who encouraged me to write this story. The idea for this book arose in a conversation I had with Governor Perdue in early 2006 as we were traveling through West Georgia and I asked him to tell me how he had decided to run for governor and challenge the incumbent who was widely presumed to be a shoo-in for reelection in the only southern state which had not elected a Republican as governor or elected a Republican majority in either house of the state legislature for 130 years. As I was just then completing a Master of Arts degree in southern history, Governor Perdue suggested to me that I might continue my academic interests by researching and recording this dramatic shift in the political history of Georgia.

I also acknowledge the support of Georgia's legislative leadership, both Democratic and Republican, who helped me to understand and appreciate how a significant political transition occurred in the Georgia General Assembly after many years of a Democratic hegemony to a dominant Republican majority in the state legislature in the early years of the twenty-fist century. I specifically thank House Speaker Glenn Richardson, Speaker Pro-Tem Mark Burkhalter, former Democratic speaker Terry Coleman and former Democratic House leaders Larry Walker, Bob Holmes and Michael Thurmond, as well as Republican state senators Eric Johnson and Tommie Williams and former state senator and now Congressman Tom Price for their participation, cooperation and frank discussions about this phase of political transition in the Georgia statehouse. I also acknowledge the roles of current state Senate Appropriations Chair Jack Hill and former state senators Rooney Bowen, Don Cheeks and Dan Lee who braved to change political parties from Democrat to Republican in November 2002 and thereby provided the newly elected governor Sonny Perdue a majority in one house of the state legislature. In addition, I appreciate state senators George Hooks, Tim Golden and others explaining why they chose to continue serving as

Democrats instead of changing political parties when invited to do so. I also thank state senators Bill Heath and Bill Jackson and state representatives David Ralston and Tommy Smith for their observations and interpretations.

A number of early Republican party leaders in Georgia also contributed either directly or indirectly to this chronicle, including Randolph Thrower, Jarvin Levison and Bo Callaway, who were active in party politics as early as the 1950's, and Paul Coverdell, Bob Irvin, Dorothy Felton and Johnny Isakson who first became active as statehouse leaders in the Republican Party in the early to mid-1970's and to former Speaker of the United States House of Representatives Newt Gingrich for his early and continuing leadership in the development of the Republican Party in Georgia and for providing a vision and a plan for the transition in Georgia politics from almost exclusively Democratic to majority Republican over the past 35 years.

Guy Millner was especially gracious in sharing the story of his early involvement in Republican politics from the late 1970's through his runs for governor in 1994 and 1998 and for the United States Senate in 1996. Many Republican party organizers tribute Guy Millner for the significant contributions he made toward advancing the confidence of the Georgia GOP that they could eventually win victories in the statehouse.

I also acknowledge and appreciate the participation of Republican Party organizers and leaders Frank Strickland, Jay Morgan, Garland Pinholster, Eric Johnson, Rusty Paul, John Watson, Alec Poitevint, and Sue Everhart for their participation in explaining party organization and strategy as background information for this history of the recent political changes that have occurred in Georgia.

Likewise, I acknowledge and appreciate the leadership and service to the State of Georgia provided by Democratic leaders including former governors Zell Miller and Roy Barnes, former Lieutenant Governors Pierre Howard and Mark Taylor and long-serving House Speaker Tom Murphy and many others in the legislature. I am privileged to have known them and thank them for their dedication to the State of Georgia.

Members of Governor Sonny Perdue's 2002 campaign team were especially helpful in the telling of the story of Perdue's victory as the first Republican governor in 130 years and his role in influencing four Democratic state senators who had served with him in the Senate to switch political parties within days after his election as governor and later how the Perdue team, working hand-in-hand with Republican legislative leadership, were able to win a majority of representation in the Georgia House in the fall of 2004. I particularly acknowledge the support and contributions of the Perdue for a New Georgia team members Alec Poitevint, John Watson, Dan McLagan, Scott Rials, Paul and Jen Bennecke, Nick Ayers, Chris Young, Trey Childress, Leigh Ann Wood Gillis, Derrick Dickey and Corinna Magelund, and Morgan Perry Cook and Hunter Towns, who served as Perdue's early legislative liaisons in his first term as governor. I also acknowledge the importance of the successful 2002 campaign of now United States Senator Saxby Chambliss and of Steve Stancil, who shared the GOP ticket with Perdue and Chambliss as the Republican Party's 2002 nominee for Lieutenant governor. In addition, I acknowledge the roles of Republicans leaders Lieutenant Governor Casey Cagle and Secretary of State Karen Handel for their successful campaigns that co-existed with Governor Perdue's 2006 reelection campaign.

I also acknowledge the participation and contributions of Dick Pettys, the veteran and former Georgia Capitol reporter for Associated Press, and of Matthew Lutts of AP who assisted me in licensing several AP photographs incorporated in this book.

My former Georgia State University history professors, Drs. Glenn Eskew, Cliff Kuhn and Tim Crimmins and Dr. Jamil Zainaldin of the Georgia Council on the Humanities were early and constant supporters of this project, and I appreciate their encouragement and suggestions. University of Georgia professors Charles Bullock and Jim Cobb were also very gracious to consult with me on the topic of partisan change in Georgia political leadership over the past 150 years, and I am also grateful for their support.

I offer special thanks to State Senator Cecil Staton and his staff at Stroud & Hall for publishing this historical account of partisan change in Georgia's statehouse and to Sherry Barbour and Patrick Price for transcribing my many interviews with the state leaders who provided me with the insight and information to be able to write this history.

Most especially I thank my wife and long-time partner Wally Gay Hills for encouraging and assisting me throughout this project, and I am appreciative of her support and toleration and that of my beloved children and grandchildren in putting up with my sometimes preoccupation with writing and editing this book over the past two and a half years.

Contents

Acknowledgments v

Introduction xi

C H A P T E R   1
The Development of the Republican Party in the South 1

C H A P T E R   2
Evolution of the GOP in Georgia 15

C H A P T E R   3
The Emergence of the Modern Republican Party in Georgia 33

C H A P T E R   4
The Republicans Gain Momentum in the 1990s 53

C H A P T E R   5
The Perdue Campaign 101

C H A P T E R   6
Governing Georgia and Taking Control of the House 159

C H A P T E R   7
Future Challenges for the Georgia GOP 197

Bibliography 207

Notes 213

Index 223

Introduction

On Election Day, Tuesday, November 5, 2002, most Georgians were surprised to learn that they had elected their first Republican governor in 130 years, becoming the last state of the old Confederacy to break the long-time Democratic lock on the governors' office and both houses of the state legislature. Former state senator and businessman Sonny Perdue, from the Middle Georgia town of Bonaire, defeated the well-financed incumbent governor, Roy Barnes. In the same election, Democrat Tom Murphy, the longest-serving Speaker of any state House of representatives in the country, was defeated in his reelection bid after forty-two years in the House, the last twenty-nine of them as Speaker. By the end of the week, four state senators switched from Democrat to Republican, giving the Grand Old Party control of a single legislative chamber for the first time since the era of post-Civil War Reconstruction. Within two more years, Georgia elected a majority of Republicans to the state House of Representatives, and they, in turn, elected the first Republican Speaker since Reconstruction.

Many political observers were astounded at Perdue's impressive five-percentage-point margin of victory. Roy Barnes, a savvy political veteran, had raised and spent more than $20 million on his reelection, compared to Perdue's rather paltry $3 million. Also, most of the pre-election prospective voter polls had indicated that Roy Barnes was likely to be reelected. Pundits proclaimed the Republican victory was unexpected and surprising, but Perdue and a few of his closest advisors had developed a growing confidence that they could win this election. In fact, the election of a Republican governor was much less of an anomaly than the press made it out to be.

The Republican takeover of Georgia's state government had been many years in the making and was the result of superior organizing at precinct and county levels by a party that had long been ambitious to gain control and streamline the operation of government in a state that was prospering from growth but had not updated many of its management processes and practices for a number of years. The observations of several political and governmental leaders document how the Republican victories finally occurred and how Sonny Perdue and the Georgia GOP were then able to introduce his vision of a "New Georgia" and quietly begin to revolutionize the operation of state government.

CHAPTER 1

The Development of the Republican Party in the South

Political partisanship developed early in the young United States of America. The first two presidents were Federalists, and the third elected president, Thomas Jefferson, was a Democratic Republican, and he is regarded as having laid the foundation for the Democratic Party when he was elected president in 1800. Andrew Jackson, the seventh president, was the first to be elected as a Democrat. In the 1830s and 1840s, control of the presidency and dominance in Congress shifted between the Democratic Party and the newer Whig Party. Democrats in this era generally did not support a strong governmental role in economic development activities, such as canal construction and road building, while Whigs advocated the national government's involvement in these types of economic activities and others, such as protective trade tariffs and the continuation of a national bank. The Whig Party began to decline in popularity following Democrat Franklin Pierce's landslide presidential victory in 1852.[1] In the South the Democratic Party gradually became more dominant and southern Democrats in Congress held several important leadership positions that they used to try to protect their system of slavery. With growing anti-slavery sentiment and greater concern over the expansion of slavery into western territories in the 1850s, a new national political party emerged to counter the Democratic Party's laissez-faire policies accommodating slavery. In Congress in 1854, southern Democrats influenced the passage of the Kansas-Nebraska Act, which declared the Missouri Compromise on slavery to be null and void.

This legislation permitted the new territories of Kansas and Nebraska to settle the issue of slavery each within its own borders, making it potentially easier for slavery to expand into these new territories. Anti-slavery forces in the North were significantly agitated by this possibility. In March 1854, a coalition of dissident Democrats, Whigs, and members of the Free Soil Party met in Ripon, Wisconsin, and formed a new Republican Party. That summer in Jackson, Michigan, Republicans held their first state convention to nominate candidates for state offices and adopt a party platform.[2] Then, in 1856 several Republicans were elected to Congress, and former army officer and explorer James C. Fremont became the first Republican presidential contender when he challenged Democrat James Buchanan but lost the presidency, running on a platform that condemned slavery. When it was organized, the new Republican Party was "strictly a northern party and made no effort to hide its regional identity."[3]

Consequently, this new party horrified Southerners, and understandably so. Just four years later, Abraham Lincoln ran as a Republican on a platform that opposed slavery's spread outside of the South, and he won the presidency in the 1860 election. The Republicans subsequently took control of Congress following the secession of eleven southern states from the Union. After the 1864 Union elections, Republicans outnumbered Democrats by more than three to one in the new Thirty-ninth Congress. Soon thereafter, the more radical Republicans in Congress began to push for freedom for all slaves and also advocated for the blacks' right to vote.[4]

At the conclusion of the Civil War and following the assassination of President Lincoln just a few weeks into his second term, slavery was abolished by the Thirteenth Amendment to the United States Constitution. Then in 1866, Congress passed the Fourteenth Amendment to the Constitution, which prohibited states from abridging the equality of any citizens and provided for a reduction in a state's representation in Congress proportional to the number of male citizens denied suffrage by that state. The new amendment also prohibited states from paying the debts of the Confederacy and proposed to bar from national or state elective office any male who had previously held federal or state office and taken an oath to support the Union and had later aided the Confederacy, thereby opening up opportunities for Unionists and other interlopers to secure most of the elective offices in the southern states.[5]

Not surprisingly, between October 1866 and January 1867, in a display of intransigence, all of the southern state legislatures except Tennessee overwhelmingly repudiated the proposed constitutional amendment. Shortly thereafter, radical Republicans in Congress responded with the Reconstruction Act of 1867 that imposed military rule on the South, denied Confederate loyalists the right to vote, and conditioned any Confederate state's readmission to the Union on the adoption by their state legislatures of the Fourteenth Amendment and the adoption of a state constitution that would essentially provide for suffrage for freed black slaves. President Andrew Johnson vetoed the legislation, but the Republicans in Congress overrode his veto, despite the opposition of most Democrats.

In response to the new federal law, radical Republicans in Congress and the northern military leaders overseeing Reconstruction of the South instituted programs that actively registered adult black males to vote, resulting in the election of many African Americans and "carpetbagger" northern Republicans to most of the high public offices in the states of the old Confederacy.[6] The emancipation of slaves also substantially disrupted the economy of the South. Reconstruction historian Eric Foner describes the attitudes of most Southerners toward the new freedom of their former slaves and the devastation to their cotton-growing economy: "The blacks' quest for economic independence not only threatened the foundation of the southern political economy, it put the freedman at odds with both the former owners seeking to restore plantation labor discipline and northerners committed to reinvigorating staple crop production."[7] In reaction to these sudden economic, social, and political changes foisted upon them by the Republicans in the federal government, most conservative southern whites banded together under the banner of the Democratic Party and sufficiently organized themselves to stamp out radical Republican elected officials in the South by the beginning of the 1870s.

A reversal of the nation's post-war economic expansion, referred to as the Panic of 1873, and a cotton market price depression slowed the pace of Reconstruction activity in the South. Eric Foner describes the effect of the economic downturn on the politics of Reconstruction: "Voters reacted to hard times by turning against the party in power. In the greatest reversal of partisan alignments in the nineteenth century, they erased the massive Congressional majority Republicans had enjoyed since 1861, transferring the party's 110-vote margin in the House into a Democratic majority of 60 seats."[8] In the 1874 national elections, Democrats reclaimed more than two-thirds of the southern state seats in the U.S. Senate and House of Representatives. Southern Democrats whose states had now returned to the

Union also reclaimed more than half the committee chairmanships in the House. In the remaining two years of the Grant administration, the federal government began to retreat from its earlier harsh Reconstruction policies.

The presidential election of 1876 resulted in an even more pronounced withdrawal of the federal government from Reconstruction of the South. In that election, the Democratic candidate, New York governor Samuel J. Tilden, ran against the Republican Party nominee, Ohio governor Rutherford B. Hayes. In an extremely close election, vote results in Florida, Louisiana, and South Carolina for Hayes were challenged by Tilden, and a bipartisan electoral commission was charged to oversee the vote recount. The commission decided for Hayes, providing him an electoral vote victory of 185 to 184. Allegedly as the result of a political compromise newly elected President Hayes made with southern Democrats, he ordered federal troops surrounding the Louisiana and South Carolina state capitols to "return to their barracks," signaling the beginning of the end of federal military over-sight of Reconstruction in the South.[9] The eventual return to "Home Rule" in the region allowed southern state governments a freer hand in managing their domestic affairs, and the national Republican Party slowly lessened its support of universal suffrage and equal opportunity for African-Americans in the South. Soon thereafter, southern "redeemers" in the Democratic Party were able to reduce substantially the political power of blacks and begin to reshape the legal systems in support of racial and economic subordination of African-Americans in the South. By the late-1870s, Republicans essentially disappeared from elective offices in the South, and the region basically became a one-party political bastion for the Democrats from which African-Americans were effectively excluded from participation in voting by poll taxes and through a whites-only primary election process.

In the mid-1890s, Republicans in the South briefly aligned with some disaffected white and black southern agrarians under the banner of the Populist Party, but the Democrats were able to decimate both the Populists and the southern Republicans by the end of the nineteenth century. As a consequence, elected Republicans became even rarer in the South.

Nationally, however, the Republican Party, which was now colloquially referred to as the Grand Old Party or the GOP, increasingly became the dominant political party in the rest of the nation in the late nineteenth century and into the early decades of the twentieth century. In the 1894 national elections, Republicans increased their representation in the U.S. House from 113 seats to 244 seats in what historian Lewis Gould labeled as "the greatest transfer of strength from one party to another in the nation's history."[10] Republicans held the White House for every term between 1861 and 1913, except for the two terms in which Grover Cleveland served as president from 1885 to 1889 and from 1893 to 1897. During the decades of Republican dominance at the federal government level, the various administrations expanded the role of the national government into many economic development activities, such as the establishment of a national banking system, imposition of a federal income tax, building a transcontinental railroad and dispersing public lands in western territories to encourage settlement there. According to Gould, by 1904 the Republican Party "stood at the pinnacle of American politics,"[11] with control of the presidency and secure majorities in both the United States House and Senate. Increasingly over time, the GOP became identified with big business interests that were leading the industrial development of the nation. In this era when "Big Business" had a strong influence over national policy, there were occasional instances of corrupt business and governmental practices in Republican-controlled administrations, and the primarily agrarian Southerners became even further alienated from the pro-business Republican Party. Although Republican Theodore Roosevelt adopted some business regulatory measures during his presidency, the national Republican Party gradually moved away from those policies and toward support of a more limited role for the federal government in the regulation of business and national economic activities in the early decades of the twentieth century.[12]

During the years of the Great Depression, the Republican Party fell even more out of favor in the South. Not only were Republicans blamed for the Civil War, the destruction of the southern economy with the abolition of the slave labor system, and the harsh Reconstruction activities of the federal government, but now they were also blamed for the failed economic policies of the Herbert Hoover administration and the massive human suffering that accompanied the nation's most severe economic downturn.[13] The solidly Democratic South became an essential building block in a new national Democratic majority in Congress that enacted many New Deal economic relief programs during the era of the Great Depression.

As the nation emerged from the Depression and World War II, the national Republican Party continued to favor a more conservative position on the role of taxation and the size of government in sharp contrast to the Democratic Party, which continued to support the Franklin D. Roosevelt-era, New Deal policies of the 1930s that called for an increasingly larger role for government. In the 1940s a conflict emerged within the Republican Party between moderate Easterners like presidential candidates Wendell Willkie and Thomas E. Dewey, who were willing to accept some aspects of the New Deal policies, and Midwesterners and Westerners who generally were more conservative in their outlook. The Dwight D. Eisenhower-Richard Nixon combination as the Republican Party ticket in the presidential elections of 1952 and 1956 and Nixon's nomination for president in 1960 represented somewhat of an effort to unify the party, but the rift between the moderate and conservative wings of the GOP became apparent again in the election cycle of 1964 when conservative Arizona senator Barry Goldwater emerged as the leading presidential candidate over several eastern-establishment candidates. The gradual drift of the Republican Party toward more conservative governmental policies was not only a reaction to the previous twenty-five years of more moderate political positions taken by party leaders Wendell Willkie, Thomas Dewey, Dwight Eisenhower, and Richard Nixon as the Republican standard bearers in mid-twentieth-century presidential elections, but also an expression of opposition to the turn toward liberalism, big government, and more expansive civil rights for African Americans and other minorities that were favored in the Democratic administrations of John F. Kennedy and Lyndon B. Johnson.

While the national Republican Party was undergoing a shift from moderate to more conservative in the 1940s, 1950s, and 1960s, the national Democratic Party was also experiencing a schism within its ranks. In 1948 when Democratic president Harry Truman supported a civil rights plank in the party platform, many southern Democrats began to separate from the national party. That year, Senator Strom Thurmond of South Carolina bolted the Democratic Party and ran for president under the banner of the States Rights or "Dixiecrat" Party, winning the majority of popular votes and the electoral votes of Alabama, Louisiana, Mississippi, and South Carolina. In the presidential elections of 1952 and 1956, the Republican Eisenhower-Nixon ticket won a respectable 48.1 percent and 48.9 percent of the popular votes cast in southern states. The Eisenhower-Nixon ticket won the majority of votes in the southern border states of Florida, Tennessee, Texas, and Virginia in 1952 and 1956 and also won in Louisiana in 1956, signaling the beginning of a gradual shift away from total Democratic dominance of the South in presidential elections. In 1950 only two Republicans represented southern states in Congress. By 1960, seven Republicans had been elected to the United States House of Representatives from the South. However, the

Democratic Party still dominated southern politics with 99 Democrats representing southern states in the House and no Republicans serving either as United States senators from or as governors of southern states. Perhaps, more indicative of the continuing Democratic domination of elective offices in the South, only 60 of almost 1,800 members of southern state legislatures were Republicans in 1960.[14]

For several years after President Harry Truman first supported a civil rights plank within the 1948 Democratic Party platform, conservative southern Democrats in influential positions in Congress managed to stave off meaningful federal civil rights legislation. Former Georgia senator Herman Talmadge explained in a press interview reported in the October 26, 1972, issue of *The Atlanta Journal* how seniority among southern Democrats in Congress, based on the one-party political system in the South, worked and thereby allowed segregationist southern congressmen to slow the progress of civil rights legislation: "Let me tell you. You don't gain influence in the United States Senate because you work hard or because you are intelligent. . . . You gain it for one reason alone—you stay there long enough to get chairmanships of committees and sub-committees. . . . That's the only way you get your hands on the levers of power."[15]

The *Brown v. Board of Education* decisions in the United States Supreme Court in 1954, casting out the separate-but-equal schools systems concept and requiring integrated schools, caused deep concern among Southerners, most particularly in the small towns and rural areas where whites felt most threatened by the possibility of black advancement through integrated schools and job markets.[16] The 1960 presidential election between liberal Democratic Senator John F. Kennedy and moderate Republican Vice President Richard M. Nixon further fragmented the once-solid Democratic Party in the South. The Republican ticket won again in Florida, Tennessee, and Virginia, and the Mississippi Democratic electors rejected John Kennedy as a candidate and cast their electoral votes for more conservative Democratic Senator Harry Byrd of Virginia. As the Republican Party shifted toward the political center and right in the 1950s and 1960s, African American voters began to gravitate more toward the Democratic Party. This change in party affiliation gained significant momentum in 1960 when blacks abandoned the Republican Party in mass in favor of John F. Kennedy as the Democratic Party's candidate for the presidency. Kennedy garnered immense black voter support when he advocated for the release of civil rights leader Martin Luther King, Jr., from a Georgia jail just before the national election.

In the early 1960s, the Civil Rights Movement in the South became much more visible to all sections of the nation, and the cause gained increasing strength and support throughout the rest of the country. So, by the mid-1960s, the conservative southern Democrats in Congress who had resisted any congressional action on civil rights were no longer able to block votes on civil rights legislation, and a rupture occurred between Southerners and other factions within the Democratic Party over the 1964 Civil Rights Act.

Increasingly, southern Democrats began to find more affinity with conservative Republicans who wanted lower taxes and a more limited role of government in their lives. In addition to their shared opposition to federal civil rights legislation, conservative southern Democrats and conservative Republicans also feared and despised the spread of Communism in the world. Journalists and editors of *The Atlantic* see 1964 as a key milestone for the American conservative movement and the modern Republican Party: "Nineteen sixty-four was the moment when the American Right came alive as a revolt of businessmen against taxation, unions and bureaucracy; anti-communists against the accomodationist center and pinkie Left; and southerners against desegregation."[17]

The conservatives in both parties found their voice in Barry Goldwater, an outspoken but well-spoken western-states veteran politician and businessman. While representing Arizona in the United States Senate, he voted against the 1964 Civil Rights Act that expanded the federal government's role in overseeing public accommodations, and he spoke out for financial reform of the Social Security System. Goldwater also organized one of the most efficient grass-roots campaign organizations in modern American politics, which enabled him to succeed in securing the Republican presidential nomination in 1964.[18] Goldwater's opposition to the Civil Rights Act naturally attracted many racist Southerners who were intent on preserving segregation. Southern historian Numan Bartley explains the appeal of Barry Goldwater and his anti-Civil Rights Act platform among Deep South conservative voters:

> The 1964 Civil Rights Act and the spread of the movement into smaller towns brought black advances into the daily lives of ordinary whites. Despite expanding economic opportunities, they remained . . . hostile to a federal government that through its war on poverty, its civil rights laws and its other Great Society pro-

> grams, seemed to lavish aid on blacks while ignoring problems of common whites . . . thus creating a new voting bloc. Lower middle income and blue collar southern whites were the most disenfranchised and politically alienated group in the nation. . . . Politically, this group voted Republican in national politics and Democratic in state elections.[19]

Senator Barry Goldwater took advantage of the resonance of his political messaging in the southern United States and won a large majority of the votes cast by whites in the South.[20] Although he was soundly trounced by Lyndon Johnson in the general election, receiving only 52 electoral votes to Johnson's 486, for the first time since Reconstruction a Republican nominee for president carried five Deep South states: Alabama, Georgia, Louisiana, Mississippi, and South Carolina. As a consequence of this election, the Goldwater campaign provided a legacy of introducing many more conservative Southerners into active involvement in Republican Party politics.

However, the Goldwater Republican candidacy also had the effect of driving the final stake of separation between African Americans and the GOP. The Lyndon Johnson-Hubert Humphrey Democratic ticket won the vast majority of black votes in the 1964 presidential election, while it alienated most white southern conservatives. Political editors Ross Douthat and Reihan Salam explain the political shifts:

> Once LBJ associated the Democratic Party with the Civil Rights Movement and racial equality . . . the Democrats effectively traded their racist constituents for the black vote and doomed their majority by the trade-off. Liberal righteousness on race enabled the GOP to tap into the racial resentments of southern whites and working class voters in the north. . . . There's no question that from 1964 on conservative Republicans abandoned any attempt to court black voters and staked out an identity as the party that opposed the agenda of the Civil Rights Movement."[21]

The politics of race proved to be an even stronger influence in the South in the 1968 presidential election. Segregationist Alabama governor George Wallace launched a third party movement under the banner of the American Independent Party and ran against Republican nominee Richard M. Nixon and Hubert Humphrey as the Democratic nominee. Wallace won the majority of votes in the four southern states of Alabama, Georgia, Louisiana, and

Mississippi, while Republican Richard Nixon carried the remaining Deep South states except for Texas. When Nixon ran for reelection to the presidency in 1972, he won the majority of votes in all southern states, as the region continued to shift toward Republicanism. Earl and Merle Black report on the large percentage of white voters needed by Republican candidates in order to win political races in the South in the late twentieth century: "With black voters permanently alienated, Republican candidates in the South have needed a massive landslide among white voters—approximately 60 percent is a useful rule of thumb—to prevail."[22] As a practical matter, this rule of thumb required successful Republican candidates to develop a broad appeal to rural and small town white Democrats in the South.

While much of the native-born Democratic South was beginning to lean toward national Republican candidates, more Republicans were also moving to the South. The post World War II economic development of the Sunbelt South brought with it a substantial influx of northerners seeking more expansive job opportunities. Many of these migrants had historic roots in the Republican Party. These new southern Republicans soon began to take active roles in the politics of their new communities and formed Republican organizations where none had existed before. Also, the economic development of the South was providing native southerners with increased prosperity, and many of the fiscally conservative middle- and upper-income whites among them became more concerned about growth of government spending and the higher tax burden on their increasing wages and salaries.[23] This more affluent group increasingly tended to identify with the national Republican Party on economic issues, such as the desire for cuts in income taxation rates and the supply side economics theories espoused by Ronald Reagan. Political scientist David Lublin observed this political shift and reports, "Continuing partisan differences over economic issues combined with growing southern prosperity could explain at least part of the Republican growth among white voters. As more white Southerners became middle class or affluent, more became likely to benefit from Republican efforts to trim taxes."[24] Many of these native southerners were also increasingly concerned about certain social issues, such as federal government-sponsored school desegregation and forced busing, while pro-life Christian conservatives in the South were disturbed by the 1973 United States Supreme Court decision on abortion practices in *Roe v. Wade,* and all of these groups tended to gravitate toward the conservative wing of the GOP.

Arguably, one of the factors that contributed most to the increasing turn of the South toward the Republican Party in the 1980s and later was the strong appeal of Ronald Reagan and his conservative political philosophy. Former screen actor Reagan was elected governor of California in 1966, based partially on his opposition to the Civil Rights Act of 1964 and the liberal bent of the Kennedy/Johnson administrations. In the presidential election of 1980, Reagan won the electoral votes of forty-four states, including all of the Deep South states except then-president Jimmy Carter's home state of Georgia. According to political scientists Earl and Merle Black, Reagan had a special appeal to southerners who had traditionally supported the Democratic Party, since Reagan had been a Democrat for many years before he became a Republican. They quote Reagan as saying to southern Democrats, "Now I know what it's like to pull that Republican lever for the first time because I used to be a Democrat myself. But I can tell you it only hurts for a minute."[25]

Ronald Reagan's defeat of Jimmy Carter in 1980 gave the Republican Party its best opportunity to use the White House to reshape southern partisan affiliations. According to Earl and Merle Black, "Reagan's presidency was the turning point in the evolution of a competitive two-party electorate in the South. . . . Reagan's presidency built the firmest grassroots base of the Republican partisans ever to appear in the region."[26] In the election of 1980, Republican candidates won enough seats to became the majority party in the United States Senate for the first time since 1955. Political historian Lewis Gould describes Ronald Reagan's impact on the GOP as follows: "Reagan transformed the Republican Party into a conservative unit with a diminishing band of moderates on its fringes. His advocacy of smaller government, deregulation, and private enterprise commanded general assent while he was in office."[27]

Reagan's primary focus on improving economic opportunity for all Americans during his presidency was somewhat transforming to the Republican Party in the South because he shifted the party's emphasis more toward economic issues and less toward racial issues. Earl and Merle Black describe this shift: "The rise of a middle and upper-middle income class has produced millions of voters with substantial incomes subject to substantial federal and state income taxation. Many of these upwardly mobile individuals, wanting to keep the lion's share of their earnings, view the Republicans as far more sympathetic than the Democrats to their economic interests and aspirations."[28] In his 1984 reelection campaign, President Reagan again won the majority of votes in all the southern states.

The increasing Republicanism of the South enabled Reagan's vice president, George H. W. Bush, to win the majority of votes in all eleven Deep South states in his successful race for the presidency in 1988. In his losing 1992 reelection bid, Bush lost the four southern states of Arkansas, Georgia, Louisiana, and Tennessee to native southerner and Democrat Bill Clinton, but Bush won the other seven Deep South states. Just two years later in 1994, however, the South provided the margin of victory needed for the GOP to win a majority of seats in the U.S. Senate and also take control of the U.S. House of Representatives for the first time in forty years. The Republican House victory that year was organized and led primarily by conservative Georgia congressman Newt Gingrich, who had been first elected to the House in 1978, and was for many of the years he served the only Republican representative from his state. In 1987, Gingrich took over the leadership of GOPAC that had been created in 1978 by then-Republican governor of Delaware, Pete du Pont, to recruit and elect Republican candidates to public office in an era in which the Democratic Party controlled the White House, both houses of Congress, and all but twelve governorships. Under Gingrich's aggressive leadership, GOPAC raised significantly greater amounts of funds and was more active in recruiting Republican candidates for Congress, whom GOPAC supported with issue briefing books, campaign strategies, and generous financial contributions.[29]

While serving as minority party whip in the House in 1994, Gingrich drafted the "Contract with America" as a party platform to define the goals of the Republican Party, including a balanced budget and term limits for congressional representatives. In the general election that fall, Republicans gained 52 seats in the House elections to obtain a 236-seat majority, and Newt Gingrich was rewarded by being elected as Speaker. Also in that election cycle, Georgia Republicans gained a majority of the state's seats in the U.S. House of Representatives for the first time ever, as did Republicans in North Carolina, South Carolina, and Tennessee. Prior to 1994, Florida had been the only Deep South state to have a majority of Republicans in its delegation to the U.S. House of Representatives. The shift of these southern states to majority Republican congressional delegations was an important factor in the GOP's victory in regaining control of the House that year. Columnist Jack Bass, a close observer of southern politics, comments on the significance of that year's elections to the Republican Party in the South:

"The 1994 elections reflected the full beginning of political realignment in the South. Republicans emerged with a 6-5 edge among governors, 13-9 in the Senate and 64-61 in the House. . . . After the Voting Rights Act, two groups—blacks and Republicans—made gains in the South. . . . The changes undermined moderate and progressive Democrats who got elected by biracial coalition."[30] In the 2000 presidential election cycle, the Bush-Cheney Republican ticket won the majority of votes in every one of the Deep South states, causing University of Georgia political scientist Charles Bullock III to label the South at that time as "the most solidly Republican area of the United States."[31] Even though majorities in most southern states voted Republican in presidential elections since the 1970s and elected majority Republican congressional delegations since the mid-1990s, most of the state legislatures in the South continued to be dominated by Democrats, at least until around the turn of the century. Even then, Georgia stood out until 2002 as the only southern state that had not elected a Republican governor or had the GOP win a majority of seats in either house of the state legislature. It was regarded as having the "weakest Republican Party in the region."[32] Consequently, it is no wonder that Sonny Perdue's 2002 victory as the first Republican governor of Georgia since Reconstruction and the accompanying GOP takeover of the state senate garnered as much public attention as it did.

CHAPTER 2

Evolution of the GOP in Georgia

Although the Democrats dominated politics in Georgia from 1872 until 2002, Georgia was not always a one-party state. Before the Civil War, Georgia had brief experience with a multi-party political system. In 1836, 1840, and 1848, the state's electoral votes were cast for the Whig Party's presidential candidates, and occasionally Whigs, Democratic Whigs, and Union Democrats were elected to the office of governor or controlled a single house of the legislature.[1] Democratic candidates provided the opposition to the Whigs in this era and gradually took control of state politics as the Whig Party dissolved in the 1850s.

Since in its formative years the Republican Party was largely a northern regional party in support of an anti-slavery political platform, the GOP never gained a toehold in Georgia before the Civil War, even among the anti-secessionist unionists living in northern regions of the state. Following the defeat of the Confederacy in 1865, then-president Andrew Johnson appointed a former unionist and lawyer from Columbus, Georgia, James Johnson, as the first provisional governor of Georgia. James Johnson had previously served as a Whig congressman from Georgia, and had sat out the war without supporting either side.[2] Under the direction of the provisional government, a constitutional convention recognized the abolition of slavery and acknowledged the supremacy of the national Constitution again. Charles Jenkins, another pre-war unionist, succeeded Johnson as provisional governor until 1867 when radical Reconstruction began and military rule was imposed on Georgia.[3]

On July 4, 1867, a small group made up primarily of former unionists and a few northern carpetbaggers organized the first Republican Party in

Georgia, and held their convention in Atlanta. The group included Foster Blodgett and Benjamin Conley, both former mayors of Augusta, banker Rufus Brown Bullock, and attorney Henry P. Farrow, all of whom were members of what was known as "the Augusta Ring." Unionist William Markham, a former mayor of Atlanta who had emigrated from Connecticut to Atlanta before the war and built the region's first rolling mill, was also a founding member of the Georgia GOP. The early Republican Party also attracted radical northerners and many freedmen who were former black slaves, and tension existed among these disparate interests. Conflict developed between "confiscatory radicals," who were mainly black, and more moderate whites who were mostly concerned with the economic redevelopment of the state.[4]

In early 1868, General George Meade, a post-war Third District military commander of Georgia, called for a constitutional convention to form a new state government to replace the military rule of the federal government. According to an early historical account, the 169 delegates to the convention included "37 Negroes, 9 white Carpetbaggers, 12 conservative whites and the majority were native whites, known as Scalawags, because they went over to the reconstructionists."[5] More recent studies have been more complimentary toward the categories of both "carpetbaggers" and "scalawags." One Reconstruction historian reports that "carpetbaggers" tended to be "well-educated and middle-class in origin (including) lawyers, businessmen, newspaper editors . . . veterans of the Union Army, teachers and Freedmen's Bureau agents," while among scalawags "the most extensive concentration of white Republicans lay in the upcountry bastions of wartime unionism."[6] Unionists in the South had been mainly concentrated in western North Carolina, eastern Tennessee, and northern Georgia.

In an April 1868 election organized under a newly adopted state constitution, Republican candidate Rufus Brown Bullock defeated the Democratic candidate General John B. Gordon for governor. Bullock, a telegrapher by trade and later a banker, was an anti-secessionist who had relocated from New York to Augusta, Georgia, in the 1850s. However, he had served in the Confederate Army quartermaster corps during the war. Henry Farrow, who had opposed Bullock for the Republican nomination, was selected as the state's attorney general. Bullock's support came primarily from radical reconstructionists, and a survey of ballots cast in that election reveals that 75 percent of the votes for Bullock came from cotton plantation counties where virtually all of the Republicans were black.[7]

Under the new state constitution of 1868, a majority of radical Republicans was elected to the state legislature, and Augustan Benjamin Conley was elected to serve as president of the Senate. The new legislature contained a mix of moderate and radical Republicans, and more than 40 percent were Democrats. Twenty-nine blacks were elected among the 172 members of the House, and 3 of the 44 senators were black. According to mid-twentieth-century Georgia historian E. Merton Coulter, "Democrats were undoubtedly shocked to see Negro members."[8] That was evidently the situation because in early September 1868, "All of the known negro members of both houses were expelled, in all twenty eight; four members of the House were so light-skinned that there was some question about whether they met the 'one-eighth Negro blood' definition, and they were left alone."[9] Purportedly, the expulsion decision was based on the premise that the recently provided right to vote did not also include the right to hold office. Obviously, race surfaced as a divisive issue early in the Reconstruction politics in Georgia. According to Eric Foner, Georgia Republicans downplayed blacks' demands in attempt to appeal to white, upcountry yeomen, and in Georgia no black was elected to any major office in state government during Reconstruction, in contrast to some other southern states, and Georgia was also one of the states with the lowest level of blacks elected to local governmental offices.[10]

In contrast to its action of expelling African Americans from elected office, the new General Assembly was progressive in many other ways and provided for several initiatives that advanced the later development of the state, including abolishing imprisonment for debt, granting Negroes the right to vote, granting full property rights to married women, and establishing the principle that the state would be responsible for public education. The new constitution directed the General Assembly to provide a thorough system of public education to be forever free to all children of the state.[11] Later in 1868, upon the expectation that Georgia soon would be readmitted to the Union, the state legislature elected moderate Republicans Joshua Hill of Madison and Homer Virgil Milton Miller of Rome to represent the state in the United States Senate. Hill and Miller prevailed over a slate of more radical Republicans who had been supported by Governor Bullock. However, when Hill and Miller arrived in Washington, the U.S. Senate tabled their credentials and neither was seated, because by that time Georgia and most other states of the former Confederacy had rejected passage of the new Fourteenth Amendment to the U.S. Constitution, and Georgia's read-

mission to the Union was stalled. In 1868, Georgians did send their first representatives to a Republican national convention, and Republican electors
were on the presidential ballot in Georgia for the first time that year.
However, Georgia and Louisiana were the only two states of the old
Confederacy that year in which the majority of voters supported the
Democratic presidential candidate, New York governor Horatio Seymour,
over Republican candidate General Ulysses S. Grant.

In 1869, Congress reinstated military rule in Georgia at the request of
Governor Bullock, based on the recalcitrance of the legislature. General
Alfred H. Terry was appointed as the new military commander in the state,
while Rufus Bullock was permitted to continue to function as the provisional
governor. In June 1869, the Supreme Court of Georgia decided that Negroes
had the right to hold office under the state constitution, and the following
January those who earlier had been expelled by the state legislature had their
seats restored to them. Military governor Terry removed a group of white
conservatives to accommodate the previously expelled black members in
what is referred to as the "Terry purge," to the satisfaction of radical
Reconstructionists.

After Georgia was finally readmitted to the Union in July 1870, three
Republicans were elected to the United States House of Representatives. The
new GOP members of Congress were Marion Bethune, an attorney and
judge from Talbotton; Jefferson Franklin Long, a merchant tailor from
Macon and the first African American to represent the state in Congress; and
Richard Whiteley, an attorney and cotton mill owner from Bainbridge,
whose election was not finally determined until early 1871 because of alleged
voting irregularities in some of the ballots cast for his Democratic opponent.
The Republicans from Georgia were not finally seated in the U.S. House
until early 1871. Also, in February 1871, both Joshua Hill and H.V. M.
Miller were finally seated by the U.S. Senate but served for only a few weeks
until the end of the term on March 3 of that year. Miller lost his next election to a Democrat, but Republican Joshua Hill was subsequently reelected
to the Senate and served until 1877. Bethune and Long did not continue to
serve, but Richard Whiteley was reelected to Congress and served an additional two terms until his defeat by a Democrat in fall 1874. According to
his biographer, "Whiteley became the incarnation of Radicalism as the most
loathed Republican in Southwest Georgia"[12] because of his congressional
vote in favor of an 1874 Civil Rights Bill that would have allowed equal
access to public accommodations for freed African-American slaves many

years earlier than when equal rights were finally legislated through the controversial Civil Rights Act of 1964.

In the state elections of December 1870, the Democrats regained control of both houses of the state legislature. Under the threat of impeachment, Governor Bullock resigned from his office in October 1871 under a cloud of alleged financial improprieties involving a state-owned railroad. Since at that time, the position of lieutenant governor did not exist in state law, the Republican president of the state senate, Benjamin Conley, moved up to become governor for the next few months.

In addition to the alleged railroad corruption charges against the Bullock administration, the cost of supporting the growth of the railroads was taking a toll on the taxpayers of the state. Between 1868 and 1872, the rail system in the South was expanded by nearly 40 percent, and operating and debt service costs rose proportionately. As property taxes increased to pay for the railroads, support for the Republican Party began to wane.[13]

In a special election in December 1871, Democratic candidate James M. Smith, a Columbus lawyer, was elected governor of Georgia, unopposed by any Republican. James Atkins, an Atlanta lawyer, had been nominated by the Republicans, but he had declined to run. James Smith had initially opposed secession, but he later served in the Confederate Army. He took office in early 1872 and thus began the era of Redemption and the restoration of Democrats to the key positions of power in state government, a situation that would continue to exist in Georgia for the next 130 years. A Republican candidate, Jonathan Norcross, did run for governor in 1876, but he was soundly defeated by Democrat Alfred Colquitt by more than a 3-to-1 margin.

New laws were passed in the Democrat-dominated state legislature to dilute the political influence of African Americans. A poll tax was imposed on potential voters, and voter residency and registration requirements grew more stringent so that black suffrage declined. According to southern historian Numan Bartley, "The Georgia Bourbons supported a stable social order based on white supremacy, a closed political system resting on one-party politics and a passive national stance that protected 'home rule.' . . . . The discredited and demoralized Republicans increasingly devoted their energies to factional party squabbles and the quest for federal patronage."[14]

Georgia College political historian Olive Hall Shadgett describes the challenges faced by the Georgia Republican Party in the late nineteenth century: "Unfortunately . . . for the Republican Party in Georgia, it was from the beginning identified with the extremes of Radical Reconstruction, with bayonet rule and the Negro voter. Add to this the corrupt administration of Rufus Bullock, Georgia's only elected Republican governor, and it is easy to see why the party no longer prospered in the state."[15]

In the latter years of the nineteenth century and early twentieth century, the Republican Party essentially ceased to have much relevancy in Georgia. The primary role of the Republican Party organization in Georgia was to dispense federal patronage jobs, like U.S. postmaster positions, whenever Republicans controlled the White House, and even this activity was carried out by a small "syndicate of party leaders, mostly residing in Atlanta and other large cities and in the mountain area of North Georgia."[16] Among the members of the "Republican syndicate" that was formed in 1881 were James Atkins, an Atlanta lawyer; Henry Farrow, the former state attorney general during Reconstruction who resettled to Porter Springs, north of Dahlonega, to open a health resort and who later ran and lost as a Republican candidate for United States House of Representatives from Georgia in 1896; and former Confederate general James Longstreet, who had retired to Gainesville, converted to Catholicism and Republicanism, and later served in various federal government patronage positions. Longstreet had been close to Ulysses Grant while they were both students at the United States Military Academy, and no doubt this long friendship influenced General Longstreet to become a Republican, for which Grant rewarded him by appointing him as surveyor for the United States Customs Office in New Orleans. Later, President Hayes appointed him as the nation's ambassador to the Ottoman Empire, and he also served as United States Marshall in northern Georgia under presidents Garfield and Arthur and as United States Commissioner of Railroads under presidents McKinley and Theodore Roosevelt.

In the waning years of the nineteenth century, the Populist threat to the rule of the Democratic Party in the South actually had the effect of strengthening one-party rule at the further expense of the Republican Party, and it also resulted in even harsher measures to diminish any potential political influence of African Americans in the South. Numan Bartley describes the Populist challenge to the one-party rule of the Democrats: "The Populists sought to create an alliance of 'have-nots' across color lines. The projected coalition threatened white supremacy by offering political power to Negroes. The white reaction led to solidification of the one-party system, disenfranchisement, and a precipitous decline in voting generally."[17] African Americans did not vote again in Georgia in any appreciable numbers until the state constitution was revised and the discriminatory poll tax was eliminated during the progressive gubernatorial administration of Ellis Arnall in the late 1940s, and most of those who did take the trouble to vote continued to support the Republican Party in presidential elections.

Despite the disempowerment of the Republican Party in Georgia, some Republican political activity did exist in the early twentieth century. It was centered mostly in the mountainous sections of middle North Georgia and in Atlanta and the other larger cities of the state. Roscoe Hays Pickett, Sr., from Pickens County in North Georgia was perhaps the most notable GOP activist. He served in the Georgia House in 1911 and 1912 and then served for several years as a Republican state senator, representing Fannin, Gilmer, and Pickens counties in the forty-first senatorial district. He was also the Republican national committeeman from Georgia for several years. One of his sons, Will Hays Pickett, later served as the Republican state representative from Pickens County in 1959 and 1960, and another son, Roscoe Pickett, Jr., ran (but lost) on the Republican ticket for the fourth district congressional seat (comprised mostly of DeKalb County) in 1966. Like his father, Pickett, Jr., also served a term in the 1960s as Republican national committeeman from Georgia.

According to the Georgia Official Statistical Registers of the 1920s through the 1950s, Republicans continued to represent the forty-first state senatorial district, composed of Fannin and Gilmer counties in the Georgia House of Representatives.[18] Most were businessmen or farmers who had roots in either western North Carolina or eastern Tennessee, where many Unionists had resided before and during the Civil War. However, according to the biographies of these state legislators contained in Georgia's Official Register, at least several of them had fathers or grandfathers who served the Confederacy during the Civil War. A biographical sketch of Charles Kiker, who served in the state House from 1929 to 1931 and then as the lone Republican state senator for several terms between 1935 and 1960, reports that his grandfather, Benjamin Kiker, represented Fannin County in the Georgia House of Representatives from 1873 to 1879, from 1884 to 1885, and from 1888 to 1889, but this official biography does not identify the elder Kiker as being either a Republican or a Democrat. The younger Kiker was able to gain some positions of influence in the Senate, as he served on the important Appropriations and Highways committees. Francis Reid Mull, a Republican merchant from Blue Ridge, represented Fannin County in the state House for twelve years between 1949 and 1960.[19] David Ralston, who has represented Fannin County in the state legislature in recent years, confirmed that the unionist heritage in the North Georgia mountains was responsible for that region's continuing support of the GOP and also reports that Atlanta was the only other area of Georgia that had any concentration of Republicans, but none of them were elected to the General Assembly until the early 1960s.[20] In the rare instance when a Republican would seek a statewide office, the candidate's only choice was to conduct a write-in candidacy against a Democrat, since there was no Republican primary held in Georgia until 1970.

Perhaps the most publicized Republican write-in candidacy was that of D. Talmadge Bowers of Hart County, Georgia. In 1938 Bowers ran as a write-in candidate for the tenth district congressional seat and lost, but he surfaced again as a write-in candidate for governor in the general election of 1946 and thereby became a cameo role player in the notorious "three governors controversy of 1946." Bowers received 637 votes as a write-in candidate and as the nominal Republican in the general election for governor that year, initially placing him third behind the winner, former governor Eugene Talmadge, and James V. Carmichael, whom Talmadge had defeated in the Democratic primary but who had still received 669 write-in votes in the general election.

When Gene Talmadge died before being sworn in as governor, the General Assembly was charged under state law at the time with choosing the next governor from the two persons who had received the most write-in votes in the general election balloting. Initial vote counts showed that Herman Talmadge, Gene's son, had received only 619 votes, placing him fourth in the vote tally. However, before final certification of the votes, it was discovered that Herman Talamdge had been attributed an additional 56 write-in votes from his home county of Telfair, giving him a total of 675 write-in votes, thus positioning him as one of the two highest write-in vote recipients. Subsequently, election authorities certified Herman's higher vote count, and the General Assembly passed over Republican Bowers as a finalist and elected Talmadge over Marietta businessman Carmichael. Herman Talmadge was then challenged for the governorship by newly elected lieutenant governor M. E. Thompson, who had not yet been sworn in when Gene Talmadge died, and incumbent governor Ellis Arnall, who objected to the apparent vote count shenanigans and refused to turn the governor's office over to Talmadge. Thompson was later designated by the Supreme Court of Georgia as the rightful governor from among the three claimants. Write-in candidacies by Republicans proved to be a rather ineffective means of getting elected.

Former United States Court of Appeals judge Elbert Tuttle described the Georgia Republican Party as he found it in Atlanta when he moved there in the mid-twentieth century. He stated that the party was comprised of three groups: business and professional leaders mostly from Atlanta, African Americans, and "post office Republicans," who were "the ones that hoped a Republican president would be elected every eight or sixteen years and they would get patronage."[21] Tuttle and others of the Republican "Old Guard" establishment were active in presidential campaigns and instrumental in drumming up southern support for the Republican presidential candidacies of Thomas Dewey in 1948 and General Dwight D. Eisenhower in 1952 and 1956. President Eisenhower appointed Tuttle to his federal judgeship in 1954.

Another mid-century Republican leader in Atlanta was businessman and lawyer Kiliaen Townsend, who later was elected to the Georgia House of Representatives in 1965 and served there for twenty-seven years. Townsend reportedly "put together the first Eisenhower for President Committee in the country and enlisted the General's good friend, legendary golfer Bobby Jones as a member."[22] Townsend's recruiting efforts paid dividends for the Georgia GOP, as Bobby Jones stayed active with the party and later assumed the role of Honorary Chairman of the Georgia Republican Party Executive Committee in 1960. The Republican establishment in Atlanta in the 1950s and 1960s consisted mostly of moderate whites and a few activist African Americans. In addition to Justice Tuttle, Kil Townsend, and Bobby Jones, other mid-twentieth-century GOP leaders in Atlanta included attorney Randolph Thrower (who was a former law partner of Judge Tuttle and later served as Internal Revenue Commissioner under President Richard Nixon), insurance executive Rodney Cook, businessmen Robert Snodgrass (who served as the Republican national committeeman in the 1960s), finance executive Bob Shaw, and auto dealer Harry Sommers. During the late 1950s and early 1960s, a number of young professionals also became active in Republican Party organization, including lawyers Jarvin Levison and Mike Egan (an associate of Tuttle and Thrower in the firm of Sutherland, Asbill, and Brennan) and dentist John Savage. Savage characterizes the appeal of the GOP in Georgia to young activists: "At the time I thought the Republican Party had a wonderful opportunity in Georgia to point out everything from the county unit system to the fact that blacks couldn't participate in government to the fact that Georgia ought to take leadership in the South."[23]

African Americans had been active in Republican politics in Georgia since Reconstruction, and many of the leaders in black Atlanta maintained loyalty to the party based on President Lincoln's freedom of slaves and the efforts of Republican Reconstructionists to provide civil rights for the freed slaves. Among the prominent Atlanta African Americans who were active in Georgia GOP leadership in the mid-twentieth century were *Atlanta Daily World* newspaper publisher, C. A. Scott, community activist John Calhoun, drug store owner Clayton Yates, who served as vice chairman of the state Republican Executive Committee in the late 1950s, and railway postal clerk and Masonic leader John Wesley Dobbs, who was the maternal grandfather of prominent Democratic Atlanta mayor Maynard Jackson. Dobbs, sometimes referred to as "the Grand" based on his position as grand warden of the Prince Hall Masons, a black fraternal organization, was a member of Georgia's Eisenhower delegation to the 1952 Republican National Convention. Journalist and author Gary Pomerantz explains Dobbs's loyalty to the Republican Party: "Dobbs admired Lincoln more than any other man, not only because he had emancipated his mother among more than three million slaves, but because he had risen from humble origins. Lincoln was the reason Dobbs was Republican."[24]

According to Numan Bartley, a majority of African-American voters continued to support the GOP enthusiastically in the 1956 presidential election when "General Eisenhower won more than 60 percent of the Negro vote in Macon and more than 80 percent in Atlanta." In that same year, black Atlantans voted more than 90 percent in favor of moderate Republican candidate Randolph Thrower, an Atlanta attorney, in his challenge of incumbent Democrat James C. Davis, an advocate for white supremacy, in the fifth district congressional race.[25]

The presidential election of 1960 rifted the black/white alliance in the Georgia Republican Party when many of the blacks decided to support the candidacy of Democrat John Kennedy over Republican Richard Nixon, based on the Kennedy family's plea to several state and local governmental officials in Georgia in fall 1960 to release Dr. Martin Luther King, Jr., from a DeKalb County jail. King had been jailed on a parole violation charge stemming from his participation in a civil rights sit-in protest at Rich's department store, located in downtown Atlanta, just before the national election. The shift of African Americans out of the Republican Party in Georgia and into the Democratic Party continued in the 1961 non-partisan Atlanta mayoral race when the Atlanta blacks overwhelmingly supported and provided a margin of victory to moderate Democrat Ivan Allen, Jr., over segregationist Lester Maddox, and in the 1962 gubernatorial race when blacks strongly supported moderate Democrat Carl Sanders over former segregationist governor Marvin Griffin. No Republican ran in this race.

Jarvin Levison relates that the Georgia GOP planned to run a candidate for governor of Georgia in 1962, but a fatal accident intervened. According to Levison, Ed Smith, a Columbus businessman and active Republican, was running for governor, but on his return trip to Columbus, after attending a GOP rally at the Biltmore Hotel in Atlanta that featured former president Dwight Eisenhower, Smith apparently fell asleep at the wheel of his automobile and was killed in an accident.[26]

In the 1950s and early 1960s, Republicans continued to represent a portion of the North Georgia mountain region in the General Assembly. Charles E. (Dink) Waters, a merchant from Ellijay who had attended the U.S. Military Academy at West Point, served the forty-first district of North Georgia as its senator in 1956/1957 and again in 1961/1962. Waters was even selected to chair the Senate Administrative Affairs Committee in his last term. In the 1960 election cycle, E. Ralph Ivey became the first Republican in the twentieth century to be identified on the ballot as a representative of the GOP in his run for the United States Congress, when he challenged Democratic representative John W. Davis to represent Cobb County and several other counties in northwest Georgia.

In 1962, Ivey again challenged Davis for his seventh district congressional seat, and again he lost. Atlanta businessman Jimmy O'Callaghan was the first Republican to run for Congress in Atlanta's fifth congressional district that year, but he lost to Democratic attorney Charles Longstreet Weltner. However, in that year's elections, insurance agent Dan McIntyre III, an Atlanta native, graduate of Georgia Tech, and World War II veteran, was elected to the state senate as the first Republican to represent Fulton County at the state House in the twentieth century.

In the early 1960s, a series of lawsuits in southern states challenged the basis on which Georgia, Tennessee, and Alabama apportioned their representation in Congress and in state legislative districts. In Georgia, a lawsuit also challenged the basis on which votes were tallied and awarded in the Democratic primary, based on the state's archaic county unit system. The case of *Baker v. Carr*[27] established the right of the United States Supreme

Court to adjudicate the fairness and equity of weighting citizen votes in state elections and in apportioning representation in legislature districts. The Georgia case of *Gray v. Sanders*[28] invalidated the state's use of the county unit system in apportioning votes in statewide Democratic primary elections, and the subsequent case of *Wesberry v. Sanders*[29] invalidated the use Georgia's county unit system in awarding votes in congressional races. Finally, the Alabama case of *Reynolds v. Sims*[30] had the effect of constitutionally invalidating the practice of determining representation in state House and Senate districts based on the county unit system. The Court ruled that representation in state legislatures must be apportioned equally on the basis of population, rather than by geographical areas. At the time, the Georgia House of Representatives was composed of 205 members who were selected as follows: the 8 counties with the largest populations were allotted 3 representatives each; the next 30 most populous counties were allotted 2 representatives each; and the remaining 121 counties were each allotted 1 representative each in the House. In the state senate, each of the largest counties was represented by only one senator, while smaller counties were grouped together in districts with populations much smaller than the largest counties. Consequently, it was virtually impossible for a small concentration of Republicans in a few sparsely populated North Georgia counties or even a sizeable minority of Republicans in large urban counties to win representation in the Georgia General Assembly under the confines of the county unit system. As a result of these lawsuits and judicial decisions, new and more equitably sized districts were drawn for both houses of the state legislature in order to accommodate the one person-one vote interpretation of the Equal Protection Clause of the United States Constitution. As a consequence, the Georgia GOP was able to increase its representation significantly in Congress and in the state legislature.

This series of court rulings was to be the first of several reapportionment decisions over the next four decades that would aid the Republican Party eventually in winning a majority of seats in the Georgia General Assembly. These Supreme Court decisions, the arrival of a number of Republican-leaning migrants from other regions of the country, and the presidential candidacy of Barry Goldwater in 1964 all contributed to the development and growth of modern Republicanism in Georgia. However, it would still be several decades before the GOP would win enough seats in the General Assembly to provide a serious challenge to Democratic dominance.

Rufus Bullock, the first Republican governor of Georgia (1868-71).
Credit: Georgia Archives, Small Print Collection, spc 17-033.

C.A. Scott, founder and editor of *Atlanta Daily World* and an early
African-American Republican. Credit: *Atlanta Daily World*/ Alexis Scott.

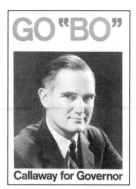

1966 "Go Bo" campaign for gubernatorial candidate Howard "Bo" Callaway.
Callaway was the first Republican nominee for governor in Georgia since 1876.
Credit: Howard "Bo" Callaway.

Bo Callaway on the campaign trail for the 1966 gubernatorial election.
Credit: Howard "Bo" Callaway.

Bo Callaway speaking to crowd with "Go Bo" signs.
Credit: Howard "Bo" Callaway.

Paul Coverdell served as Georgia Senate Majority Leader from 1974 until 1989.
He was elected to the U. S. Senate in 1992 and served until his death in 2000.
Credit: Georgia Archives, RG 37-1-104, file ah01224.

In 1986, Democrat Michael Thurmond became the first African-American elected
to the Georgia General Assembly from Clarke County since Reconstruction. He was
elected Labor Commissioner in 1998. Credit: *Creative Loafing*/Joeff Davis.

Republican gubernatorial candidate Guy Millner and
his wife Ginny during the 1994 campaign.

State senator Sonny Perdue with Lt. Governor Pierre Howard in the 1990s.
Credit: Georgia Archives, RG 37-1-104, file ah01226.

Jack Hill and Sonny Perdue in their early years in the State Senate in the 1990s, when they were roommates in Atlanta during the legislative sessions. Credit: Jack Hill.

CHAPTER 3

The Emergence of the Modern Republican Party in Georgia

As Georgia and the rest of the South recovered from the Great Depression and World War II and began to experience greater economic and job growth in the 1960s, many transplants from northern and midwestern states moved to Georgia. A large number of these relocating new citizens were Republican in their political orientation; as they moved into the Atlanta suburbs, they began to affiliate with the existing party structure centered in Atlanta. Georgia Republican U.S. senator Johnny Isakson describes how this occurred in his home district:

> Well, in Cobb County its growth has probably been spurred by . . . new-comers from outside the state of Georgia that moved from areas where Republicans and Democrats ran competitively, and this whole business of having one-party politics they weren't used to. . . . They would go to the polls and cross over. They would turn out and vote in the Republican pri-mary. This was a major contributing strength. Even though we won some races, sustaining those in re-election only took place if you built a party base. And that party base was built primarily by newcomers.[1]

However, in some districts these newcomers were not always immediately welcomed into the Republican "old guard" establishment. Former state representative Dorothy Felton, who later was the first Republican woman to be elected to the Georgia General Assembly, describes her early experience with the Georgia GOP after moving from Oklahoma: "I moved to Atlanta as a Republican. . . . I had always voted Republican. . . . I came from a Republican family, and I had gone to some Republican things, but it was kind of a closed party. There was an attitude they didn't want too many people involved. It was a closed shop situation."[2]

It was the presidential election campaign of 1964 that seemed to energize the various segments into the modern Georgia Republican Party when Arizona senator Barry Goldwater successfully challenged the moderate policies of the Republican eastern establishment. Goldwater was the first Republican presidential candidate ever to win a majority of the votes in Georgia. The abrupt rightward shift of the GOP in Georgia that year resulted in the final transition of most African Americans from the Republican Party of Lincoln to the new and more liberal Democratic Party of Lyndon Johnson. Former Republican state senator and party activist Rusty Paul puts the 1964 Goldwater campaign in perspective: "You have to go back to the early 1960s and the formation of the modern Republican Party. Goldwater came in. The civil rights era, obviously, changed a lot of the dynamics of politics in the South. The Republican Party was sort of a backlash against that."[3]

The white backlash against the Civil Rights Movement had been gathering momentum in Georgia and the other states of the Old Confederacy since the *Brown v. Board of Education* series of decisions that effectively overturned the "separate-but-equal schools" doctrine in public education. Racial tensions were further exacerbated by the sit-in movements in Atlanta, the forced integration of public schools and colleges, and demonstrations like the 1963 Albany Movement in which local groups of protesting African Americans in the heart of the "Black Belt"[4] in Albany, Georgia, were joined by representatives of the Student Non-Violent Coordinating Committee from across the state and the South in an extended protest for the desegregation of public facilities and for equal employment opportunities. In 1964 the United States Congress responded to the Civil Rights Movement in the South with the passage of the Civil Rights Act of 1964, disallowing further discrimination in public accommodations. Senator Goldwater voted against passage of this legislation and thereby secured a dedicated following of supporters in the Deep South, including Georgia. Goldwater's opposition to the civil rights legislation resonated most strongly among rural and other less affluent southern whites who seemed to feel most threatened by the prospect of blacks obtaining equal rights.[5]

Barry Goldwater's anti-civil rights platform, in contrast to the strong pro-civil rights and "Great Society" platform of the Democratic Lyndon Johnson-Hubert Humphrey ticket, resulted in Goldwater winning the majority of popular votes in Georgia and four other southern states. Many traditional Democratic voters voted Republican for the first time in 1964. Long-serving Democratic state senator George Hooks concurs in this assessment: "The Goldwater Republican surge was the direct result of civil rights. What you had was a disagreement with Lyndon Johnson on civil rights and many felt like he had overstepped." Historian Numan Bartley further describes this change in traditional political alliances in the South:

> The Goldwater candidacy disrupted normal partisan patterns in the state. In the countryside Goldwater ran best in the South and Central Georgia lowlands, past citadels of Democratic strength. More than 60 percent of the voters in the black belt in the South marked their ballots for the Republican candidate. . . . Not surprisingly, there was a high correlation (.9516) between the Goldwater vote in 1964 and the vote for the Dixiecrat ticket in 1948. Both appealed strongly to citizens residing in the lowlands.[6]

In contrast, black voters in Georgia overwhelmingly supported the Democratic Johnson-Humphrey ticket.

As a consequence of the breakdown of the county unit system, the resulting reapportionment of congressional and state House districts, and the Goldwater candidacy, the Georgia GOP was able to field a much broader slate of candidates in the 1964 elections than they had at any time since Reconstruction. Republican candidates challenged Democratic contenders in five of the ten congressional districts. Bo Callaway ran from the third in southwest Georgia, Roscoe Pickett ran from the fourth in DeKalb County, Jim O' Callaghan ran from the fifth district in Atlanta, Ed Chapin III ran from the seventh in northwest Georgia, and Jack Prince ran from the ninth in the northeastern part of the state. Third district candidate Howard "Bo" Callaway, scion of a prominent Georgia textile mill family and developer of Callaway Gardens Resort, was the sole GOP winner and became the first Georgia Republican to serve in the United States House of Representatives in the twentieth century. He defeated former Democratic lieutenant governor Garland Byrd by a vote of 45,545 to 33,737. The Republican Party of Georgia also ran many more candidates for the state House in 1964 and in a special state legislative election in 1965 than they had since Reconstruction. Riding on the Goldwater coattails, nine Republicans were elected to the Georgia Senate, and eight were elected to the House.

For the first time since Reconstruction, Republicans were elected to General Assembly from regions of the state other than the mountains of

North Georgia or Atlanta. They came from Augusta, Macon, Columbus, Savannah, and Thomasville, from Fulton, Cobb, and DeKalb counties in Metro Atlanta, and even from Wadley in rural east Georgia. Among those elected to the state senate in 1964 were engineer Joe Tribble of Savannah, who chaired Georgia's Draft Goldwater Committee and was then serving as chair of the state Republican Party; East Point attorney and decorated World War II pilot Fletcher Thompson, who would later serve three terms as the only Republican to represent Atlanta in Congress in the twentieth century; Perry Gordy from Columbus, who was selected by a Democratic Senate to chair of the Senate Administrative Affairs Committee for a two-year term; and Roy G. Foster, a highway contractor from Wadley who had chaired the Republican Party of Georgia from 1944 to 1952 and was an ally and supporter of Senator Robert Taft of Ohio. Among the eight elected to the House that year were G. Paul Jones from Macon, a future state party chairman, and DeKalb newspaper publisher Jim Bowen. Frank Troutman from Augusta was elected as party chair. In 1965, Republican candidates also swept city elections in Savannah, Georgia's second largest city, winning the office of mayor and all six aldermanic positions. Julius Curtis Lewis, a broadcasting media mogul, served from 1966 to 1970 as that city's first Republican mayor.

Building on his third district congressional victory and the momentum of Goldwater conservatism, two years later Bo Callaway ran for governor of his home state as the first strong Republican gubernatorial candidate in almost a century. He was also the only Republican candidate to run in a statewide race that year. Callaway ended up in a three-man race when prominent segregationist Lester Maddox won the Democratic primary and second-place finisher and progressive former Democratic governor Ellis Arnall entered the general election field as a write-in candidate. Although Callaway won a plurality of the popular vote with 453,665 ballots cast for him versus 450,626 for Maddox and 45,603 written in for Arnall, he failed to win a majority with only 47.75 percent of the vote. Callaway won the majority of the votes of upper-income whites and blacks, while Maddox ran strongest among lower- and low middle-income whites in Atlanta and rural Georgia. Elllis Arnall polled the overall greatest percentage of black votes.[7]

Since Callaway failed to win an absolute majority of all votes cast, the final election determination for selecting a governor was thrown into the Democratic-controlled state legislature. Not surprisingly, in a January 10, 1967, joint session of both houses of the Georgia General Assembly, with only a few Republicans serving, Maddox was elected governor with 182 of

259 possible votes. This unanticipated turn of events for the Georgia GOP surely set back the pace of their progress toward becoming a more viable second party alternative in state politics. The Callaway gubernatorial candidacy apparently did inspire greater Republican participation in the General Assembly races in 1966. GOP candidates ran in twenty-one of the fifty-four state senate districts and won seven of them (five of them reelected for their second term), and Republican challengers contested in seventy-one House races and won in twenty-two of them. Surprisingly, only two of those victories involved the reelection of Republicans previously elected in the class of 1964. Notable among the Republicans first elected to the House in 1966 were Atlanta insurance executive Rodney Cook, who later served as state party chairman and then ran as the GOP standard bearer for Congress in 1972 and for governor in 1978, and attorney Mike Egan and hospitality executive Kil Townsend, both of whom would represent Atlanta in the Georgia General Assembly for many years thereafter.

The Republican Party organization also showed greater geographic diversity in its leadership in 1966. G. Paul Jones of Macon served as state party chair; Frank Troutman, an Augusta businessman, served as vice chairman; and Atlanta attorney Jarvin Levison served as one of the general counsels.

The party did achieve some success in the 1966 congressional races. The GOP fielded candidates in eight of the ten congressional districts and was victorious in two. Fletcher Thompson won the fifth district City of Atlanta-Fulton County seat, following the decision of popular Democratic congressman Charles Weltner not to run on the Democratic ticket that year, rather than sign an oath of support for all of the other party candidates. Weltner objected as a matter of personal principle to endorsing a slate that included arch-segregationist Lester Maddox as the Democratic nominee for governor.[8] Also, attorney Ben Blackburn narrowly won a seat in Congress that year in the fourth district that was comprised primarily of populous DeKalb County, when he defeated long-serving Democratic congressman James C. Davis. Among the Georgia Republican candidates who did not win a seat in Congress that year was Mack Mattingly from St. Simons Island, who would later be elected to the U.S. Senate. 1966 was the first year that that Georgia's Official Statistical Register provided a record of Republican candidacies and victories. Up until 1966, all GOP candidates for office were chosen through a system of caucuses and a state party convention. Republican Party legal counsel Jarvin Levison explained that in the early years of the Republican Party formation, the party simply could not afford to pay for a statewide primary. Instead, candidates for local and legislative offices were chosen in caucuses organized by precinct level, county level, and congressional district level. Statewide candidates were selected at the state convention.

In 1968, both Fletcher Thompson and Ben Blackburn were reelected to Congress, but former Republican Party chair and state senator Joe Tribble lost his bid for the first district seat. In that election, a humbled GOP offered candidates in only three congressional districts. However, for the first time in the twentieth century, a Republican qualified to run for a U.S. Senate seat from Georgia. Atlanta businessman Earl Patton challenged incumbent senator and former governor Herman Talmadge, who had just survived a historic Democratic primary challenge by future Atlanta mayor Maynard Jackson, the first African American to run in a statewide race in Georgia. Patton lost his race, polling only 22.5 percent of the total votes cast in the general election. Republicans did retain seven seats in the state Senate of the eighteen they contested that year and also won twenty-seven House seats among the sixty-two they contested. Representatives elected for the first time in 1968 included Bob Bell from DeKalb County, who would later chair the state party and run for governor, and Herb Jones from Savannah, who would later serve as House minority leader. The Georgia GOP achieved notable success in the decade of the 1960s. The party began the decade with no congressmen, one state senator, and two representatives. They closed out the decade with two congressmen, seven state senators, and twenty-five state representatives.

The GOP also managed to win a few notable municipal elections in the late 1960s. In addition to their 1965 victory in the Savannah mayor's race, jewelry store owner and gospel singer Ronnie Thompson was elected mayor of Macon in 1967, and Republican candidates also won mayoral races in Columbus and East Point.

Perhaps the most exciting development for the Republican Party in Georgia in 1968 involved five influential Democratic statewide office holders (referred to as "the Capitol clique") switching to the Republican Party. Comptroller General Jimmy Bentley, Agriculture Commissioner Phil Campbell, State Treasurer Jack Ray, and Public Service Commissioners Alpha Fowler and Crawford Pilcher all bolted the Democratic Party as part of a more rightward swing in political attitudes in Georgia and a rejection of the candidacy of liberal Minnesotan Hubert Humphrey as the Democratic nominee for president. Then-governor Lester Maddox also distanced himself from the Humphrey Democratic presidential candidacy. According to Numan Bartley, "Humphrey's Georgia campaign dramatized the disintegration of the National Democratic Party's position in the state. Humphrey received little assistance from the state Democratic Party sources."[9] Indicative of the almost reactionary bent of many Georgians that year, American Independent third-party candidate for president, segregationist George Wallace, the former governor of Alabama who had resisted integration of the University of Alabama, won a plurality of popular votes and all of the electoral votes in Georgia and in four other southern states.

In the 1970 election cycle, three of the five party switchers (Bentley, Ray, and Fowler) were defeated in their statewide races two years after changing parties. Phil Campbell accepted an appointment in Washington in the new Nixon administration and did not run for public office again. Crawford Pilcher's term on the Public Service Commission did not expire until 1972, and after watching the defeat of his fellow party switchers, he chose not to run again. TV broadcaster Hal Suit defeated Jimmy Bentley in the first ever Republican primary contest for governor that year, but he, in turn, was defeated in the general election by state senator and peanut farmer Jimmy Carter from Plains in southwest Georgia. Carter positioned himself as the "common-man's candidate," beating former governor Carl Sanders (whom he dubbed "Cufflinks Carl") in the Democratic primary race.[10]

Suit polled a respectable 40.6 percent of the votes in the general election (which was the highest percentage of the vote that any Republican gubernatorial candidate in Georgia would receive for the next twenty years), but he lost to the Carter coalition of the urban working class and rural and small-town white voters. Veteran political journalist Dick Pettys, who covered the Georgia Capitol for Associated Press from 1969 to 2005, comments on Hal Suit's relatively strong appeal to the voting public: "Hal [Suit] had a lot of credibility going for him He'd been on the air for years and years, a very likable guy, and he was a good solid presence on the ballot. . . . On TV he conveyed that he was somebody you could trust. He was kind of like a Walter Cronkite in a lot of ways, I think."[11]

In that election cycle, Republican candidates for lieutenant governor, secretary of state, commissioner of agriculture, comptroller general, and commissioner of labor all lost their statewide races also. Republicans ran for five of Georgia's ten congressional seats, but won only the seats of incumbents Fletcher Thompson and Ben Blackburn. In the 1970 state legislative races, Republicans won only six state senate seats out of fifteen they contested. Notable among the senate victors that year were insurance executive and future U.S. senator Paul Coverdell, Buckhead businessman Earl Patton, who had run as the Republican Party nominee for the U.S. Senate in 1968, and electrical engineer and World War II army veteran Jim Tysinger from DeKalb County, who would continue to serve in the state legislature for many years to come. Republicans won only 22 seats in the House that year among the 58 they contested. The number of seats in the Georgia House was reduced to 180 in this election, but the state senate increased its seats from 54 to 56.

Republican Party insiders sometimes refer to the decade of the 1970s as "the Dark Years." The party ended the decade with fewer representatives in Congress and both houses of the General Assembly than they had in 1970. Those candidates who were victorious in that decade won primarily because of their ability to organize a coalition of staunch supporters within individual state House and Senate districts, populated mostly by higher-income, politically active Republican voters. The best thing that can be said about the 1970s by the Georgia GOP is that several of its most outstanding future leaders were first elected to office in that decade. Perhaps the greatest benefit the party experienced in those years was the opportunity to plan and organize more effectively for the future.

When asked about the condition of the state Republican Party organizational structure in Georgia in the mid-1970s, when he was first running for office, current U.S. Senator Johnny Isakson replied,

> It was non-existent. . . . The Republican Party in the late sixties and early seventies was a handful of folks in Atlanta that were pretty much involved in Fulton County Republican politics. The state party came to life about six months before every presidential election because it got a little money out of the national campaign, enough to open a storefront office and to put some volunteers in, and then it went out of business until the next presidential election.[12]

Another early Republican leader is Bob Irvin, who was first elected to the state House of Representatives in 1972 while he was an Emory Law School student, and he was among those who worked most diligently to begin to organize the party and especially the elected Republicans within the General Assembly. Irvin was elected from a new district in North Fulton County, after working in the campaigns of Barry Goldwater, Congressman

Fletcher Thompson, and State Representative John Savage. When he was asked about the Republican organization within the state House of Representatives, Irvin described the situation as follows: "The caucus was so small, and Republicans were rare. . . . There was a Republican caucus . . . but they really didn't think in terms of trying to elect more Republicans; and they didn't think in terms of trying to do things during the legislative session to set up issues for the next election."[13] Bob Irvin further explains how the Republicans began to organize to make a difference in the legislature in the mid-seventies: "I wrote a paper and circulated it among the Republican leadership about how we ought to take on an issue that would position us to beat Democrats. . . . The first one I got us to take on was open meetings. There were a lot of closed meetings in those days." Dorothy Felton, who was first elected to the General Assembly in 1974 (and served for twenty-six years) also remembers the importance of this issue to the party: "When I first went into the state House . . . open meetings was the issue at that point in time."[14]

This type of issue orientation for the GOP activists and their few elected representatives provided the framework for an even more intense planning process. Both Bob Irvin and Paul Coverdell describe the formation of a Republican Party long-range planning committee in the mid-seventies. Irvin reports, "The long-range planning committee—it was Mack [Mattingly, an office products sales executive residing in coastal Georgia] as chair, Paul, and Newt [Gingrich] and me and [John] Linder and Bill Amos, who had been Bo Callaway's campaign manager, and Nora Allen, who was the national committeewoman, and Don Layfield, who was the vice vhair, and what we did was kind of built on the model we used in the 1975 session." Irvin further enumerates the long-range benefits of their planning efforts:

> The first is that we really did establish the expectation that the Republican Party was going to engage on a kind of persistent, ongoing systematic campaign to do things that were necessary to elect Republican candidates. . . . The second thing is that we actually did develop some issues for the 1976 session and for the 1977–1978 cycle that were helpful. Welfare reform was one. The third thing accomplished is that it really established the core group that built the party through the seventies and eighties and the nineties—that is, Mack and Paul and Newt and me and John all together on the same page working for things. It made a team out of us."[15]

Irvin served as chair of the Republican caucus in the House from 1976 to 1978.

Coverdell described the planning process similarly in a 1989 interview:

> Mack Mattingly was elected chairman of the Republican Party in 1974–1975. He formed a long range planning committee. I was invited to participate. That led to even deeper involvement in the Republican Party, which by the year 1980, was almost total immersion. . . . That brought Mattingly, Gingrich, and Coverdell together and that is a thread that goes through this era. That coalition led to the election in 1981 of Fred Cooper as party chair, which led to a new financial base. . . . It was this concept of planning and identifying the major functions of a party, which are administration, finance, candidate-recruitment, and party development. Those fundamental building blocks are still in place and have gotten stronger and stronger. That was the turning point. . . . It did create a coalition powerful and intelligent enough to move the party to a new era.[16]

Prophetically, Coverdell went on to say in this interview that "We are moving on to the era of actual power. I am not exactly certain, but we are coming close to becoming a different animal."[17] In 1992, Coverdell was elected to the U.S. Senate, and two years later Newt Gingrich was elected Speaker of the U.S. House of Representatives.

Newt Gingrich was active in Young Republicans while an undergraduate student at Emory University in the early 1960s. He earned a doctorate in history from Tulane University and returned to Georgia in the late 1960s to teach history at West Georgia College in Carrollton. He quickly stepped into a leadership role in the newly organizing Georgia GOP. According to one of his biographers, "Gingrich viewed the Republican leadership in Georgia as 'a disaster,' . . . and he was fiercely determined to build a Republican Party in Georgia and the region based on organizational strength, long-range strategy and patience."[18] Certainly, he needed patience, as he ran for a congressional seat from Georgia and narrowly lost to conservative incumbent Congressman Jack Flynt of Griffin in 1974 and 1976, and it was 1978 before he eventually was victorious and won his first of his ten terms in Congress. In that race he defeated Democratic state senator Virginia Shapard, a member of a prominent Griffin textile family, by winning 54 percent of the votes.

Even with all their planning and organizational efforts, Republicans in Georgia experienced limited electoral successes in the 1970s. The Georgia

GOP was somewhat stymied in this decade primarily by two factors. President Richard Nixon's Watergate scandal and his eventual resignation from office certainly cast the Republican Party in a bad light. As a consequence of Nixon's disgrace, former Georgia Democratic governor Jimmy Carter emerged from the pack of contenders to secure both his party's nomination and the presidency in 1976. Two Republican stalwarts in Georgia have commented on the adverse effects of the Carter presidency on the Georgia GOP and their party's meager electoral successes in that era. Longtime Republican Party activist and several term chair of the Georgia party, Alec Poitevint, comments about how the Carter presidency factored into the GOP's limited successes in the seventies: "We were trying to survive. It was post Watergate; Jimmy Carter was president. . . . After Carter was elected president and there was euphoria in Georgia, it really did set Georgia back versus the change going on in other southern states. . . . It stopped Newt Gingrich from getting elected in 1976."[19] Former GOP executive director Jay Morgan labeled the era as the "Carter Curse, which retarded the growth of the party."[20]

No Republican candidates for statewide office were successful in the 1970s. The GOP came close to winning a U.S. Senate seat from Georgia in 1972 when fifth district Republican congressman Fletcher Thompson ran for the seat vacated by the January 1972 death of long-serving Democratic senator Richard B. Russell. Then-governor Jimmy Carter appointed his close confidante, prominent Democratic attorney David Gambrell, to fill the seat temporarily. In a hotly contested Democratic primary race with several prominent contenders, state representative Sam Nunn of Perry claimed the victory and subsequently defeated Thompson in the general election, although Thompson won an impressive 46 percent of the votes cast and won 40 percent of the votes in the traditionally Democratic strongholds of rural Georgia. Thompson ran on a platform opposing the busing of students to achieve racial integration in the schools and also rode on the coattails of Richard Nixon's presidential reelection campaign. An analysis of the voting patterns in this race reveals that Republican Thompson actually won a majority of votes cast by Georgia's white voters in this election. According to political scientists, Earl and Merle Black, "Nunn became Georgia's first Democrat to win a Senate election despite losing the white vote."[21]

In the 1974 gubernatorial election, former Macon mayor "Machine Gun" Ronnie Thompson lost convincingly to popular state representative George Busbee of Albany by a vote total of 646,797 to 289,113.

Representative John Savage lost the lieutenant governor's race to former state senator Zell Miller by a similar wide margin. In 1978, Republican chairman and state representative Rodney Cook was soundly trounced by incumbent Governor Busbee, who captured almost 81 percent of the votes in his second term bid. Republicans managed to gain only a toehold on the Georgia electorate in the "dark years" of the 1970s. In the three primary elections in the 1970s, 93 percent of Georgian voters still cast their ballots in Democratic primaries, and only 7 percent voted in Republican primaries.

It wasn't until the 1980s that the GOP's fortunes begin to improve again. A particularly bright spot for the Republican Party of Georgia occurred in 1980 when former party chairman Mack Mattingly was elected as the first Republican United States senator from Georgia since Reconstruction. He won 50.8 percent of the votes to defeat four-term Democratic senator and former governor Herman Talmadge, who had recently experienced a highly publicized divorce, a Senate reprimand for financial misconduct for failing to report contributions adequately, and apparent bouts of alcoholism, perhaps the cause of his many absences from Senate voting.[22]

To some extent, Mattingly was also aided by riding the coattails of Ronald Reagan who defeated Jimmy Carter for the presidency in that election. Native son Carter still carried Georgia as one of only six states that he won in the 1980 presidential election. Former state representative and 1974 GOP candidate for lieutenant governor John Savage rather ungraciously attributed Mattingly's victory simply to being "at the right place at the right time."[23] To a large extent, Savage's explanation is credible. In 1980 there were still many more Democrats than there were Republicans among likely voters in Georgia, and according to Earl and Merle Black, "Republican breakthroughs (in the South) were generally a result of temporary disarray within the Democratic Party, rather than the inherent grassroots strength of the Republicans."[24] Nevertheless, Mattingly won by more than 27,000 votes, and his victory provided a ray of hope for further GOP victories in Georgia. Former party counsel Frank Strickland observed, "It was absolutely dramatic in 1980 when Mattingly was elected to the Senate. It was not expected and was an eye-opener. You know, maybe we can do this."[25]

In a setback for the GOP in Georgia, Mattingly served only one term and was defeated in his 1986 reelection bid by Democrat Wyche Fowler who won by 22,503 votes out of 1,224,948 cast. Mattingly still won 59 percent of the votes cast by white Georgians in this election, but Fowler won overwhelmingly among black voters and also won the majority of votes in 102 counties. He was successful in portraying Mattingly as a "country club Republican" who favored business interests over consumer interests.[26]

Newt Gingrich continued to serve in the United States House of Representatives during the entire decade of the 1980s. Although Republican candidates ran in most congressional districts in Georgia during the decade, only one additional Republican was elected to Congress, and that was Pat Swindall who represented the then heavily Republican fourth district centered in DeKalb County. Swindall was elected in 1984 and reelected in 1986 but ignominiously lost his reelection bid in 1988 and later served a jail term for lying to a federal grand jury regarding a home refinancing scheme.

The Republican Party dutifully drafted and enlisted candidates for key statewide offices in the 1980s. Bob Bell ran against Joe Frank Harris for governor in 1982 but won only 434,496 or 37 percent of the votes. The same year, Zell Miller and Max Cleland defeated Republican opponents for the offices of lieutenant governor and secretary of state, respectively, by even greater margins of victory. In the 1984 U.S. Senate race, incumbent Sam Nunn thoroughly beat a relatively unknown Republican challenger, Mike Hicks, by taking 80 percent of the votes, and in 1986 incumbent governor Harris handily defeated Republican challenger, Sandy Springs attorney Guy Davis, by winning 70.5 percent of the votes. Davis did not win the majority of votes in a single county in that election. Although the Georgia GOP lacked success in electing many candidates to Congress and to statewide offices in the 1980s, these results were in direct contrast to the voting patterns of Georgians in the national presidential elections in the 1980s. In 1984, Georgians voted by a wide margin to reelect Ronald Reagan to his second term. Reagan was popular in Georgia, especially among the higher and middle-income voters that benefited from his supply-side economic policies and lower taxation rates.

Most importantly for the Republican Party in Georgia, Ronald Reagan, a former Democrat himself, made voting for Republican candidates for office somehow seem more acceptable for lifelong Democrats. According to Earl and Merle Black, "Reagan's successful presidency was the central development that eventually established favorable conditions for the Republican's southern breakthrough in the 1990s. . . . By and large, the Reagan presidency made the Republican Party respectable and preferable to many southern whites who had never before thought of themselves as

Republican."[27] In 1988, Reagan's former vice president, George H. W. Bush, easily won Georgia's electoral votes in his race for the presidency.

Because of the contrasting voting patterns between national and state elections, Johnny Isakson reports there were several attempts made by Republicans in the General Assembly to change the Georgia election cycles and laws to allow for the gubernatorial elections to be held in the same year as presidential elections; there was hope that this would give Republican candidates for governor and other statewide offices a better chance to ride the coattails of popular national Republicans.[28] Earl and Merle Black comment on this issue: "In the South, splitting state and national elections places an additional burden on the Republican Party, since it deprives that party of the surge of white voters who might be attracted by a conservative Republican nominee or repelled by a presidential candidacy of a northern liberal Democrat."[29]

From 1978 through 1996, voter registration and voter participation both declined in years in which the governor and other state constitutional officers ran for office, but both increased again in presidential election years.[30] Democrats in the General Assembly always managed to defeat the proposals to elect governors in the same year as United States presidents. However, Georgia Democratic House Speaker Tom Murphy did allow the passage of legislation that discontinued straight-party ballots in Georgia so that winning Republican candidates for federal offices did not sweep Republican candidates into state House victories. Terry Coleman elaborates on Murphy's motives: "Speaker Murphy wanted to split the ticket and take the president off the ticket. . . . I think he really felt like he was helping conserve his number one interest besides Georgia, and that was the House of Representatives."[31] Coleman remembers the process as a two-step change in which the presidential election was taken off the straight-party ticket first, and later the General Assembly removed the U.S. Senate and House of Representatives races from the straight-party ballot. Former Democratic state legislator Larry Walker remembers this second phase of removing candidates for Federal office from the straight-party ticket: "I think if you'll check into it, it was Wyche Fowler's defeat [in 1992] that made them go away from the straight-party ballots because Republicans were more popular [in federal elections]."[32]

During the decade of the 1980s, the Republican Party leadership in Georgia continued to refine and enhance its organizational strength through a number of measures. Two-time Republican nominee for governor Guy

Millner relates how he and the Coverdells and others started a Young Republican organization: "I was involved with Paul Coverdell. Paul and Nancy (Coverdell) would come by my office on Piedmont Road, and we would do the Young Republican thing, the 120 Club. It was $10 a month, $120 a year. We would be on the phones calling, signing people up." Coverdell also organized an intra-party communications network within each congressional district, which he called the "point person list." He maintained a catalog of three to five Republican leaders in each of the state's congressional districts and engaged in periodic issue-oriented teleconference calls originated from his insurance business office on Peachtree Road in south Buckhead.[33]

In the mid 1980s, Coverdell served as the Republican Party chairman for Georgia. His chosen party executive director, Jay Morgan, discusses how Coverdell functioned as a party organizer and leader in these years: "Coverdell was an interesting guy. He loved this stuff 24/7. He realized what we were doing at the state party was . . . bringing a lot of things that I had learned from working at the Republican National Committee (RNC) to Georgia for the first time—telemarketing and some of the grass roots organizing—the targeting of legislative races and that kind of thing." Morgan named the party's targeting tool ORVIS for Optimal Republican Voting Strength, and it was modeled after a successful effort in Texas to recruit and run Republican candidates in every election district that was deemed winnable by the database in ORVIS. The Georgia database initially contained election results from the ballots cast in the 1984 and 1986 presidential and U.S. senatorial elections, two partisan statewide Public Service Commission races, several state legislative races, all of the state's congressional races, and certain county commission races. This tool helped the party identify legislative districts that were deemed likely to elect a Republican.

In Morgan's 1987 report to Coverdell as party chairman and to the executive committee, he identified three congressional districts, ten state Senate districts, and twenty-seven state House districts where the data suggested that Republicans had a better than even chance of winning in the next election cycle or future races.[34] As a result of this data-based research, Morgan and the party leadership attempted to recruit candidates to run as Republicans in these districts. According to Morgan, essentially all of these districts are today served by Republican legislators. University of Georgia political scientist Charles S. Bullock III studied the ORVIS district targeting process as it was employed in the late 1980s and 1990s and validated Morgan's findings. He states, "ORVIS, a measure of partisan strength, calculated from the precinct level vote share in previous statewide elections, has been used since 1988 to target Republican efforts in Georgia state legislative contests. The top-down approach implied in the use of this targeting device has paid dividends. Successful Republican challengers come disproportionately from districts with high ORVIS scores."[35]

Although the Georgia GOP experienced only limited success in electing Republican candidates to statewide offices in the 1980s, the party did manage to make meaningful progress in winning more seats in the General Assembly and in electing several senators and representatives who would become leaders in their party in future years. Between 1980 and 1990, Republican members of the state Senate increased from five to eleven, and the number of GOP representatives in the House grew from twenty to thirty-six, a new record-high level for House Republicans.

Among the future Republican state leaders elected in this decade to the state Senate were Cobb County business owner Carl Harrison, elected in 1982; attorney Skin Edge from West Georgia, who defeated Arthur Bolton, the former Democratic state attorney general in 1986; Sallie Newbill from North Fulton County, who became the first Republican woman to serve in the state Senate when she was elected in 1986; Chuck Clay with a long family history in Cobb County, elected in 1986; and future U.S. congressman Mac Collins from Middle Georgia, also first elected in 1986. New Republican leaders elected to the state House in the 1980s include former House minority leader Paul Heard (first elected in 1982), Gwinnett County Commission chairman Charles Bannister and Congressman Jack Kingston from Savannah (both first elected in 1984); and Steve Stancil and Earl Ehrhart (first elected in 1988). Senator Johnny Isakson reports on GOP progress and how the number of Republicans in the state legislature increased from when he first served in 1977 until the end of 1980s:

> There were only nineteen out of a hundred and eighty. We were outnumbered ten to one in the General Assembly. So the reality is you lose on any vote. . . . And when I left fourteen years later, instead of being outnumbered ten to one, it was six to one. Thirty-six, actually it was five and a half to one. We had thirty-six Republicans, and we formed some coalitions that could get us enough votes to sometimes block things. So from a practical standpoint, our victories were few and far between.[36]

Despite Republican gains, Democrats continued to dominate both houses of the General Assembly by substantial margins. The relative dearth of Republicans inspired long-time Democratic House Speaker Tom Murphy periodically to mock the House Republican caucus members. Former GOP House member Tom Lawrence comments on Murphy's taunting attitude when Lawrence first served in 1983: "At that particular time, there were only twenty-five Republicans down here. And the Speaker used to announce the meeting of the Republican caucus and then parenthetically put that it will take place in the phone booth in the east annex or something like that. We were generally ignored."[37]

State labor commissioner and former legislator Michael Thurmond relates a humorous anecdote about the House Republican Caucus in 1987. Thurmond, a native of rural Clarke County who was serving his first term that year and was the only African American in the General Assembly at that time representing a majority white district, reports, "One of my best memories when I first arrived in the General Assembly—there was this sign posted somewhere that said 'Minority Caucus.' And I went. I opened the door and they were all Republicans. But there were fewer Republicans than there were African Americans when I was first elected."[38]

Former representative Steve Stancil, who served as House minority leader from 1992 to 1994, recalls how Speaker Murphy on several occasions would wave his hand around his face as if swatting at gnats flying around him when Republican members would come forward to speak on proposed legislation from the well of the House. When asked about the role of Republicans in the House while Tom Murphy was Speaker, long-serving House member Bob Holmes, a political science professor at Clark-Atlanta University, observed, "Actually he treated them [Republicans] worse than he did urban legislators, and of course they didn't get any kind of things. . . . Their bills would never go anywhere."[39] Terry Coleman, who succeeded Murphy as Speaker, comments on Murphy's attitude about the minority party in his House: "You know, Murphy used to say 'we don't really need a Republican Party; it's a duplication of government. We've got liberals, moderates and conservatives in the Democratic Party, and it's just a waste of taxpayer dollars.'"

In fact, some analysts of the rise of Republicanism in the South have observed that it was because of the similarity in political philosophy between state-level Democratic leaders and their Republican counterparts in the legislature that the GOP was slow to win control of state Houses. David Lublin elaborates on the concept:

> In order to explain why the Democrats retained dominance of the region's politics for so long after the racial conflicts of the 1960's, one must look . . . to the interrelated roles of elites, institutions and issues. White Democratic elites adapted to the enlarged electorate by adopting conservative to moderate stands on racial issues. The conservative to moderate positions of most Democratic candidates made it extremely difficult for Republican candidates to capitalize on the issues for decades. . . . The lack of difference between Republicans and Democrats on social issues in rural areas worked to the advantage of Democrats and stalled partisan change toward the Republicans in the rural South.[40]

State senator George Hooks concurs with Lublin's assessment, at least as it pertains to Georgia: "The old-line Democratic Party in Georgia was very conservative. When I say conservative, I couch that in taxpayer, money-type terms. . . . Truthfully, there was not a great deal of difference in the philosophical outlooks of the leadership of the two parties." In Georgia, most rural Democrats in state House leadership positions were careful to distance themselves from any liberal national party platforms and from left-wing candidates for national office.

Alec Poitevint also notes that Democratic elites in Georgia controlled much of the funding for campaigns and therefore funds were not made available to Republican candidates in meaningful amounts until recent years: "We had the additional problem that a lot of the old rich money and the business community in this state were in line with the Democratic machine. . . . Maybe some of them thought they had no alternative. . . . It was a culture that we had in Georgia, and maybe some other states did not have it to the same degree."

The lack of well-known and experienced Republican candidates in many races in the years before 1990 also contributed to the slow rise of Republicanism in Georgia. There was a limited base of Republicans with extensive political or governmental service from which to recruit. Bob Irvin explains why it was difficult even in the seventies and eighties to recruit candidates from the business and civic communities: "Community leaders—they just want to get elected, and they want to serve. So, we had a real hard time recruiting people to run as Republicans because they didn't think they could win. . . . Even though they weren't particularly Democrats, they ran as Democrats." Because the field of potential state legislators was limited, for many years Republicans lacked sufficient numbers of committed potential candidates to make much progress in winning elective offices at the local government level, and this situation, in turn, limited the pool of candidates for the state legislature. Political scientist David Lublin observes that "candidates who have previously won a lower office are almost always the stronger candidates for higher office than political novices." He further notes that "even at the end if the 1980s Republicans still did not attract candidates for over eighty percent of county offices in the South."[41] Certainly, that was the situation in Georgia.

The GOP experienced some success in electing candidates to municipal and county leadership positions in the 1980s and early 1990s in some of the larger cities and in the larger suburban counties in Metro Atlanta. Following in the footsteps of Julius Curtis Lewis, the first Republican mayor of Savannah from 1966 to 1970, Republican Susan Weiner served as Savannah mayor from 1991 to 1995. In Macon Ronnie Thompson served two terms as the Republican mayor from 1967 to 1975, and while he was serving as mayor he was defeated in runs for U.S. Congress in 1972 and for Georgia governor in 1974. Current Georgia Chamber of Commerce president George Israel also served as a Republican mayor of Macon from 1979 to 1987. Republican Lillian Webb served as mayor of Norcross from 1974 to 1984, and was the first Republican and first female chair of the Gwinnett County Commission for two terms from 1984 to 1992. Earl Smith was elected as the first Republican chairman of the Cobb County Commission in 1985 and served until 1989. Still, Republicans lacked sufficient numbers of locally elected officials to provide a meaningful base of likely candidates for state House races. Political scientist Charles S. Bullock III surveyed Republican officeholders at the county level in Georgia in 1989 and determined that they composed only 153 or 5.8 percent of the officeholders at the time. County commissioners were the largest group (57) constituting a mere 8.1 percent of the total county commissioners in the state, and they were limited to only 28 of 159 counties, with a majority of them in the Atlanta Metropolitan Statistical Area.[42]

Even when Republicans were elected to the state legislature, they were rarely given meaningful positions of leadership that they could use to induce more Republican candidates to run or to provide significant benefits to their communities. Democrats jealously guarded their positions of influence, earned from long service in the legislature, and they used their monopoly on state House power tenaciously and fervently to hold on to their control of the state legislature for as long as they could. They employed their considerable influence to support other Democratic candidates for open seats, and where possible, they managed reapportionment processes to protect incumbent Democrats and overpopulate areas with Republican leanings.

CHAPTER 4

The Republicans Gain
Momentum in the 1990s

The 1990 election cycle provided only limited successes for the Republican Party in Georgia. Popular state House representative and minority party leader Johnny Isakson decided to run for governor that year, since the incumbent, Joe Frank Harris, was not eligible to seek a third term. Isakson's opponent was long-serving lieutenant governor Zell Miller, who defeated former Atlanta mayor and congressman Andrew Young in the Democratic primary election.

Isakson campaigned aggressively and ran the most successful Republican gubernatorial campaign since Bo Callaway's near victory in 1966. However, Miller also ran an aggressive campaign with perhaps the most professional campaign organization ever assembled by a Georgia gubernatorial candidate up to that point in time. He hired James Carville, an experienced political strategist, and they formulated an impressive platform including provisions for a state lottery to raise money for merit-based college scholarships and a four-year-old pre-kindergarten program, a promise to remove sales taxes on groceries, and a Marine-type boot camp for young first offenders in the criminal justice system. In the end, Isakson lost by a pretty sizeable margin, garnering only 645,625 votes or 44.5 percent of the total to 766,662 votes or 53 percent for Miller, with 2.5 percent of the ballots cast for the Libertarian candidate.

Also, in that election, Democratic candidate Pierre Howard, a DeKalb County lawyer, state senator, and scion of a prominent political DeKalb County family,[1] convincingly defeated Cobb County Republican attorney

and printing executive Matt Towery in the race for the lieutenant governorship by a vote margin of 63 percent to 34 percent. Towery was later elected
to the state House of Representatives in 1992.

Republican candidates ran in all of Georgia's ten congressional districts
in 1990, but all new challengers lost their races. Even Newt Gingrich, the
only Republican then serving in Congress in the Georgia delegation, almost
lost his reelection bid. David Worley, a Democratic Party activist, challenged
Gingrich in his South Atlanta district that was rapidly changing in its voter
composition. Gingrich only narrowly won with 78,768 votes, or 50.3 percent, compared to 77,794 for Worley. Alec Poitevint, who was then the state
party chairman, comments on the election challenges that year: "Newt was
in trouble. He was really in bad trouble. . . . In 1990 he was still in the district south of the airport. It was a very, very close race, and he almost lost it.
Our focus was to save his seat, the only seat we had. We were building, and
we were already working on redistricting for 1992." The Republican candidates for Congress, in aggregate, received only 37 percent of the votes cast in
1990.

At the request of Republican Party leadership, Jay Morgan analyzed the
votes in the 1990 election cycle and concluded that Isakson was a victim of
low voter turnout, particularly in the Republican bastions of Gwinnett,
Clayton, and Cobb counties. He calculated that 360,000 fewer Georgians
voted in the 1990 governor's race than voted in the 1988 presidential election. Morgan attributed Zell Miller's victory primarily to his promise of a
lottery for funding the improvements to education. Isakson carried only 18
of Georgia's 159 counties. However, those counties were geographically dis-
persed around the state, and that dispersion provided a hopeful sign for
future GOP statewide races in Georgia.[2]

Once again, redistricting became crucially important for the Republican
Party's success in the next election cycle. Political scientists Michael Binford
and David Sturrock, joining with journalist Tom Baxter, describe the significance of the 1991 reapportionment to the Georgia GOP:

> The process that started the fundamental transformation of the Georgia
> Congressional delegation from staunchly Democratic to overwhelmingly
> Republican began with the 1990 census. As a result of strong population
> growth, the state was given a new district, the eleventh. Court rulings made
> it clear that at least one new black majority district, joining John Lewis'
> fifth district in Atlanta, would probably have to be a part of the new map
> to meet the requirements of the amended Voting Rights Act. . . . The

newly drawn districts offered substantial opportunities for Republicans, who had worked closely with African-American state legislators in drawing new lines. . . . The process [of concentrating blacks] also reduced the number of African-American voters in surrounding districts, substantially raising the proportion of whites there (a result sometimes referred to in the elegant language of the politicians as "bleaching") and possibly tipping those other districts in the Republicans' direction.[3]

Former party legal counsel Frank Strickland also comments on the 1991 redistricting process: "In the 1990's redistricting cycle, the state party decided it was going to carefully monitor the redistricting activities . . . and there was some litigation filed by others—we were not parties to the litigation—but we were monitoring it. . . . And we ended up filing an amicus brief in that case. . . . It was filed on behalf of John Lewis and Newt Gingrich," (who were then the only African-American and the only Republican members of the Georgia congressional delegation). While serving as party chairman, Alec Poitevint saw the potential benefits to the Republican Party of actively supporting the creation of more majority African-American congressional districts in Georgia and thereby more Republican districts, and worked hard to raise the necessary funding for the Republican Party to participate in the reapportionment challenge.

The politics surrounding the 1991–1992 reapportionment litigation caused quite a bit of dissension within the ranks of the Georgia Democratic Party. AP journalist Dick Pettys describes Speaker Murphy's challenge in the early 1990s redistricting disputes:

Increasingly, Tom Murphy faced many challenges in keeping order in the House. He rose to most of them, I think. But he had—as Republicans started gaining power—he then had problems keeping his own Democrats in line because there were fewer Democrats in the majority. So the black Democrats needed more tending; women Democrats needed more tending, and of course the white Democrats who were used to being tended and taken care of, you had to take care of—it was like a father with children competing for his attention; you have to try and satisfy all of them. That was a specific challenge for Tom Murphy that he seemed to accommodate pretty well until you got to things like reapportionment. Then, all hell would break loose. . . . Well, it was the black and white Democrats unable to reach accord, largely because neither of them was powerful enough to do it on their own. Neither one of the groups could steamroll the other because there were so many Republicans. . . . Well, you know, one of the most chilling quotes I've seen up here—chilling in the sense that it's one of those defining moments when you really see what's happening—was Tyrone Brooks [an African-American Democratic representative from Atlanta] saying "no permanent friends, no permanent enemies," and forging that coalition between black Democrats and white Republicans.

Rural and small town Democrats found themselves at odds with urban African Americans who advocated for a reapportionment plan that would provide for the largest black electorate in Congressional and state legislative districts so that it might be more likely for African-Americans to win. Their plan was dubbed by its advocates as "max-black." State representatives Cynthia McKinney and Tyrone Brooks have been identified as the chief advocates for this plan among the black legislators. Representative Bob Holmes who chaired the Legislative Black Caucus in Georgia in 1990 explains the plan as "an alliance over the common mutual interest that we could create these districts . . . to enhance the possibilities of electing minorities. . . . So, if you put more African-Americans in districts where they could elect more black representatives, then you would have more opportunities for Republicans, as well. We saw it as a mutually beneficial thing.

However, not all members of the Black Caucus agreed with the concept of the "max-black" plan. Bob Holmes describes being in the middle of the controversy: "I was kind of in between. It was basically Tyrone and Cynthia who kind of led 'max-black,' and there were others like Michel [Thurmond of Clarke County] and Calvin [Smyre of Columbus] who were kind of at the other end." Michael Thurmond discusses his objections to the plan:

> At that point I was the chairman of the Legislative Black Caucus. And if you want to know hell on earth, serve as chair of the Legislative Black Caucus during reapportionment. That was quite a year. Cynthia McKinney and a group of blacks proposed something called the "max-black" plan. That strategy was to create as many majority black districts as possible concentrating the African-Americans. And I opposed the "max-black" plan because . . . I thought that would lead to increased Republican members in the House because by creating and concentrating the blacks in one district you created more majority white districts. I just saw it as not in the best interest of the Democratic Party. We also created the new Congressional district. They used the same strategy in creating the old 11th District. I ran against Cynthia—I ran for Congress in 1992—and one of the things she used against me was my opposition to the "max-black" plan

in a majority black district. There were five people in the race and I always say I came in sixth.

Thurmond further explains that he had formulated his objection to the "max-black" strategy while he was a summer student at Harvard University in the early 1990s: "I spent a summer at the Kennedy School, and one of my professors was a Republican strategist. One day at lunch he was explaining to me that the real strategy the Republicans were going to use to their benefit was 'bleaching' as many white districts as possible and concentrating blacks. It worked. . . . At this point the federal judiciary and the Attorney General's offices were all basically Republican."

The new redistricting guidelines essentially set up the scenario that Michael Thurmond predicted. Two new majority black districts were created, but the new reapportionment plan also resulted in three new Republicans being elected to the U.S. House of Representatives in the 1992 elections. Jack Kingston from Savannah, John Linder from the northeast Atlanta suburbs, and Mac Collins from Middle Georgia joined Newt Gingrich in Washington in January 1993. In this election cycle, Gingrich took advantage of the opportunity to move from South Atlanta to a much safer seat in the new sixth district comprised mostly of Cobb and North Fulton counties. The two new African-American Democrats from Georgia were Cynthia McKinney and Sanford Bishop, who joined John Lewis in Congress for that term. Consequently, only four white Democrats remained in the Georgia delegation, two of whom were newly elected that year. Georgia political scientist Charles Bullock III provides a reflective analysis of the 1991 congressional redistricting: "The gerrymandering devastated white Democrats' office-holding ambitions in Georgia's Congressional districts following the 1992 Voting Rights Act arguments by the Department of Justice to expand black political influence. The direct impact resulted from concentrating black voters, the most loyal Democrats, so that the adjacent bleached districts became more Republican."[4]

The most significant Republican victory in Georgia in 1992 was Paul Coverdell's defeat of Democrat Wyche Fowler in the U.S. Senate race. Coverdell had left the state Senate in the late 1980s to serve in Washington under President George H. W. Bush as director of the Peace Corps. In his race against the incumbent Fowler, Coverdell hired a team of professional consultants including Tom Perdue as campaign manager and Whit Ayers as pollster. Tom Perdue had previously served as Governor Harris's chief of staff and was a conservative strategist now turned Republican. In a series of television ads, Coverdell employed a rural, grandmotherly type to sing a political ditty that effectively tarnished Fowler as too liberal for Georgia. Paul Coverdell also campaigned tirelessly in all parts of the state and not only attracted the traditional Republican base of upper-income metropolitan whites but also many rural and small town white voters in both the northern and southern parts of the state. He polled 35,000 votes behind Fowler in the general election, but a Libertarian candidate on the ballot forced a runoff, since Fowler failed to get the majority of all votes cast, as was then required under Georgia law.

Only slightly more than half the number of citizens who had participated in the general election voted in the runoff race, and Coverdell came from behind to win. He carried 74 counties and won 635,114 votes or 50.6 percent of the total cast in the runoff, a margin of only 16,237 votes more than Fowler received. Bob Irvin offers an explanation for Coverdell's success in the runoff election: "We [Republicans] had always had a long history of being able to mobilize to win special elections, and Paul was able to do that." Dick Pettys offers a more succinct journalistic analysis of the Coverdell victory. "I think there was buyer's remorse with Wyche. He was not the moderate that people thought they were electing. He was liberal, and so Coverdell dispatched him." In the 1992 general election, Republican Bobby Baker also won a seat on the Public Service Commission, thereby becoming the first Republican to be elected statewide to a constitutional office in Georgia in the twentieth century.

In this same election year, Republicans won fifty-two seats in the Georgia House, an impressive and record gain of seventeen new representatives. The GOP also picked up six more seats in the state Senate, giving them a new high of seventeen senators. However, Georgians once again demonstrated their propensity to split tickets, as a majority of voters cast their presidential ballots for a Democrat and fellow southerner, Bill Clinton, the former governor of Arkansas, in his race against the incumbent President George H. W. Bush. 1992 was the first presidential election year since 1980 (and the last to date) in which a Democratic candidate carried the state of Georgia.

1994 turned out to be the most important year for Republican victories in the Georgia congressional delegation, but it was a year for another defeat of the GOP in the governor's race. Three members of the GOP won new congressional seats that year—Saxby Chambliss, a Moultrie attorney; Bob Barr, an attorney from the northwest Atlanta suburbs; and Charlie

Norwood, a dentist from Augusta—and these victories gave the GOP a majority in the Georgia congressional delegation for the first time in the history of the state. Two of the defeated Democrats, Buddy Darden of Cobb County and Don Johnson of Augusta, had voted in 1994 for a President Clinton-sponsored tax increase, and their Republican opponents successfully used that issue again them. Most importantly for Georgia, Newt Gingrich was elected Speaker of the U.S. House of Representatives on the strength of his leadership in drafting a Republican Party "Contract with America" and for engineering a Republican takeover of the House after forty years of Democratic rule. The GOP won fifty-four additional seats in Congress that year, and many were from southern states. Rusty Paul, who served from 1995 to 1999 as chairman of the Georgia Republican Party, describes these victories as "the culmination of, at the time, 30 to 35 years of changes that had been occurring in the State of Georgia."[5]

In addition to recognizing Newt Gingrich's leadership in the Republican House victories, professors Earl and Merle Black attribute much of the GOP success in winning a majority in Congress in the early 1990s to the foundation for victory laid by Ronald Reagan during his presidency.

> In the South the Reagan realignment of the 1980s was a momentous achievement. By transforming the region's white electorate, Ronald Reagan's presidency made possible the Republican Congressional breakthrough in the 1990s. . . . Reagan's optimistic conservatism and successful performance in office made the Republican Party respectable and useful for millions of southern whites. Reagan attracted a majority of white conservatives into the Republican Party and persuaded many conservatives to think of themselves as 'independents," rather than as Democrats.[6]

When the 104th Congress convened in early 1995, Democratic representative Nathan Deal from northeast Georgia and four other southern Democrats switched parties. According to former House Republican minority leader Steve Stancil, Deal was influenced to make the change by Newt Gingrich, who had already recruited the popular Stancil to run as a Republican and oppose Deal in the next congressional election.[7] Deal was apparently sufficiently convinced by Gingrich's influence and the threat of Stancil's competition that he did switch parties, even though he had won his 1994 race with 58 percent of the district vote. The mix of Georgia's House delegation had changed dramatically in less than three years from one white Republican, one African-American Democrat, and eight white Democrats to no white Democrats, three African-American Democrats, and eight white Republicans. State representative Bob Holmes describes his personal reaction and that of the Georgia Democratic Party: "It was a major shock, honestly, to me and to the political system. I thought there would be a more gradual and evolutionary kind of development and emergence, but this was just a quantum leap. . . . Of course it didn't affect Georgia as much in terms of the state. We were still in the top two or three most Democratic states in terms of elected officials."

Republicans did continue to make significant gains in the state legislature in the 1994 election cycle, however. The GOP picked up an additional fourteen seats in the House for a total of sixty-six. Republicans won four more seats in the Senate to claim a new high total of twenty-one. The GOP also picked up two other significant wins in 1994 when Republicans Linda Schrenko and John Oxendine defeated Democratic candidates to win stateside victories as State School Superintendent and Commissioner of Insurance. Also, Nancy Schaefer, the Republican candidate for lieutenant governor, polled 42.5 percent of the votes (the strongest showing to date by a GOP candidate for this seat) in her race against the popular incumbent, Democrat Pierre Howard. 1994 was the first election year in which Republican candidates filed for and ran in every congressional district and for every state constitutional office that was elected on a statewide basis.

Also in the 1994 election cycle, the well-liked and respected and thrice-elected Democratic attorney general Mike Bowers switched to the Republican Party, apparently in anticipation of making a future run for governor. John Watson, who later served as Bowers's campaign manager in his 1998 gubernatorial election bid, explains Bowers's strategy: "Mike Bowers was the Democratic longtime attorney general. He had been appointed by Arthur Bolton as a 34-year-old attorney general. Then he ran successfully three times, and then before standing for election the fourth time, he switched in 1994. So, Mike came in on that wave. That was an orchestrated switch in prelude to a gubernatorial run in 1998."[8]

The great disappointment for the Georgia GOP in 1994 was the loss of the governor's office by a slim margin. Wealthy businessman and longtime Republican financial supporter, Guy Millner, challenged incumbent governor Zell Miller. Millner was raised in Florida in a Democratic family, as most southerners were. According to him, "Goldwater turned me Republican."[9] Millner had a long history of supporting Republican candidates. He was active as a primary fundraiser for Mack Mattingly in his two Senate campaigns and served as finance chair for Republican businessman Bob Bell in his 1982 gubernatorial race. He also worked closely with Paul Coverdell to grow the party in the 1980s and was a leading fundraiser in Coverdell's 1992 senatorial campaign. Millner won an impressive victory in the four-candidate Republican primary contest, besting the largest field of GOP contenders to date.

In addition to running against the rising Republican tide, Zell Miller had alienated a number of Georgia voters in his advocacy for a new state flag without the St. Andrews cross, an emblem also displayed in the flag of the Confederate States of America. In a 1993 press conference, Miller explained his reason for wanting to change the state flag: "The present Georgia flag with its stars and bars was adopted in the dawning days of the civil rights era. What we fly today is not an enduring symbol of our heritage, but the fighting flag of those who want to preserve a segregated South in the face of the civil rights movement. It is time we shake completely free of that era."[10] Miller himself admits to the political damage: "The flag flap almost did me in. . . . In 1993 I gave it my best shot. I called the legislative leadership in and made my pitch. They said I was crazy. . . . I then spoke to different groups of legislative leaders, veteran legislators, rising stars, Republicans and freshmen. . . . I failed to persuade them. I just made them mad."[11] On the other hand, Miller had successfully passed the new lottery for education to fund merit-based scholarships for college students and established a statewide four-year-old pre-kindergarten program, and these programs made a lot of Georgia voters happy.

Millner mounted an aggressive campaign for governor and came as close to winning the governor's office as any Republican had since Bo Callaway in 1966. Millner captured 756,371 votes, or 48.95 percent of the total, to Zell Miller's 788,926 votes or 51.05 percent. Perhaps most significantly, Millner garnered support from a much broader geographic territory than Isakson did in 1990, as he won in seventy-five counties. In his own assessment of the campaign, Guy Millner states, "Zell was, you know, a very good campaigner, and I was green as a gourd, and you got a real novice against a real pro. The truth is I probably should not have gotten as close as I did." While most people attribute Miller's narrow margin of victory to the popular HOPE scholarship program that he created from the proceeds of the new Georgia lottery, state senator Jack Hill provides an additional dimension to the analysis of Miller's victory: "The thing I think really helped Zell was the (Flint River) flood of 1994. In this huge crisis, Georgia really shined. The state departments really came together and clicked. There was absolutely no criticism. . . . I think Zell's popularity started to turn a corner here. His fortunes turned because of the way he handled that."[12]

Arguably, Zell Miller and the leadership of the Georgia Democratic Party also moved toward more conservative political positions on some social issues during his first term as governor. As an example of this shift in policy, the Georgia General Assembly passed SB441, the Sentence Reform Act of 1994, which provided for a minimum sentence for any person convicted for the first time of any of seven serious violent felonies. The law further provided that any person convicted by a jury of a second serious violent felony would serve a mandatory minimum sentence of life in prison with no parole. Governor Miller approved and signed this new "tough-on-crime" law. Miller vividly recounts his reasons for backing this legislation:

> The sentence "life in prison" has long been one of the biggest frauds in our judicial system. The so-called "life sentence" actually amounts to eleven to thirteen years behind bars, and in some states even fewer. Victims and their families deserve better than this. Justice demands better than this. That is why I created in Georgia the nation's only two strikes law for violent felonies. That's right—two, not three, like the feds have. Three strikes is for baseball, not for those who commit violent crimes.

In addition to this tough–on-crime law, the Miller administration also supported the Clinton administration's welfare reform initiative. In addition and in cooperation with the legislature and the federal government, the Miller administration also developed a new state health insurance program called "Peachcare for Kids," designed to help children whose families could not easily afford traditional commercial health insurance. These more conservative political actions quite likely helped Miller to retain broad-based support in Georgia as he sought a second term.

One of Zell Miller's biographers reports that the Miller campaign surveyed Georgia citizens before the election and that the survey showed Miller had a 70 percent approval rate for the job he was doing as governor. This Miller biographer also quotes a national political journal that reported Miller "was writing the book on how a Democratic governor can flourish in a new Republican state."[13] As a result of his popularity and the desire of the Democratic Party to maintain control of the state political apparatus, most state Democratic Party leaders and elected officials rallied around Miller in his reelection campaign.

The close race between Miller and Millner was expensive for the candidates and their parties that year. Reportedly, the two candidates spent a record combined $9.2 million.[14] State Senate leader Eric Johnson comments on the benefits of Millner's substantial investment in his own campaign: "It was nice to have a guy who could self-fund, and the closeness of his race showed that a good [Republican] candidate with sufficient resources could win. . . . He came damn close to Zell."[15] Party chairman Rusty Paul also comments on Millner's importance to the GOP electoral efforts: "He [Millner] made a huge, huge contribution to the Republican Party. . . . Guy brought wealth to the Party, and he basically raised a lot of money for his campaign. He was able to self-fund his campaign, so it gave us a tremendous amount of freedom and flexibility. Since he was funding the governor's race . . . we could take the resources that we developed and target the legislature." When asked about his investments in his own campaign, Millner acknowledged that he had indeed invested several million dollars of his personal wealth, but he had a somewhat different perspective on the state party's role in providing campaign funding in this race: "The Georgia Republican Party was not, in these elections, ever equipped with a lot of funds. It was funds coming out of the national party, and I was always supported to the maximum extent they could."

Representative Bob Holmes provides a Democratic perspective on the first Millner candidacy: "Well, I think anyone who can self-finance his campaign is a threat because if you can get your message out . . . you're going to win some support. And I think he reflected a sense to some people, even some Democrats, that maybe we do need to have a more business-oriented type of government. . . . You knew he had the base, but did he have the crossover appeal?"

Dick Pettys provides a new reporter's perspective on Millner's first run for governor: "When he was running for office I was on him like white on rice because there was no real reason for him to run other than the fact that he had money. And he never made the case there was anything beyond that. Although I suspect that if he had been elected governor he would have been a pretty good governor. 1994 was the high-water mark. They ran a good campaign, but Miller ran a better campaign."

In 1996 Guy Millner again emerged as a statewide candidate, this time for a U.S. Senate seat. Veteran Georgia Democratic senator Sam Nunn decided not to seek reelection, and so his seat all of a sudden became an open one. Johnny Isakson planned to run as a Republican for this seat, and apparently he thought he had a commitment from Guy Millner to assist in his campaign. Then Millner decided that he would also run for the seat. Isakson loyalist Jay Morgan explains the reaction in the Isakson camp: "He [Millner] committed to be Isakson's finance chairman for the Senate race in 1996. That race was probably more hurtful than any race I recall for all of us that were Isakson people. It was because Guy really betrayed us." Millner defends his decision to run by arguing that he was recruited by several party officials to seek the open Senate seat. "I was recruited by Billy Lovett [who served as the Republican Party Chairman in Georgia from 1992 to 1995]. That was the race where, you know, Sam Nunn stepped down unexpectedly or said he wasn't going to run. . . . So I was the obvious person to step in, having just run." No doubt Millner's willingness to substantially self-fund his own campaign also gained him some support among other of the party leaders at the time.

Millner placed first in the six-person primary race, winning almost 42 percent of the ballots cast, and Isakson polled second with almost 35 percent of the votes. Despite the competitiveness of a contest between two strong candidates in the Republican primary, few Georgians bothered to vote that year. Only 12.9 percent of the electorate cast votes in the GOP primary, compared with 19.9 percent of the state's registered voters participating in the Democratic primary, for a total of roughly 33 percent voter participation. In the runoff, Millner outpolled Isakson by some 18,000 votes to win 52.8 percent of the total. To a large extent, the Republican primary battle revolved around abortion rights issues and which of the candidates was the most conservative one to represent Georgia in the Senate.

Nevertheless, the Republican Party once again failed to secure a victory. In the general election, Democrat Max Cleland, Georgia's popular former secretary of state, outpolled Millner by 30,024 votes out of almost one and a quarter million votes cast to win 48.9 percent to 47.6 percent over Millner, with a Libertarian candidate receiving the remaining votes. Following Wyche Fowler's defeat in a runoff in 1992, the voting laws had been changed so that a 50 percent majority was no longer required, and Cleland was declared the outright victor. For Millner it was another expensive race in which he spent some $9.8 million, of which he invested approximately $6.4 million personally. Cleland spent only $2.9 million.[16] As in his 1994 gubernatorial race, Millner's largely self-funded Senate campaign allowed the party to divert resources it might have otherwise used to contest the Senate seat to support other congressional and state legislative candidates, thus broadening the party base. Then party chairman Rusty Paul explains, "Millner put a lot of his own wealth into it, and this freed me up to raise resources . . . to devote strictly to legislative races. We were able to put about a million dollars each cycle into legislative races. Without Guy we would not have been able to do that."

In 1996, former Republican Party executive director David Shafer, who later was elected as a state senator from Gwinnett County, ran for the secretary of state position that opened up when Max Cleland resigned to run for the U.S. Senate. Governor Miller had appointed Lewis Massey as the Democratic secretary of state to replace Cleland, and Massey also ran for election to the seat for the two-year remainder of the term. Following a four-person Republican primary race Shafer was cast into a bitter runoff with former state representative Willou Smith. Shafer won the runoff but lost decisively to Massey, who captured 53.8 percent of the votes in the general election.

During the decade of the 1990s, the Georgia House, the Senate, and the Republican Party organization each developed initiatives to recruit and train candidates for the state legislature and other elected offices. The party continued to make good use of the ORVIS technology to identify House and Senate districts where a majority of the voters supported Republicans in congressional elections but were still represented by a Democrat in the General Assembly.

In 1993, House minority leader Steve Stancil asked his longtime family friend, Representative Garland Pinholster, to serve as vice chair of the Republican caucus and specifically to step up the pace in recruiting Republican candidates in those districts that had been identified through the ORVIS technology. Pinholster, who was called "Coach" by his close associates, was a fitting choice for the job. In his younger life, he had been a successful high school and college basketball coach and later was a successful grocery merchant. Party chairman Rusty Paul describes Pinholster's suitability for this assignment: "Garland Pinholster was basically the recruiter. He was briefly an old college and high school basketball coach and believed that recruiting was key to your success. Garland was the best recruiter that ever lived on the face of the Earth." The "Coach" called his new recruitment program "91 in Y2K," a name reflecting the Republican ambition to become majority party in the Georgia House of Representatives by the year 2000. Pinholster and Stancil were joined in their recruitment efforts by Bob Irvin, the newly chosen House minority leader who had been reelected to the

House in 1992 (after he had taken a break in service of several years to earn a Harvard MBA and begin a new business consulting practice), and by Representative Mike Evans of Forsyth County who was elected to the House in 1992 and was selected as GOP caucus chairman in 1995.

The program was remarkably successful in that the party ultimately achieved its goal, although it took four years longer than Y2K. Pinholster expressed that he preferred to recruit candidates who were already successful in business or professions and who had already attained some level of self-confidence and recognition for their life work before becoming legislators, based on his theory that legislators who had already been successful in a career would be better able to deal with the considerable pressures of the General Assembly.[17] He also reported that the candidates he recruited were provided substantial assistance in their campaigns, including guidance and advice on organizing a campaign team, voter lists and telephone numbers, speech-making aids, signage and promotional material, guidance in operating a campaign office, research on the opposition, and assistance in fundraising and getting out the votes.

The 91 in Y2K program in the House also reached out to Republican candidates to help them understand key legislative issues and formulate party position statements regarding those issues. Pinholster acknowledges that the GOP leadership in the House would set up floor debates on certain controversial issues in targeted legislative districts by proposing amendments to bills on the floor of the House pertaining to issues where a local community position and the Republican position might be at variance with the opinion of Democratic House leadership. Stancil called these "sucker votes" since all votes were registered on public record, and the vote of an incumbent Democrat lining up with House leadership in opposition to local community interests could be used against a Democratic incumbent by a Republican challenger in the next general election. As an example, Bob Irvin relates that the 85 percent sentencing proposal developed by Attorney General Mike Bowers (after he switched to the Republican Party) was one such issue that Republican candidates were able to use against incumbent Democrats in the 1990s. Essentially, the 85 percent rule provided that individuals convicted of the most serious felonies could not be eligible for parole until they had served at last 85 percent of their judicial sentence. According to Irvin, the Democratic leadership of the House initially opposed the legislation and urged their members to vote against it. Irvin explains that several Republican winners in 1996 legislative races were aided in their victories by running against incumbent Democrats who voted against the 85 percent rule.

Mid-'90s state GOP party chairman Rusty Paul explains how the Republican Party in Georgia further assisted the House and Senate candidates they recruited:

> We put together what we called a Republican Entitlement Program. . . . We took a group of young men and women, mostly college kids, and we trained them how to manage campaigns. We gave them ten things to do. It was everything from submitting a campaign plan to raising "x" amount of dollars to meeting weekly with their party's campaign manager. We had existing legislators serve as mentors, and they had to talk to them so many times during the course of the campaign and get advice and counsel. . . . We could promise for a House seat up to $15,000 and for a Senate seat $15,000 to $20,000 in goods and services and reduced costs. . . . We forced candidates to go out and really engage voters. That was the most successful thing we did. We had a threshold of a certain number of houses that you had to go out and knock on a certain number of doors before we would consider funding.

In 1995, Rusty Paul recruited John Watson onto the staff of the Georgia Republican Party. Watson was a northern Virginian and Wake Forest University graduate who had known Paul when they were both working for different congressmen in Washington, D.C. Watson recalls some of the Republican Party activities in the mid 1990s, as they strategized and organized to run against Democrats:

> We were doing grass-roots, organizational block and tackle politics. The Democrats were continuing to win but they were an atrophying political machine. They weren't exercising their muscles. They weren't working to have an organizational structure that could get out and run a grass roots campaign. . . . The Republicans weren't winning, but they were working out. They were building the lists. They were building the donor base. They were building county chairmen. They were doing things that ultimately would reap victory.

Among those current congressional or state legislative representatives that Pinholster identified as having been supported by the Republican caucus and/or recruited into the General Assembly during the years of the 91 in Y2K program are current Speaker Glenn Richardson, state House majority leader Jerry Keen, Congressman Lynn Westmoreland, state representatives Vance Smith, Amos Amerson, Ron Stephens, Ben Bridges, and Roger Williams, and Public Service commissioner Doug Everett. House Speaker Glenn Richardson recollects that while he received support from the Republican Party and the House recruitment team in his first House race in 1996, the assistance he received was seemingly more meager than Rusty Paul implies was available to new GOP candidates: "I think they wanted to help, and their hearts were in the right place, but I don't recall getting any financial support that amounted to anything, maybe $1,000. They did assign me a person who was going to help me run my campaign, and that was John Watson."[18] Richardson does commend the mentor system that the Republican Party provided to new House members when he took office in early 1997, saying, "Earl [Ehrhart] was my appointed mentor, and he showed me where everything was and told me what to do, which is the basis for our strong friendship."

By the late 1990s the tide began to turn in the direction of the Republican Party in Georgia after many years of organizing for success. Bob Irvin recollects his impressions of when the changing tides first became evident to him: "I always remember the 1995 state Republican convention was in Savannah. It was the first convention that I ever saw lobbyists come to . . . all of a sudden hosting hospitality rooms. That was the year after the congressional sweep of 1994. We picked up fourteen seats in Georgia in 1994." The chart below summarizes the considerable progress made by the Republican Party in gaining seats in the Georgia General Assembly in the early and mid-1990s:

YEAR	REPUBLICAN HOUSE MEMBERS	REPUBLICAN SENATORS
1991	35	11
1993	52	17
1995	66	21
1997	79	22

The state House of Representatives made the greatest strides with the GOP picking up seventeen seats in the 1992 election, fourteen in 1994, and thirteen more in 1996. Among future leaders elected in 1992 were current Speaker Pro-Tem Mark Burkhalter, representing a newly created district in North Fulton County; Mike Evans of Forsyth County; future congressman Lynn Westmoreland, a real-estate development and construction company owner from Coweta County; and current Senate President Pro-Tem Eric

Johnson. Johnson was first elected to the state House seat formerly held by his close Chatham County associate Jack Kingston, who successfully ran for Congress that year. Former House minority leader Johnny Isakson and current Senate Rules Chairman Don Balfour were elected to the state Senate that year. In 1994, current House Appropriations Chairman Ben Harbin of Columbia County was first elected, and Lieutenant Governor Casey Cagle and Eric Johnson were elected to the Senate. In 1996, Speaker Glenn Richardson and Representative Austin Scott of Tifton were first elected to the House, and Congressman Tom Price was elected to the state Senate.

Rusty Paul also indicates that while he was party chairman in the 1990s, the party apparatus began targeting more electoral opportunities for local offices and started providing more help to Republican candidates for municipal offices: "We tested our theory in mayoral races around the state. We picked seven or eight cities just to test—there were several cities—Savannah, Newnan, Dalton, and Macon. A lot of municipal elections are odd-year elections. We tested our concept in some of those cities, totally under the radar. . . . We won a majority of these mayoral races."[19]

Political scientists point to two trends that emerged in the mid-1990s that also helped the Georgia GOP elect more of their candidates than ever before. One was the surge in voting in Republican primary elections. As described by political scientist David Sturrock, "Many more people began to vote in Republican primaries in the South because they began to think of themselves as Republicans."[20] At the same time, there were an even greater number of Republicans moving into Georgia and the South in the 1990s. The growth of the Republican base in the suburbs of Atlanta and in Coastal Georgia provided more potential candidates as well as more Republican voters.

As the Republican Party began to grow and experience greater success in .Georgia, Senator Paul Coverdell continued to provide leadership in the development of the party infrastructure. One of his most enduring contributions was the creation of a leadership training program for Republicans, which former party executive counsel Frank Strickland describes: "Just on a gradual basis you had more and more people become interested in running for the state House or Senate, and then Paul Coverdell began a program . . . now called the Coverdell Leadership Institute . . . for the purpose of developing a cadre of people and really training them for public service, and a fair number have carried out that mission." On its website, the Coverdell Leadership Institute describes its mission as strengthening political and leadership skills; securing better government and successful candidates; broadening the knowledge of government and political processes in Georgia; and increasing the participation of Georgia Republicans in and promoting their leadership of government at the state and local levels. The first class was convened in 1996, and since then several hundred emerging GOP leaders have participated in the institute.

In the minds of many Republican stalwarts, 1998 was supposed to be the year that the momentum of the Republican Party, as reflected by its gains in the Georgia congressional delegation and in both chambers of the General Assembly, was going to catapult the party to victory in the governor's race. At the time, Governor Zell Miller was completing his second term and was ineligible to run again. Popular and appealing Attorney General Mike Bowers, who had switched to the Republican Party in 1994, was thought to be the leading GOP candidate for governor. Bowers, a West Point graduate and retired major general in the Air National Guard, was first appointed as attorney general in 1981 and ran successfully three times as a Democrat before he changed parties and was reelected for the fourth time as Georgia's first Republican attorney general since 1868. It was presumed he would run against well-regarded two-term Democratic lieutenant governor Pierre Howard. According to UGA political scientist Charles Bullock III, Bowers was considered to be the strongest GOP gubernatorial candidate since Bo Callaway, and many Republicans also dared to hope they might win other constitutional offices and perhaps even gain control of one house of the legislature.[21] However, the Bowers team had barely begun their campaign in June 1997 before the popular candidate was obliged to admit to a ten-year extramarital affair with his former legal secretary who had also been a former Playboy Club waitress. He immediately lost his edge in the GOP primary.

Bowers stayed in the Republican governor's race, but in a hotly contested primary campaign he lost to Guy Millner, who for the third time in four years once again stepped forward to become the Republican Party standard bearer. Millner won 50.4 percent of the vote with Bowers polling 40 percent and conservative candidate Nancy Schaefer getting 7.7 percent of the vote in a four-person primary contest. John Watson, who served as Bowers's campaign chair, describes how Guy Millner ended up as Bowers's rival in the primary election:

> Prior to Mike making his announcement [about his extramarital affair], it was as big a love fest as I had ever seen. We had donors upon donors lining up to max out. . . . Mike personally is very gregarious, incredibly smart, a

West Pointer. It was just a fairy tale description of a governor and a candidate. After the revelation of Mike's marital problems is when Guy got into that race. Rightfully, he saw an opportunity, a weakness in a candidate. . . . We lost by a thousand votes of getting Bowers into a runoff.

In the Democratic campaign for the gubernatorial nomination, the presumed frontrunner, Pierre Howard, dropped out of the race in January 1998, and respected Democratic legislator Roy Barnes jumped into the contest and won the greatest number of votes in the June primary among a field of six candidates, including recently elected Secretary of State Lewis Massey and well-known former labor commissioner David Poythress. In a move toward party unity, Massey dropped out of the primary runoff, handing the Democratic nomination to Barnes. Roy Barnes proved to be an effective campaigner and defeated Guy Millner in the general election, taking 52.5 percent of the vote to Millner's 44.1 percent. Millner actually won in only forty-one counties, far fewer than the seventy-five counties he swept in his first race for governor in 1994. The governor's election that year also turned out to be the most expensive ever at just over $27 million, with the Barnes campaign raising and spending $10.9 million and the Millner team expending over $16 million with the candidate himself again funding a significant portion of his costs. Much of the money was spent on expensive television advertising messaging.[22]

Although Guy Millner was able to garner significant support from the traditional Republican base in the suburban counties of Atlanta and other urban centers around the state, he was simply unable to connect sufficiently with rural voters to earn the additional votes he needed to win a statewide majority. No doubt he had diminished his appeal to rural Georgia voters in his first run for governor when he told a group of university students, "You are not going to see me in parades on a Saturday down in Vidalia because that is not where the votes are and that's not where the fundraising will be."[23] Not surprisingly, Guy Millner lost Vidalia/Toombs County to Roy Barnes in the 1998 gubernatorial election, and he failed to win the majority of votes in most other rural areas of Georgia that were critical "swing districts" needed for a statewide victory.

Although Republicans John Oxendine and Linda Schrenko handily won their reelections, the GOP was further frustrated in 1998 by the failure of Republican candidates to win any new constitutional offices that were open seats in that year. GOP challengers lost to Democratic opponents in races for the posts of lieutenant governor, secretary of state, attorney general, and commissioner of labor. The GOP also failed once again to win a majority of either house of the state legislature and in fact actually lost a seat in the House, retaining only seventy-eight seats. Republicans made no further gains in the state Senate but retained their twenty-two seats. Notably, two future Republican Senate majority leaders, Bill Stephens and Tommie Williams, were first elected that year. Williams was the first Republican to be elected to the state Senate from the Democratic rural area of Southeast Georgia.

Political scholar Charles Bullock attributes the Democratic sweep in 1998 to a "record black turnout" and notes that African Americans were candidates in three statewide races: for attorney general, which Democrat Thurbert Baker won; for commissioner of labor, which Democrat Michael Thurmond won; and insurance commissioner, which Henrietta Canty lost to John Oxendine.[24] Guy Millner shares Bullock's opinion about the high black turnout being a significant factor in the 1998 statewide races, stating, "In that year, you recall, that was a Democratic year across the country. If you look at the breakdown on votes, you'll find that the minority vote in Georgia went from 360,000 in 1994 to 540,000 in 1998, and I lost 92 percent of that vote." Millner actually received a smaller percentage of the general election vote in the 1998 governor's race than he had in 1994. He self-critiques his 1998 campaign for governor by commenting, "You know you do wear out your welcome, and in that third race . . . there was probably an element in the party that suggested, well, he's run twice and lost, let's find somebody who can win."

Michael Thurmond attributes much of the strong showing by Democrats in statewide races in 1998 to the overall strength of the ticket with Roy Barnes, Mark Taylor, Cathy Cox, Thurbert Baker, Michael Thurmond, Henrietta Canty, Tommy Irvin, Joe Martin, and Michael Coles. Only Canty, Martin, and Coles lost, all to incumbent Republicans. Thurmond comments, "The ticket helped—just the fact that we ran as a ticket. We had a strong one with Cathy Cox, and we had rural and urban, black and white, men and women, and I just think we had a strong ticket and everybody benefited from each other being on the ticket more than anything else in 1998." In addition, overall voter registration increased in Georgia in 1998 with almost 300,000 more voters registered for the general election that year than were registered for the 1996 presidential election.

The most significant Republican victory in 1998 was Paul Coverdell's reelection to the U.S. Senate. He outpolled cookie entrepreneur Michael Coles, taking 52.4 percent of the votes. Paul Coverdell thus became the first

Republican U.S. senator from Georgia to win a second term since the days of Reconstruction. In contrast to Guy Millner, Paul Coverdell was able to generate sufficient support among the voters in rural Georgia to win a majority of the votes in a large number of "swing districts" around the state, including a number of rural counties that Democrat Roy Barnes won in the gubernatorial race that year. Coverdell spent $6.9 million in the Senate race, compared to $5.3 million spent by Michael Coles. According to a vote analysis, Coverdell won approximately 70 percent of the white vote but only 10 percent of the black vote. He carried the Republican-rich Atlanta suburbs but also won many rural counties in North and South Georgia.[25]

One notable achievement for the Georgia Republican Party in 1998 was state senator Sonny Perdue's decision to switch from the Democratic Party to the Republican Party just before the qualifying date in the spring of that year. Perdue, a successful businessman from Houston County in Middle Georgia, first served in public office in 1980, when he was appointed to the Houston County Planning and Zoning Board, and he chaired the board for the last five years of his term of service. In 1990 he was successful in his bid to be elected to the state Senate from the eighteenth district to represent Houston, Bleckley, Pulaski, and a portion of Bibb counties.

Perdue's keen intellect and strong leadership qualities were quickly recognized by his Democratic brethren in the Senate, and he rose rapidly through the ranks. In 1993 he was appointed as chair of the Senate Higher Education Committee, two years later he was selected as Senate majority leader, and in 1997 he was elected president pro-tempore of the Senate. In the legislative directory for 1999/2000, Perdue was described as "one of the body's most effective consensus builders."[26] As a Democrat he also served on the powerful Appropriations, Rules, and Ethics Committees and was appointed to represent Georgia on the prestigious Southern Growth Policies Board.

State senator George Hooks, now the "dean of the Senate," based on his long service in the legislature, assesses Perdue's rapid rise through the ranks of the Senate: "Sonny was popular, he was low-key, he was from the right part of the state [not surprisingly, Perdue's district was adjacent to Hooks's district!], he got along with everybody, and frankly the man that took him forward was Pierre Howard. Pierre adopted him, so that's how he got where he was."[27] Perdue comments on his close working relationship in the state Senate with Pierre Howard: "Pierre and I came from different perspectives. Pierre was from Decatur, and I was from Bonaire . . . but I came to frankly respect and love Pierre because I thought he was a compassionate person who cared about people mostly. . . . So I found myself being his primary implementer in the Senate. . . . He empowered me to speak for him. Lewis Massey, obviously, was his closest aide, but in the body I think I became his closest ally."[28]

In the late 1990s, Perdue became somewhat disquieted about some of the compromised decisions the state Democratic Party had to make in order to maintain the fragile coalition among mostly conservative rural whites, liberal urban whites, and the blacks who were becoming an increasingly important political force within the Democratic Party. Perdue elaborates on his thought process:

> I had become increasingly concerned about the direction of Georgia. The Democratic Party was, I thought, fractionalized in reaching the broad interests of our state. The African Americans in our state—due to redistricting and due to the efforts of really mandating districts in which they could get elected—had an interesting hold on the Democratic Party, in that they were a minority of the Democratic Party, but every Democrat needed the African-American vote—in the General Assembly and otherwise—to be successful. And so they used that very astutely and very wisely, in order to take the state in a direction that I didn't think the mainstream of Georgia was. I expressed this to my colleagues. . . . I cautioned them that if they continued allowing a minority of the majority to determine the agenda, then it would be to the detriment of those people in conservative areas. You had a lot of conservative Democrats still left at that time, of which I included myself. I thought it would be to the detriment of those conservative Democrats who could not go back home to their districts and justify some of the things that they were doing.

Perdue was particularly troubled by the apparent self-dealing of Senator Charles Walker, who succeeded Perdue as Senate majority leader. When asked why he thought Perdue had changed parties, Senator Jack Hill, who was a close friend and confidante of Perdue's and shared an Atlanta apartment with him during several legislative sessions, replied, "There had been some pretty serious problems. It was just obvious that Senator Walker wasn't somebody anyone could keep their finger on. Sonny Perdue, being the kind of person he is, felt a lot of responsibility for the Party and for the leadership. He was unable to control that [Walker]."

When Perdue was selected by the Senate Democratic Caucus as president pro-tem, he had nominated and supported Jack Hill to succeed him as majority leader in the Senate. To the surprise of many, Charles Walker put together a coalition of supporters and defeated Hill for this influential position. Perdue comments on his opinion of Charles Walker's election: "I thought it was an unwise decision from a Senate perspective. It was very disappointing for me to see the Senate choose Charles Walker over a very honorable man like Jack Hill for that position. Well, I probably think I hurt Jack Hill, in that they felt like Jack and I were too close, and they didn't want both of us to have those two positions."

Labor Commissioner Michael Thurmond comments on his perception of the disagreements between Perdue and Walker: "I knew about the war—at least the disagreements—he [Perdue] was having with Charles Walker in particular. It was almost legend, their dislike for each other . . . that's what was generally understood—just two strong personalities in a relatively small geopolitical, geographic area which is the Senate." Veteran AP reporter Dick Pettys assesses the Walker-Perdue conflict from his vantage point:

> It was obvious that he and Charles Walker were just at loggerheads. And it wasn't just policy, and it wasn't politics—clearly, it was personal. Charles apparently knew how to push all Sonny's buttons and did with glee and great satisfaction. And Sonny just had a belly full of it. I mean this is me assuming these things. . . . It's like two magnets when you get a positive and a positive, you going to have sparks fly. I'm sitting here visualizing Charles, and I see him. He had a particular way of grinning after he had just gutted you, and I can just visualize or imagine him doing that to Sonny.

In their comments, both Thurmond and Pettys overlook Perdue's primary concern with Charles Walker, which was the use of his leadership position in the Senate to self-deal for personal gain, for which he was later indicted and convicted of several crimes. As Jack Hill notes, he and Perdue were concerned that Charles Walker was using his leadership position in the state Senate to arrange improper and undisclosed service contracts between his personal business interests and various governmental entities. As president pro-tem of the Senate, Perdue was certainly in a position to observe any suspicious business arrangements between governmental agencies and Walker's personal interests; and although he was not alone in the Senate in suspecting untoward activity by Walker, no doubt he was frustrated by the lack of consensus among the Democratic Party leadership in Georgia about the need for a concerted investigation into Walker's business arrangements to the end result that changing political parties may have seemed the most rational alternative for him personally in order to deal with this moral dilemma.

As a social and fiscal conservative, Perdue also experienced discomfort with some of the more liberal positions adopted by the national Democratic Party, such as that on abortion. Political scientist David Lublin comments on how the abortion rights issue played out in the late twentieth century: "More recent scholarship points to rising social issues as spurring greater identification with the Republicans among southerners. Many discussions on social issues focus almost exclusively on abortion rights because it is a highly emotional issue for advocates on both sides of the intense debate surrounding this topic."[29] Perdue's close aide Morgan Perry Cook, who worked with him in the Senate and later became his first legislative affairs director when he was elected governor, suggests that the abortion debate may have been a strong influencing factor in Perdue's decision to switch parties:

> One of the reasons Sonny Perdue left the Democratic Party was that the bigwigs in the national Democratic Party came to him and said "we know you're the bright rising star here, but you've got to change your position on abortion to meet the national platform." And he said "I'm not going to do it." It was one of the straws that broke the camel's back with him. He wasn't going to change his position on abortion, and they said "well, there's not room for you on our national level,"and he said "Well, forget it, and maybe by the way there's not room for me in this party."[30]

Perdue elaborates on the discussion he had with Democratic leaders on party platform in the late 1990s:

> I had these Democratic consultants come to me and just kind of go down almost a litany litmus test of the things I would have to believe and do and say if I were going to be a Democratic governor. . . . I realized after this litmus test that I had to question really what I believed and which party more closely represented what I believed. . . . I had been a conservative Georgia Democrat . . . we called ourselves Sam Nunn Democrats. . . . But I finally concluded that I could not go back and continue because of the conflict of convictions that I had experienced in some of the things and the direction we were going.

Chris Young, who first worked with Sonny Perdue as a legislative intern in the Senate during the winter of 1998, supports Morgan's opinion but also provides a deeper understanding of the factors may have influenced Perdue to become a Republican:

> The governor's father was very ill. . . . I will never forget going down to Warner Robins to the hospital there, and the governor—they had been so gracious, they gave him a conference room—and he was working. He literally shifted both his personal business and political business to a conference room so he could stay in vigil with his father. And he began to talk about how when he was born the Democratic Party was stamped on your birth certificate . . . but it wasn't so much that he had changed, but the Democratic Party had changed and had left him. And he talked about the White House—and not just the White House but the Democratic Party more largely in Washington had kind of targeted him as a potential rising star in Georgia politics . . . and they essentially said "Okay, if we're going to support you, you have got to have the following positions in your plank." And among them were ones that are very strong that the governor is against—the abortion litmus test being one of those. . . . They said "you've got to change." And of course the governor likes to say, "I did change—I switched parties." And it wasn't just a position here or there, and it wasn't just this idea that Washington Democrats had gotten away from the Zells and the Sam Nunns, but it was more that he began to observe . . . that it had become increasingly difficult to hold together the fractious caucus that the Democrats were. . . . And he just became convinced that he could do things better from the other side.[31]

State Senator Eric Johnson, an architect and real-estate developer from Savannah, served as Senate minority leader in 1998 and was Perdue's initial contact in the GOP as he explored a possible jump to the Republican Party. Johnson describes their first party-switching discussion during the 1998 legislative session and some subsequent developments:

> I was the Republican leader. It wasn't apparent on the floor, but inside the (Democratic) caucus, there was a real war going on; and people like Jack Hill and Sonny Perdue hated Charles Walker. At one point Sonny was presiding and just on the spur of the moment I went up and sat down on the chair next to him and said, "At some point I would like to talk to you about switching parties." He turned to me and said, "I would like to do that." I almost fell out of my chair. At that conversation I said, "Well, this needs to be a deep dark secret. We need someone to be a go-between that we both know and trust." It ended up that [Johnny] Isakson became the person that Sonny talked to and I talked to.

As state party chairman at the time, Rusty Paul was also a key partici-pant in the early discussions about the possibility of Perdue switching to the Republican Party. He describes his remembrance of how Johnson related the Perdue conversation to him: "I was sitting in my party office one day. The phone rang, and my secretary told me it was Eric Johnson. Eric was at that point the minority leader in the Senate. Sonny was the president pro-tem. He [Eric] said, 'I have a question, and this is a serious question. What would the Republican Party's reaction be if Sonny Perdue were to switch parties?' I did not hesitate. I said ' it would be very positive—we would take him in a heartbeat.'" When asked about the Republican Party's reaction to Perdue's party switching, former party chair Alec Poitevint commented on Perdue's political courage in making the decision to switch parties by himself: "In Sonny's case he was coming from an area of Georgia that elected a few Republicans, but it was not a Republican area. He had lot of power and a lot of prestige, and he was giving it all up to stand on principle. Those sorts of conversions are very helpful to the party."[32]

Perdue's intern Chris Young describes a day in spring 1998 when Perdue began to meet with Republican Party leaders to discuss his plan to switch parties:

> The day after the session ended—it was still a cold day in March and I remember coming into work and the place was quiet. So I thought it was an interesting day because there was a parade of people either calling or coming in and out that day—Johnny Isakson, Newt Gingrich, Eric Johnson—and it just seemed to be incongruous with a normal day. About 4:00 Mary [Perdue] came and both of them were in his office on the third floor of the Capitol, and he said, "Chris, I've got something to tell you," and he said, "I am going to switch parties."

Yet, Perdue did not make a public announcement right away, because he had work to do first, and there was also an intervening family tragedy. He hoped to convince other state Democratic senators to switch parties at the same time he did, so that they could bring a Republican majority to the Senate and simultaneously retain their positions of power and influence on the var-ious committees. According to Chris Young, "The governor and I were in his single engine Maul airplane going around the state different places and meet-ing with people about switching parties or meeting with people about joining a governing coalition—Hugh Gillis we talked to—Tim Golden, Jack Hill, and then some."

Perdue discusses how he envisioned the team of rural and small town Democrats that he wanted to induce to switch parties when he did:

> Well, it was Paul Broun [father of Georgia's current tenth district congressman], Hugh Gillis, Rooney Bowen, Tim Golden, Jack Hill, and Don Cheeks. I knew those people's hearts, and I knew that they were solid conservative-hearted people—and those were the folks that I went to and told them respectfully what I planned to do—that I planned to qualify as a Republican, and I wanted to ask them to come with me because we can essentially have a bloodless coup here in respect of changing Georgia in this way. . . . And I solicited them. After I had made my announcement I went to them and solicited them to come register as a Republican with me, and they chose not to.

Quite understandably, Jack Hill was a likely candidate for Perdue to want to join him in party switching both because of their close personal relationship and because Perdue had sponsored Hill to be Senate majority leader in 1997 when Charles Walker beat Hill for that position of influence. Hill reports on their discussions about changing parties:

> I wasn't all that surprised when he [Sonny] first brought it up. It was probably something we talked about on an ongoing basis, and to some degree the lack of direction in the Democratic Party in the business world sense and the fact that there was nothing in their agenda that promoted small business. . . . I think we felt the Republican agenda and philosophy fit our philosophy a whole lot better. . . . We talked about it. The whole idea was we would like to switch without losing any power. We identified five senators. . . . It got out, and one or two Democrats blew the whistle. It all fell apart, and Sonny's father was deathly ill the week before qualifying.

Hill further discusses why he made the political decision to remain a Democrat at that time: "I had a decision to make, and frankly I made it for purely political reasons. I cannot be outside the budget process. No matter how strong the principle, I could not do that. Sonny was a little bit freer because he had Larry Walker in his district. Larry looked after the district."

Tim Golden, a printing executive from Valdosta, was another potential convert to the Republican Party that year. At the time, Golden was still serving in the House to which he had been elected in 1991, but he was planning to qualify that spring to run for the Senate seat becoming vacant as a result of long-serving state senator Loyce Turner's retirement. According to

Golden, Perdue had been one of those who encouraged him to run for the open Senate seat. Golden relates that Perdue called him in Valdosta just after the session had ended in March 1998 and asked to meet with him. Golden suggested that they meet in Tifton, halfway between their hometowns, which they did. Perdue revealed to Golden his plans to change parties and asked Golden to consider doing so. However, Golden decided that he owed too much loyalty to his Democratic mentors, former senator Sam Nunn and Congressman Charles Hatcher, both of whom Golden had served as a congressional aide, and retiring state senator Loyce Turner, and so he decided to proceed with his original plans and qualified as a Democrat.[33]

Senator Don Cheeks of Augusta was another potential convert. Cheeks, who eventually switched to the Georgia GOP in 2002, describes his 1998 discussions with Perdue, Hill, and others about a possible party change: "Five of us were supposed to switch to the Republican Party. Jack Hill called me, and we met at the Partridge Inn in Augusta to talk about how we were going to switch together and give control to the Republicans Party in the Senate. . . . Tim Golden was one of them that had promised. Eddie Madden [a pharmacist from Elberton] talked about it. . . . Sonny switched and let the cat out of the bag, and we couldn't swing it."[34] Perdue's father was terminally ill at the time of the party-switching discussions, and when his father began to fail and then die, Perdue was understandably unavailable to keep the coalition together and effect the wholesale change the GOP had hoped for.

Eric Johnson corroborates these accounts of the plan for other senators to join the GOP in the Senate: "The plan was for Sonny, after the session, to switch and bring six Democrats with him and bring a majority with him. That is when his father had the heart attack and went into intensive care. Sonny got locked down, and it leaked out. Somebody leaked within that six, and of course Zell Miller and Pierre Howard came down quick, and it all fell apart. Sonny was left out there by himself."

Analysis reveals, however, that although the plan for a number of state senators to switch parties in 1998 was not widely known, in fact, a number of Democratic Party and press insiders were aware of the possibility. From the standpoint of the news media, Dick Pettys recollects his thoughts about Perdue's party change: "It was a widely believed rumor up here at the time . . . and it really made sense because here he was—he was pro-tem. You don't get any higher than that in the Senate unless you are lieutenant governor. And this is a big deal to throw away unless you have a plan . . . so it made sense that what he really was trying to do was to lead a revolt." Senator

George Hooks discloses that he was generally aware of the party-switching conversations between Perdue and some other state senators at the time: "He didn't call me at the time. He visited with Senator Gillis, and Senator Bowen, and I think we all talked or they called. He visited, encouraging them . . . but I don't think anybody would have really switched at that time."

Chris Young comments on Perdue's decision to proceed to qualify as a Republican in mid-April 1998 even though none of the other Democratic senators with whom he had discussed party switching were willing to join him at the time: "It just wasn't in the cards in 1998 for any number of reasons. People were still used to voting 'D,' and there was no anti-incumbent mentality. . . . But the governor, you know, it was his conscious decision. I won't say it was right or wrong, but he just chose to qualify as a Republican. He made the conscious decision not to run as a Democrat, get elected, and then change." Sonny Perdue declared his decision to qualify for reelection to the state senate as a Republican on April 13, 1998, in an exclusive interview at the hospital in Warner Robins with journalist Nancy Badertscher, who was then a reporter with the *Macon Telegraph*. One of the first contacts Sonny Perdue made to discuss his decision to change parties was Lieutenant Governor Pierre Howard. They met at Eagles Landing Country Club in Henry County for Perdue to let his formerly strong supporter in the state Senate know about his plans to switch parties. Perdue reports, "I gained a lot of respect for him, and I think the feeling was mutual. . . . I purposely did not seek his counsel ahead of time because I didn't want . . . people to beg me to stay. That was not my intention."

Perdue's announcement about his decision to convert to the Republican Party surprised many of his longtime Democratic allies. Perdue's close family friend and the former Democratic majority leader Larry Walker of Perry, who represented part of Houston County in the House while Perdue represented most of the same district in the Senate, remembers his reaction to the news: "He called me and told me he was switching parties. . . . You could have knocked me over with a feather. I was astounded. I had no hint whatsoever. My assessment is that Charles Walker had a lot to do with it." Democratic House leader and future Speaker Terry Coleman of Eastman shared representation of Bleckley County with Perdue and describes his reaction to the news: "I thought he was crazy," but then Coleman offers his own explanation as to why he thinks Perdue switched, saying, "When Charles Walker became majority leader, I think they almost shut Sonny out. . . . Anyway, the Democrats in the Senate got to be almost militant in some of the issues that they chose. And some of the issues they chose were perceived as very liberal positions . . . and Sonny seemed to want to take things in a different way."

Democratic state representative Bob Holmes, who had already served in the state House for twenty-four years by 1998 but who was not close to Perdue gives a more detached but now ironic appraisal of how Perdue's switch from Democrat to Republican was viewed by the broader constituency in the state Democratic Party of Georgia at the time: "He [Perdue] was not looked on as a prominent political threat. He was looked upon as sort of a disgruntled person who, in part, was seeing changes that were occurring in the state, at the national level, and feeling that the evolutionary process was clearly evident; but he was just looked at as someone who was going over to the other side—hey, that's the last word we'll ever hear of him."

In November 1998, Perdue was reelected to the state Senate in his home district, but this time as a Republican. He, of course, lost many of the privileges he had enjoyed as a ranking Democrat when the General Assembly convened in January 1999. Senator Jack Hill comments on how the newly elected lieutenant governor, Mark Taylor, and the Democratic leadership in the Senate tried to punish Perdue for switching parties: "There were a hundred ways they tried to put the screws to him, and this culminated of course in the 2001 reapportionment which basically put him out of his district. I think the other Republicans rallied around him." Chris Young amplifies the story:

> Obviously, he was exiled. . . . They took his parking spot, his committee assignments, his staff—and they moved him to a "broom closet." . . . I'll never forget Patsy Bailey and the governor and me—well, Senator Perdue at the time—walking across from the Capitol to the legislative office building carrying plants and pictures. . . . It was over in the LOB [legislative office building], third floor, tucked away well off the elevator. They didn't even let him put his name on local legislation.

Even though Perdue was not treated with much respect by his former Democratic colleagues after he switched parties, Perdue was appreciated by his new Republican cohorts and quickly assumed a major role among the Republican leadership team in the Senate. Perdue worked along with Senate minority leader Eric Johnson and senators Tom Price and Bill Stephens to design a cogent strategy for a near-term Republican takeover of state Senate by the year 2000. Eric Johnson comments on their planning efforts: "We began to really focus on winning and taking over and stopped trying to fight the Democrats on everything and focus on issues and come up with a better idea for a new Georgia." Perdue reports on how he approached his new role in the Senate as a Democrat-turned-Republican:

> I purposely tried to teach my new colleagues about the rest of Georgia. We didn't have a lot of rural members at the time, and I wanted to convey to them that the rest of Georgia was just as conservative as they were, but they'd been Democrats by birth and by nature, rather than by choice, and that there were a lot of Democrats across the state that would vote Republican if they communicated the right way and presented it in the right way.

On several occasions, Perdue, Price, Johnson, his state Senate aide Morgan Perry, and Republican Party political director Scott Rials (a former Newt Gingrich congressional staffer who was appointed to this party position by Georgia GOP chairman Chuck Clay), flew around the state on Perdue's airplane to recruit Republican senatorial candidates for the next election cycle. Rials describes one particular candidate recruitment trip during the summer of 2000, "We created a 'Better Ideas for Georgia' tour Sonny went on it. Eric and Tom Price went on it. I think Casey [Cagle] went. The guy who is now a federal judge from Columbus, Clay Land, was a state senator then and he went. We rented this bus and went around to all of our targeted Senate districts."[35]

Although the GOP efforts to win a majority of the seats in the state Senate picked up momentum in 1999 and 2000, the Republicans won only two new seats in the Senate in the 2000 election cycle and fell short of achieving a majority with only twenty-four Republicans and thirty-two Democrats. Eric Johnson notes the GOP was far closer to winning control of the Senate in 2000 than the final seat tally indicates. Johnson explains, "We lost five seats by a combination of 1200 votes. I mean we almost took the Senate in 2000, and that is why they [state Democratic Party leadership] did the gerrymandered redistricting in 2001."

University of Georgia political scientist Charles Bullock III analyzed the voting results in state Senate races in 1998 and 2000 and reported that Republicans as a total group of candidates running for state Senate seats in those years actually outpolled the Democratic group of candidates in both years. He observes, "In the 1998 general election 75,000 more votes were cast for Republican than Democratic state Senate candidates, even though

Democrats emerged with a 34 to 22 seat edge. . . . In 2000 once again Republicans outpolled Democrats, taking 55 percent of the vote for the Senate but winning only 45 percent of the seats."[36]

Bob Irvin, who served as state House minority leader from 1994 to 2001, made a similar observation about election voting for House candidates: "The Republicans got more votes for the state House in every election from 1996 on, and more votes for the Senate in every election since 1998. So, it was gerrymandering that kept the Democrats in control." Irvin, Garland Pinholster, Steve Stancil, Mike Evans, and other House members continued to recruit candidates in targeted House districts, but without net gains in 1998 and 2000. In fact, when the Republicans ended up net losing three seats in the 2000 election cycle, Representative Lynn Westmoreland, a contractor and real-estate developer from Coweta County, challenged and ousted Bob Irvin as House minority leader for the 2001–2002 session of the General Assembly.

While the Republicans were being stymied in their quest to gain greater influence in and control of state government, the Georgia GOP experienced significant setbacks when it lost the two most influential members in its congressional delegation in Washington. After being elected to his eleventh term in the U.S. House of Representatives in November 1998, Speaker Newt Gingrich was challenged within the Republican House Caucus and resigned not only the Speakership but also his seat in Congress just before beginning his next term in January 1999. Later that year, Johnny Isakson was chosen to fill Gingrich's seat in Congress in a special election, but the Georgia delegation had lost control of the most influential position in the U.S. House of Representatives.

Then, in July 2000, U. S. Senator Paul Coverdell died suddenly and unexpectedly from a cerebral hemorrhage. Governor Roy Barnes appointed popular former governor Zell Miller to fill Coverdell's seat until a special election could be held. Once again, the Georgia GOP had no representation in the U.S. Senate. In that fall's election for the remaining four years of Coverdell's unexpired term, Zell Miller defeated former Republican senator Mack Mattingly by a margin of 58.2 percent to 37.9 percent to retain the Senate seat for the Democrats. Scott Rials, who was then serving as political director of the Georgia Republican Party, relates how Mattingly was chosen to represent the GOP in that Senate race and how Sonny Perdue was also considered:

When Coverdell died, the Georgia Republican Party, by its executive committee, had to put somebody on the ballot. We got together at Fred Cooper's house. [Eric] Tanenblatt, [Fred] Cooper, Joe Rogers [Waffle House CEO], and Isakson were there. We had Newt on the phone. We had Alec [Poitevint] on the phone. It was what we called the grand poobahs. Mack Mattingly was a safe bet. He had been a senator, and he would not embarrass the party. But Alec said, "I am fine with going with Mattingly, but remember we might want to consider our number one rising star, Sonny Perdue."

In the end, the group asked Mattingly to run, which he did, but he lost to Zell Miller. All eight Republicans and the three Democratic incumbents in the Georgia delegation to the United States House of Representatives were reelected that year.

In the 2000 presidential election, Georgia, as well as all the other Deep South states, voted convincingly for George W. Bush for the presidency in a close election in which the Bush-Cheney ticket actually had fewer popular votes than the Gore-Lieberman Democratic ticket nationally, but the Republicans won the most electoral votes by a slim margin. In Georgia, the Bush-Cheney ticket won 55 percent of the popular vote, compared to 43 percent of votes for the Democrats. The number of citizens who registered to vote in Georgia in 2000, as a percentage of those eligible to register, increased from 58.36 percent in 1990 to 64.1 percent in 2000. In addition, 69 percent of all registered voters in Georgia actually voted that year, indicating an increasing interest in national politics. Because the Republicans had been unsuccessful in winning either the governorship or control of either chamber of the General Assembly, the party was not well positioned to influence the 2001 reapportionment process. Republicans became increasingly focused on how the imbalanced state House and Senate districts had a detrimental effect on their party's ability to win new seats, and the GOP leadership was aware of the desire of Democrat stalwarts to maintain their power base. This conflict set the stage for a fierce battle over the redistricting process in the upcoming General Assembly sessions.

The 2000 census required a reapportionment and remapping of all the state's congressional districts, as well as all state Senate and House districts. Georgia's growth earned it two new seats in the U.S. House of Representatives for the new decade. In August 2001, the Georgia General Assembly convened in special session to draw up the new congressional and state House districts. According to several participants, Democratic governor

Roy Barnes and his chief of staff Bobby Kahn played heavy-handed roles in developing the legislative redistricting maps that were ultimately adopted by the majority Democratic General Assembly. Barnes and his cohorts seemed to be especially determined to draw boundary lines that would preserve, as best they could, a majority of districts that would continue to elect Democratic candidates to the General Assembly for most of the decade ahead. Charles Bullock explains what he believes was the logic of the Barnes team: "If Republicans captured the majority in a legislative chamber, one of the biggest losers might be Governor Roy Barnes, who could be the first Georgia governor to experience the challenge of divided government. With the stakes so high, Barnes played an unprecedented role during the 2001 Special Sessions to redraw Georgia's districts."[37]

Both houses of the General Assembly convened in special session in early August 2001, and the first order of business was for each house to draw its own reapportionment maps and select a plan by majority vote. Morgan Perry Cook, who was then aide to the minority Republican Party in the state Senate, describes the environment as very partisan and comments, "It was as nasty a political battle as I have ever seen. We had been working hard, drawing all of these maps, working with the Black Caucus thinking there was room to repeat 1991-92 [when Republicans and black Democrats aligned to gain greater representation for each group], but there was a chink in the armor." The GOP soon learned that the Barnes administration and Democratic leadership in the state legislature had already formed their own coalition of whites and blacks within the Democratic Party to the exclusion of Republicans. Michael Thurmond explains why the African Americans in the General Assembly backed away from another coalition with the Republicans in 2001:

> I wasn't there in the House then, so I was looking at it from afar, but one thing was different. Tyrone and some of the others had backed away from the "max-black" strategy and were now moving toward a more moderated view of reapportionment, recognizing that as far as the Democratic Party was concerned, that they had to look at a broader agenda, not just what's in the best interest of black politicians.

According to Republican representative Bob Irvin, Representative Kathy Ashe, who in 1998 switched to the Democratic Party after serving many years as a Republican representative in the state House, freely admitted to him that the purpose of the partisan reapportionment was to create a

Democratic majority for the next ten years.[38] Press reporter Dick Pettys also relates how transparent the state's Democratic leaders were in undertaking reapportionment in 2001: "That was clearly an incredibly partisan effort. . . . The Democrats made no bones about it. They acknowledged 'yeah, we are doing this for partisan reasons. We've gotten this interpretation of the law that says, yeah, it's okay to gerrymander politically.' And the problem was that they took it way too far."

The Senate was first to act. Their committee was chaired by Senator Tim Golden and was composed of twenty Democrats and only four Republicans appointed by House leadership. Minority Leader Eric Johnson requested assignment to the committee but was declined. Golden appointed a five-member subcommittee, made up entirely of Democrats and chaired by Senator Robert Brown of Macon. Its purpose was to review alternative maps and report back to the full committee. On the first day of the session, Golden, joined by Senators Charles Walker of Augusta and Terrell Starr of Clayton County, introduced Senate Bill 1EX1 as the legislative vehicle to offer a Democratic map that eventually would be proposed to define the new districts. In response, Eric Johnson introduced five bills that could serve as alternative vehicles for carrying Republican-drawn maps.

Former Republican Party executive counsel and longtime party activist Frank Strickland was involved in the special session and ultimately served as plaintiff's attorney in the lawsuit to overturn the 2001 and 2002 reapportionment legislation. He relates his observations about the committee processes in the Senate:

> The chair of the Senate Committee was Tim Golden—those Committees—the reapportionment committees in each house would convene meetings, and they would sort of look around and say, "Well, does anybody have a map?" The Senate was particularly bad about this. "Does anybody have a map?" "Nope." "Alright, we are adjourned." And that happened a couple of times. And then the third time around they convened a meeting and Tim Golden said, "Does anybody have a map?" And Senator Brown said, "I have a map." It appeared out of nowhere. Nobody on the committee had seen the map, and I think it was drawn offsite. And the Republicans of course said, "Wait a minute. We have never seen this map." "I move do pass." Bam! The map's out of the committee. But the map was clearly drawn offsite, and it's hard to say whose hands were on it because you couldn't observe the process.

Senator George Hooks explains from whence the maps were derived:

> A fellow named Karinshak was drawing the maps over at the Democratic
> Party headquarters. . . . He was a computer wizard, and he was the go-to
> man. . . . He said "I'm just the messenger." The Barnes administration had
> made up their mind legally that they were going to redraw the legislative
> districts—House and Senate. . . . Lieutenant Governor Taylor . . . went
> along with, more or less, the command of Governor Barnes and Bobby
> Kahn. They proceeded to draw all these districts on their own without any
> input from members of the Senate.

Senator Hooks disclosed that he was bitterly opposed to the maps as drawn
for his district, as were several other Democratic senators, but the
Republicans had the most reasons to be upset. Morgan Perry Cook reports
on the reaction of Republican senators: "The plan was beyond our compre-
hension the day the maps were unveiled. They had these snake-like fingers all
over." The Federal District Court eventually overturned the maps and ruled
that partisanship to protect incumbent Democrats was too much involved in
drawing the maps when it reported in its 2004 decision, "The Senate plan
splits eighty-one counties into 219 parts. The plan also paired twelve incumbents, including ten of the 24 incumbent Republicans, but only two of the
32 Democrats."[39] Basically, the districts seemed to be designed so as to overpopulate Republican-leaning districts in high-growth areas of the state and
underpopulate Democratic-leaning districts in low-growth regions.

Republican Senator Tom Price delivered a fiery Minority Report for the
GOP on the morning of August 9, 2001, after the Senate Reapportionment
Committee had passed out a bill with the egregious map attached. He stated,

> I believe it violates the Fourteenth Amendment to the United States
> Constitution, the Voting Rights Act, and the principles of redistricting.
> The map adopted is a blatant violation of the one person-one vote rule of
> the Fourteenth Amendment's Equal Protection Clause. The greatly under-
> populated districts are generally all held by minority Democrats, while the
> overpopulated districts are generally held by Republicans. We were to con-
> sider political subdivisions. This map splits 81 counties, many of them into
> several pieces. It splits 189 precincts, nearly 25 percent more than the cur-
> rent map. The map completely ignores the citizens who begged us not to
> split their counties and the election officials who diligently attended every
> public hearing to urge us not to split precincts. This map destroys commu-
> nities of interest.

As an additional defensive strategy in the special session, the Republicans drew up a set of redistricting guidelines that required adherence to more traditional reapportionment criteria, such as district compactness and contiguity, but the GOP-proposed guidelines were rejected by the Democrat-controlled House and Senate Reapportionment Committees.[40] During the special session, Senator Eric Johnson also tried on a number of occasions to call for a vote on Senate-drawn redistricting plans, but his bills were never put on the calendar for discussion or a vote. Among the Senate districts that were most radically altered was the eighteenth, which was represented by party-switching Sonny Perdue. Senator George Hooks indicated that in one version of the bill, Sonny Perdue's house in Bonaire was actually redistricted into his adjoining district and out of the old eighteenth.

Subsequently, the Senate approved the committee maps by a vote of twenty-nine to twenty-six. Upon receipt of the Senate reapportionment legislation, Governor Barnes hurriedly signed the bill on August 24, 2001. The governor then sent the Senate plan to the U.S. District Court, D.C. Circuit, for validation of its constitutionality. It was found to have slight defects, and it was returned to the General Assembly so that minor modifications could be made in the 2002 session of the General Assembly, when it was passed again. Governor Barnes then quickly signed the corrected Senate redistricting bill into law.

Veteran representative Tommy Smith, a pine tree and blueberry farmer from Bacon County in South Georgia, chaired the House reapportionment committee and explained that the redistricting process worked somewhat differently in the House than it did in the Senate. According to Smith, Speaker Murphy refused to accept the map initially urged on the House by Governor Barnes and Bobby Kahn, much to their displeasure. However, Smith disclosed that the Speaker was intimately involved in drawing the new House maps and he states that he (Smith) was the quarterback but Speaker Murphy was the coach who called the plays.[41]

Frank Strickland relates how the newly elected House minority leader Lynn Westmoreland became closely involved in analyzing and finding opportunities to object to the Democrats' maps: "In the special session, Lynn Westmoreland became an expert in drawing maps and dealing with statistics and so on. When the House map was released, he found a potential minority district issue within one of the multi-member districts and word got circulated, and in about 24 to 48 hours—that district had been redrawn in the process to cure that problem." Westmoreland had discovered that the minority vote had been diluted in one of the multi-member districts, arguably in violation of the United States Department of Justice guidelines. A reapportionment bill realigning House districts was passed in the first special session of the General Assembly, but Governor Barnes was apparently concerned about a potential legal defect with the plan and vetoed the bill. Barnes then recalled the General Assembly into a second special session to redraw the House districts and also to draw up new congressional districts. The second session convened on August 22, and on the first day Tommy Smith, who chaired the House committee, introduced a bill that was co-sponsored by Democratic Majority Leader Larry Walker, Speaker Pro-Tem Jack Connell of Augusta, and Representative Jimmy Skipper of Americus. The House quickly passed HB14EX2 on August 27, just five days later, and rapidly transmitted it to the Senate where it passed by a vote of twenty-nine to twenty-two, despite efforts of Senate Republicans again to substitute a different bill with less disruptive districting. Glenn Richardson vividly describes his feelings about the 2001 reapportionment experience in the House: "It was tough to be sitting there. We were like sheep to the slaughter. And you were never consulted; you just kept seeing maps come out. Maps would come out, and multi-member districts and the +4.99 percent population deviations in all Republican districts. . . . Stuff like that. It was tough."

Former House minority leader Bob Irvin also describes his reaction to the 2001 House maps: "It was the most partisan and most outrageous reapportionment that anybody had ever seen." He was particularly aghast at the split of so many counties. Irvin also criticized Roy Barnes for the plan. "There had never been a reapportionment session where the governor had gotten so involved. . . . This was directed from the governor's office."

After the state Senate and House redistricting plans were approved in special session, the remaining task for both chambers of the General Assembly was to pass a bill with new congressional district lines, including the two new districts that Georgia's growth over the last decade of the twentieth century had earned. In the 2002 elections, Georgia would have thirteen seats in the U.S. House, compared to only eleven before. HBEX2 was quickly passed by the Georgia House and transmitted to Senate, where parliamentary debate ensued and dragged out final action on the bill until September 28. Morgan Perry Cook dramatically describes the state Senate's last day activities as the final votes were taken on the congressional redistricting maps drawn by the Democrats:

We were in that little Room 121—sitting and staring at those maps—they had set us back by ten years—and Sonny Perdue stood up in front of that caucus meeting and he said, "We're going out of here with our heads held high, and we are coming out of here knowing one thing: it's more important than ever that we don't give up and we don't let Georgia down." The entire Senate [Republican] caucus marched out of that room and marched up the stairs singing the Battle Hymn of the Republic. . . . When we got to the entrance to the Senate chamber, Eric Johnson turned around and said, "The strength of the warrior is in the tribe. Nobody break rank." We entered that chamber for the most heart-wrenching few hours of debate, and it was an excruciating debate. After they took the votes—I believe Mark Taylor called for a vote around 2 or 3 that afternoon—we went back downstairs—Eric Johnson, Tom Price, Bill Stephens, Sonny Perdue, and myself . . . and we had a prayer . . . that we were going to stay focused on what we believed was our righteous calling . . . to help Georgia. And I guess it was in a couple of months later that Perdue declared he was running for governor.

The new congressional redistricting plan was passed by a 33-23 vote in the Senate, and Governor Barnes signed both the state House and congressional reapportionment bills on October 1, 2001. Sonny Perdue describes his personal feelings about the 2001 reapportionment actions taken by Democratic Party leadership: "They severely overreached. . . . It was not necessarily for political gain. It was really punitive. . . . For instance, and I was still being 'taught a lesson,' they took my district from Kathleen to Covington, a hundred miles long and twenty miles wide. . . . It had no cohesiveness, and it had no commonality about it. And they did it all over the state. My sense of morality, my sense of government, my sense of righteousness got offended."

In retrospect, Perdue and the Republicans in the state Senate were not the only groups that objected to the new district lines. Former state representative Bob Irvin comments on some of the disaffected constituencies: "In rural areas and with the white rural establishment voters and with elected officials in those counties, this was a big deal and a big problem. The white rural voters and their elected officials—the sheriffs, the county commissioners, and the election supervisors were really ticked off." Even Senator Tim Golden, who chaired the Senate Reapportionment Committee, realized at the time that the new maps were, as he described them, "overreaching." Golden admits that Bobby Kahn brought him the maps to be introduced into the redistricting process.

Former Democratic Speaker Terry Coleman agrees with Golden's assessment of the Barnes/Kahn reapportionment maps. "Barnes got too deep into it. We told him he went too far. . . . He pushed it to the max. . . . The reapportionment thing was too aggressive for the tastes of moderate Democrats and conservative Democrats, or moderate to conservative Republicans either." Former House majority leader Larry Walker corroborates the concern of the Democratic leadership in the General Assembly about the redistricting plan as approved. "Roy Barnes told me that people don't care about reapportionment, and I said 'we made them care about it.' . . . It was rubbed in people's faces too much." However, Walker does acknowledge the full complicity of the Democratic leadership in both houses of the legislature in supporting the maps they were given by the Barnes administration. "I think that Roy and Bobby were driving it, but I think it was a collaborative process to some extent. I mean, I think the House leadership and the Senate leadership were probably going along with it." Reportedly, House Speaker Tom Murphy refrained from drawing the boundary lines of his own district for his personal political benefit, as was recently recounted by former Republican state representative and publisher Matt Towery:

> In the last redistricting in which Murphy would participate, there came a fateful day. Murphy's own team had drawn the Speaker into a perilous (and indeed politically fatal) district. By the last years of his speakership, he had grown to distrust the political maneuverings of Governor Barnes' chief of staff, the omnipresent Bobby Kahn. To their credit, Barnes and Kahn attempted to save Murphy by drawing their own House map that would have assured the Speaker a Democratic district for at least several more terms. When an emissary from Barnes and Kahn presented Murphy with the new map, he rejected it. He is quoted as saying to the emissary, "I can't do it. It would leave two fellow Democrats at too much risk. I know you are trying to help me, but tell Bobby and Roy I know they are trying to help me, but I had just as soon go out there and lose straight up.[42]

Murphy's words turned out to be quite prophetic as a year later he was defeated in the newly drawn district.

President George W. Bush with gubernatorial candidate Sonny Perdue and
U. S. senatorial candidate Saxby Chambliss on a campaign trip to Atlanta on
Saturday, November 2, 2002. Credit: Associated Press/Gregory E. Smith.

94

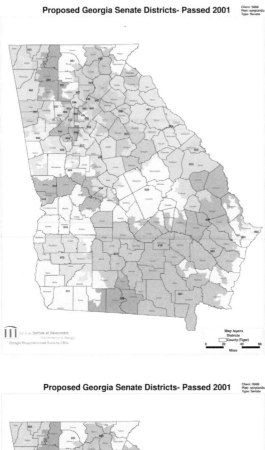

Redistricting map proposed
by Sen. Golden, passed by the
General Assembly, but rejected
by the Department of Justice.
Credit: Georgia Redistricting
Services Offices.

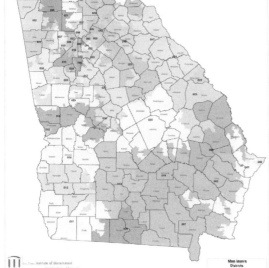

Redistricting map adopted
in 2002, pre-cleared by Justice,
and used for the 2002 election.
Credit: Georgia Redistricting
Services Offices.

Gubernatorial candidate Sonny Perdue addressing the Association of College Republicans in Athens in 2001. Many of his young campaign staff came out of this organization into his campaign. Credit: Jen Bennecke.

Candidate Sonny Perdue with campaign staffers Nick Ayers, Trey Childress, Chris Young, Scott Rials and Marty Klein on November 5, 2002. Credit: AP Photo/*Atlanta Journal-Constitution*/Rich Addicks.

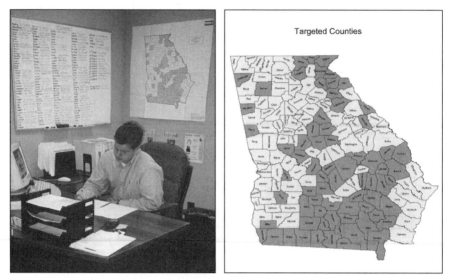

Paul Bennecke on Sonny Perdue's 2002 campaign staff, sitting at a desk in the campaign office with a map of targeted counties (in blue) and traditional Republican counties (in yellow) on the wall. Credit: Jen Bennecke.

Gubernatorial debate featuring incumbent Democratic governor Roy Barnes, Libertarian candidate Garrett Michael Hayes, and Republican candidate Sonny Perdue at Georgia Public Broadcasting on November 3, 2002. Credit: Associated Press/Gregory E. Smith.

2002 Fourth of July parade in Cobb County. Among the young staffers in the photo with candidate Sonny Perdue are Jen Bennecke, Chris Young, Lee Ann Wood Gillis, Nick Ayers, Meredith Barrs, and Dan McLagen. Credit: Jen Bennecke.

2002 campaign photo in Cordele at the Watermelon Festival. Campaign team riding in the wagon behind the tractor in the festival parade. Credit: Jen Bennecke.

2002 campaign photo of candidate Sonny Perdue with Brian and Brett Upson at a dove hunt hosted by Alton and David Knight in Bibb County, Georgia. Credit: Chad McClure.

Sonny Perdue waits for election results at his headquarters with State senators Bill Stephens, Rusty Paul, and Tom Price and campaign consultant John Watson and former Georgia Attorney-General Mike Bowers. Credit: AP Photo/*Atlanta Journal-Constitution.*

After the concession of Governor Roy Barnes following the 2002 gubernatorial election with former U.S. Senator Mack Mattingly, Scott Rials, Alec Poitevint, Chris Young, Nick Ayers and Dan McLagan. Credit: AP Photo/*Atlanta Journal-Constitution*/Rich Addicks.

2002 photo of Governor-elect Sonny Perdue, taken from his transition office in the Georgia Pacific Building in downtown Atlanta, overlooking the State Capitol, before his inauguration as governor. Credit: AP Photo/*Atlanta Journal-Constitution*.

CHAPTER 5

The Perdue Campaign

The Primary Election

The inequities of the redistricting plan approved in the 2001 Special Session of the General Assembly significantly influenced Sonny Perdue to join with other party leaders, including Alec Poitevint and Eric Johnson, to seek out and find a strong Republican candidate to oppose Roy Barnes in his upcoming gubernatorial reelection bid. Reportedly, Sonny Perdue initially did not consider himself to be the candidate. Morgan Perry Cook describes how this small group of Republican leaders sought to influence Congressman Charlie Norwood to run against Barnes:

> We tried so hard to get Charlie Norwood to run, because Charlie had been real involved. If there was a congressman who got his hands dirty, it was Charlie Norwood. And we did everything we could to get Charlie to run for governor, and he just wouldn't. Sonny flew down there a couple of times. I think he didn't want to give up his congressional seat, and I think he probably he knew he was sick, and it probably had to do with Gloria [Norwood's wife] not being comfortable with it.

Senator Eric Johnson comments on Perdue's involvement with him in recruiting a gubernatorial candidate: "The redistricting drove us crazy. Tom Price, Sonny and I went and sat down with Johnny Isakson in his district office and tried to convince Johnny to run. And when he said no, Sonny basically said well all right, I've just got to do it." Congressman Price confirmed that the team of senators visited with Isakson and Norwood and in fact admitted that they also visited with all the other members of Georgia's Republican delegation in Washington in the hope that one of them would oppose Roy Barnes for governor. Sonny Perdue also discloses that he tried to get many others to run for governor before he decided to do so and also refutes the assertion of others that he had initially considered running for lieutenant governor:

> I tried to get people—all of our Republican congressmen—to come back and run for governor, particularly Charlie Norwood and Saxby, and none of them would consider it at all. I frankly did not consider—a lot of people thought I was considering lieutenant governor and wanted me to run for lieutenant governor, but I didn't have any aspiration to run for lieutenant governor. . . . When the Republican colleagues in the General Assembly came and said, "Would you run for governor?" most everybody had no idea Roy Barnes could be beat. . . . I can remember a meeting with the Republican establishment where they as much as told me they just wanted somebody who wouldn't embarrass Saxby Chambliss because they wanted to beat Max Cleland, and they wanted a gubernatorial candidate who would just kind of give a good presence for Saxby. And that was their reason for soliciting me.

Former Party Chair Rusty Paul's comments perhaps typify the prevailing thought among Republican leadership at the time: "I encouraged him, not because I thought he could beat Barnes. He was known to the Republican establishment, but the rank and file, grass-roots Republicans did not know him that well. I thought that by running now, he would get introduced to the grass-roots organization and network, and that would really stand him in good stead four years hence." Perdue's close campaign advisor and later chief of staff John Watson relates how Perdue analyzed the prospect of running for governor and how he eventually decided to run: "Perdue soon recognized that if no one else was going to run for governor, he would. . . . What he saw was a vulnerable governor, Roy Barnes. . . . What he also sensed was that it was apparent that nobody else had the guts to take Roy on. He was not going to let Roy have a free pass. I certainly think that he and Mary were meditative and thoughtful and prayerful about that process and determined—why not us?"

Bainbridge businessman and Republican Party leader Alec Poitevint was also a close confidante of Perdue's during his deliberations. He recounts their ongoing discussions:

> I remember it being September a year before the election. It was at an early football game. We ran into Sonny and Mary in the alumni suite. The con-

versation led to he was thinking about running for lieutenant governor. I told him, "Sonny, I hear you want to run for lieutenant governor. If you do that I will support you. If you run for governor, I will do anything you ask me to do." About a month and a half later I was in South Dakota helping to remove some pheasants. I noticed my cell phone had a message on it. So, I called him and he said, "You remember back in September when we met at the Georgia game, you and Doreen, you said if I would run for governor you would do anything you could to help me." I said "yeah." He said "Chair my campaign for governor."

Scott Rials, who was political director of the Georgia Republican Party in 2001 and had worked closely with Perdue in recruiting GOP candidates to run for state office, was also an early advisor to Perdue as he considered his political future. He tells about the personal side of Perdue's decision to run for governor: "Sonny and Mary and I went to a Ruby Tuesday's in Warner Robins, and he [Perdue] said I am not running for anything. Mary did not want him to. Then, Mary went off to a church retreat and came back and said she was ready. He called me on October 4, 2001, and said we are in." Sonny Perdue himself describes his and Mary Perdue's spiritual journeys as they considered undertaking the race for governor and how they finally determined to do so:

There's a spiritual component to this, and it happened over a long period of time. . . . I knew that God was working in my heart and life to do something. . . . Mary and I became convinced that God was calling us to do something, and I really didn't know what, honestly. We used the phrase "get out of our comfort zone," and literally I didn't know what it meant. It became clearer and clearer. Running for governor was absolutely out of my comfort zone. . . . I frankly thought God had in mind another big dose of humility in my life—get out here and put your heart on the line for a whole year and then suffer defeat and then I can use you. So, I thought it was a part of His washing and cleansing process to be used for something else. I also realized that if I didn't do it I believe I would have been disobedient. . . . It became a joint decision, or it would not have happened. That was on September 11, 2002. . . . Mary and Leigh were scheduled to go to a women's conference at Pine Mountain—just a few days afterward. . . . Mary got back and I said, "Well Mary, what did the speakers talk about?" and she said, "Virtually every one of them talked about getting out of your comfort zone." And that was our affirmation.

After Perdue finally decided to run for governor, he made his initial announcement in Macon in November 2001 and then followed up with a rally in Atlanta. In order to devote full time to his campaign, and on general principle, Perdue immediately resigned his seat in the state Senate.[1] Several members of the state legislature also encouraged Perdue to run for governor. The most notable support came from his fellow Republican state senators, as all but one of them signed a statement of support for his candidacy after he announced. Chris Young reports on their endorsement of Perdue:

> All of the members of the Republican caucus in the Senate, minus one Joey Brush, I believe because he and Linda Schrenko were close friends, and Linda Schrenko was his constituent over there [in the Augusta area]— signed a letter asking Sonny Perdue to run for governor. It was twenty people. There was a similar letter in the House, but there were fewer in the House because they didn't know him as well. But he used that letter to kind of springboard initial fundraising—"they want me to run out of the Senate"—but I remember most of the senators—in fact I think they all gave to his campaign right away. And some of them really worked.

According to Dan McLagan, Perdue's communications director, some of the legislative leaders of the Republican Party quickly became supportive of Perdue's candidacy because they did not consider Linda Schrenko or Bill Byrne, the other announced contenders for the GOP gubernatorial nomination, to be strong enough leaders to beat Governor Barnes.[2]

Perdue began immediately organizing his gubernatorial campaign. He chose Scott Rials as his campaign manager, and he was successful in persuading Alec Poitevint to chair his campaign committee. According to Rials, Poitevint was chosen for the following reasons: "(1) he is a smart business person; (2) he thinks like Sonny; (3) he is from agriculture, and (4) he was the former party chair in 1992. In addition, he was the current national committeeman from Georgia, and when Newt was Speaker, he was treasurer of RNC. He had those working connections up in D.C." Perdue also signed up Leigh Ann Wood Gillis of Macon to organize fundraising for his campaign. Gillis had assisted Perdue in fundraising for his 2000 Senate reelection bid, and she officially joined his campaign staff as finance director in January 2002.

Early on, Perdue enlisted several college Republican leaders for his campaign. Paul Bennecke, Nick Ayers, and Derrick Dickey were important early recruits. Paul Bennecke distinguished himself as a young leader while still in college. He served as president of the student body at Dalton College and organized a chapter of College Republicans there. After he obtained his associate's degree, he interned for Congressman Nathan Deal in his Washington office for several months before matriculating to the University of Georgia to complete his undergraduate degree.

He quickly became involved with the College Republicans at UGA, which he reports was the largest chapter in the country at the time. While at the University of Georgia, Bennecke first served as executive director of the College Republicans organization and later became state chairman, two positions that enabled him to meet many of the top Republican elected officials in the state and also to form a network of other similarly convicted college students across the state, several of whom formed the nucleus of the Perdue for a New Georgia campaign team. Bennecke reports on his experiences: "When I became chairman of the College Republicans, Nick [Ayers] came in as a freshman, and Derrick Dickey introduced me to Nick. That's where I met Nick, and got Nick involved. Marty Klein, Tony Simon, Jay Walker, Derrick Dickey, Chad Holland—all of the guys that were somewhat of a nucleus (of the campaign staff)—we were all in College Republicans together."[3]

As chairman of College Republicans, Bennecke trained and provided student volunteers to various Republican candidates in the 2000 election cycle in a program organized by Scott Rials, who was then serving as political director of the Republican Party of Georgia. About the same time, he also met and got to know Sonny Perdue on two occasions when Perdue was speaking to Republican groups in Athens. Bennecke explains how he was later enlisted into the Perdue campaign:

> I was on lunch break with my girlfriend (who is now my wife). We were in Athens. It was my last semester at the University of Georgia, and I got a phone call on my cell phone, and it was Scott Rials and Sonny Perdue. And Sonny said, I am thinking about running for governor, and I would like to talk to you about it. . . . I went to Atlanta and met him and Scott Rails at a Waffle House, and it ended up being a job interview. . . . And he asked me about volunteer grassroots systems, how I would harvest contacts, how would I go about building county organizations, what was my experience on campaigns. . . . It was about a two- or three-hour interview. . . . And I left that Waffle House just amazed that I was a senior in college and was actually being considered for a position in a governor's race. . . . I would say about a day later I got a call from Scott and Sonny and they

said, "We want you to be political director on my campaign for governor. And we really need you to start now." And by the end of the week I had moved to Atlanta.

Nick Ayers, who served as Perdue's "body man" during the first gubernatorial campaign and as his campaign manager in the second race for governor, similarly reports his experiences in working in politics with other College Republicans and how he became involved in the Perdue campaign shortly after Rials and Bennecke did:

> I was at Kennesaw State, and I ran for state chairman of the College Republicans after Derrick Dickey and I started the local chapter of the College Republicans at Kennesaw. They did not have one. We grew the local chapter to probably 400 members on campus, and Derrick and I would sit around at night and think of these wild and crazy ideas. He and I both became very interested in state politics and started talking about, literally, I mean it sounded so goofy at the time, but leading a Republican revolution in the state. . . . This was 2000–2001. The timing could not have been worse, since the Democrats were at the peak of power. Barnes was a powerful incumbent governor. . . . We started going to the state organization of the College Republicans where all the state chapters come together. Paul Bennecke was the state chairman. Well, Paul had similar ideas, so he and Derrick and I and a guy named Jay Walker, and Tony Simon all started running around together. Sonny Perdue, as a state senator, came and spoke to us at our state convention of College Republicans. Later, Paul called me one night and said, "I know you are in school, and I know you have a full time job, but this guy Sonny Perdue called me, and he is really interested in putting a team of young people together because he is thinking of running for governor.[4]

Ayers also tells about his next meeting with Perdue and how he was invited to join the campaign:

> Sonny flew his plane into PDK. I have always been fascinated by aviation, and I thought it was the coolest thing in the world. It was Halloween Day of 2001, and he and I sat down on the floor at PDK in an empty, barren office and just started talking for about two hours. We had a real conversation and just hit it off. He said "I need someone to travel with me everywhere and be my right hand guy." He told me what it was going to pay, and I thought that is half of what I was making now. . . . But I really felt it was the right thing to do, I almost felt called."[5]

The industrious Ayers had been working at Georgia State Bank in Cobb County ever since he had been in high school in Cobb County, and following his graduation, his managers at the bank had convinced him to enroll in Kennesaw State and study finance and even provided him scholarship funds for his college expenses. Ironically, Governor Roy Barnes was one of the primary owners of the bank for which Ayers worked until he joined Perdue's campaign. Ayers describes the reaction of his banking sponsors to Perdue's job offer:

> It was so surreal. . . . They chastised me. . . . I thought this is a problem. . . . They literally took it as if Roy doesn't deserve to have to run against anyone. . . . I knew I never could be looked at the same now that I had even gone and spoken to Sonny, so I thought strategically, I have to fish or cut bait, and it makes more sense to cut bait. I called Sonny that afternoon after I met with them, and I said "I am driving back to the campaign office. I just walked away from a job of four and a half years." I had literally been with the bank since I was fifteen. I said, "We have to win now. I have just been shunned from my hometown."

Ayers further discusses the earliest days of the campaign and what it was like building the team:

> By January we had assembled a few other staff members. Sonny himself devised the plan on targeting counties. It was more strategic. He came up with this plan that said we are going to target these seventy-one counties during the primary. We are only going to travel them. We are going to be very disciplined and very strategic in the way we scheduled each other, and those were the counties we organized from grass-roots standpoint. I think the staff was shocked that a candidate put together such a strategic targeting plan. . . . He directly tasked Paul Bennecke with implementing this plan.

Perdue explains how he derived the targeted county strategy: "Well, winning elections is really about numbers. You've got to figure out where you have to go to get the votes. And we looked at the presidential elections and what people's predilections of voting Republican were. We looked at all the statistics and the races where Coverdell had won and things like that. And that's how we narrowed it down."

Bennecke expounds on why the targeted county strategy was so fundamentally important to the Perdue for a New Georgia campaign:

The Republican Party hadn't nominated a candidate [for governor] who could go into those swing areas in rural Georgia and build a coalition with suburban Republicans—the base of the party, what was considered the base at the time—and be able to go to farmers and rural Democrats and really bring them into the fold to give that winning coalition. Coverdell did it. . . . There were about 70 to 72 counties that were outside the metro area that voted for Coverdell and Roy Barnes. Most of these places were in Northeast Georgia, Middle Georgia, and then going all the way across the state from east to west in South Georgia. These were places where the Republican nominee for governor just could never break through . . . so one of the things we had to do was to figure out was how could you add these seventy-plus counties into the fold? Basically, we needed to build our county organizations there first. We needed to get Sonny Perdue to visit those counties on a regular basis—they had to be a priority, because we could maximize our Republican vote in Metro Atlanta and still lose. If we could maximize our vote in Metro Atlanta and at least break even in these seventy-plus counties in rural Georgia, then we were going to be in the ballgame.

A map provided by Bennecke shows the geographic distribution of the seventy-one strategic counties spread around the state. Mostly, these counties were not in the Black Belt of Georgia, which contained the counties with the highest percentage of African-American voters. Analysis of the voting history in these targeted counties reveals why Perdue possibly considered them to be critical to his campaign plans.

In the 1990 gubernatorial election, Republican Johnny Isakson won the majority of votes in only nine of them, and in 1992 Republican Paul Coverdell won thirty-four of these counties in his successful U.S. Senate race, and in 1994 Guy Millner carried thirty-six of them in his close race against Zell Miller. In the 1996 presidential election, Republican senator Bob Dole carried forty-five of these counties when he outpolled Bill Clinton in Georgia, but Democratic senatorial candidate Max Cleland carried most of them in his victorious race that year. The swing nature of the voting patterns in these counties was even more dramatic in the 1998 and 2000 election cycles. Republican Paul Coverdell won the majority of votes in all seventy-one of these counties in his senatorial reelection campaign, but Democrat Roy Barnes won in seventy of these counties in his race for the governorship. He outpolled Guy Millner by almost 50,000 votes in these seventy-one counties, and lost only in Madison County by a mere six votes. Then, in the 2000 presidential election, Republican George W. Bush carried seventy of these counties (all but Terrell County) and outpolled Al Gore by over 110,000 votes in these strategic counties. However, in the same year popular Democrat Zell Miller won the majority of votes in all but two of these counties in his Senate reelection campaign against Republican Mack Mattingly.

In organizing the grass-roots campaigns in the seventy-one strategic counties, Perdue and his team elected to broaden their campaign organization beyond the traditional Republican county organizations. Ayers explains why:

> Sonny really pushed Paul not to go through the typical Republican establishment, because he said, "We need them, but they have not been able to get it done. We are going to think outside the box. We are going to have to bring in new people." We had to bring in new people in every county because the Republican establishment was solely focused on federal politics. As Paul would make these calls [on the Republican establishment], probably nine times out of ten, he was told, "Well, we signed up with Saxby Chambliss," [who was running against incumbent Democratic Senator Max Cleland for the U.S. Senate seat from Georgia that year].

Dougherty County campaign co-chairman and Bonaire native Don Cole also describes the statewide organization that Perdue and his campaign staff assembled.

> He identified and recruited chairpersons for each congressional district. Those chairpersons then identified and recruited chairpersons for each county within their districts. Finally, county chairpersons identified, recruited, and organized teams within their counties. Internal communications with campaign teams would consist of telephone contact, team meetings, and internal e-mail updates. . . . Paul Bennecke, political director for Perdue for a New Georgia sent e-mail updates to district and county chairs and others on a regular basis.[6]

Bennecke estimates that the campaign maintained a database with e-mail addresses or telephone numbers for approximately 7,000 volunteers.

Early in 2002, Perdue hired media consultant Fred Davis of Hollywood, California, to guide his campaign communications after interviewing several candidates. Davis previously had worked as a media consultant for Mike Bowers in his 1998 gubernatorial bid and for Paul Coverdell in his 1998 U.S. Senate reelection campaign and already had a strategic understanding of the political landscape in Georgia. Davis was also instrumental in bringing Dan McLagan into the Perdue campaign as the fulltime communications director. McLagan, who later served as director of communications in Governor Perdue's first administration, describes how he was recruited:

> I was doing a lot of health care consulting at that time, and it basically dried up. In 2002 I was flying down to meet with Jeb Bush who wanted to hire me as his communications director for his reelect. On the way back I swung by at the request of Fred Davis whom I had worked with in 1998. He wanted me to come and meet with this guy named Sonny Perdue. I called a good friend of mine, Whit Ayers, who had been a pollster. . . . Actually, he was working for Bill Byrne at the time, and he was one of Sonny's primary opponents. I asked him what the odds were. He was pretty candid with me. . . . He said Sonny was probably not going to get the nomination and beat Bill Byrne. He said it would be a good one to do as a relationship builder because if Sonny ran again the time might be more propitious. Sonny offered me the job, basically the money that I wanted or needed, whereas Jeb had been a little bit stingier, so I flew home and loaded up my car and my dog from Washington D.C. and came down and started the campaign.

McLagan joined the campaign as communications director for a consulting fee of $8,000 a month. McLagan admits that in the early days of the campaign he was concerned not only about Bill Byrne's candidacy in the Republican primary but also about the candidacy of twice-elected state school superintendent Linda Schrenko. McLagan comments, "No one thought we could possibly win. Most people thought Linda Schrenko, who had the bigger name ID, and as a woman, she had a better chance in the primary than we did. Basically, we got no respect."   Fred Davis was also instrumental in recruiting John Watson into the Perdue campaign. Watson essentially had suspended his political consulting practice in 1998, following Mike Bowers's loss to Guy Millner in the GOP primary that year, and joined his father-in-law's commercial concrete construction firm. Watson, who joined the campaign on a part-time basis for a consulting fee of $5,000 a month, describes how he was recruited to help Perdue:

> I got a phone call from Fred Davis. Fred Davis is the governor's creative or media strategist. . . . Fred did the ads in the 1998 Mike Bowers campaign. I left the scene. Fred, however, had begun a relationship with Sonny Perdue. I got a call from Fred saying, "What are you doing?" It was ironic

because the person that I was helping at that point in time was Bill Byrne. He was personal friends with my father-in-law. Then I got a call from Sonny Perdue who said, "I've got a campaign manager, but what I need is someone who has a little more of a strategic ability to consult with my campaign manager and just be more of a consultant than a day-to-day person. . . . So I was the general consultant for the 2002 campaign.

In spring 2002, several more key staffers joined the campaign. In May, Chris Young completed his first year of law school at the University of Georgia and took a sabbatical to work with Perdue in a campaign coordinator role. While he was still in law school in the previous fall and winter, Young had stayed in close touch with Perdue and assisted in developing some of the campaign themes. He also helped in recruiting Trey Childress to serve as policy director for the campaign. Childress and Young had known each other as students at Georgia Tech, and Childress had been working in the State of Georgia Office of Planning and Budget under Governor Barnes.

Childress joined the campaign on a full-time basis in May 2002 after he was awarded his Master's in Public Policy degree from Georgia Tech. Former College Republicans Derrick Dickey, Julie Smith, and Jen Englert (Bennecke) also joined the campaign staff that spring. Later in the summer, Corinna Magelund joined the staff as office manager and volunteer coordinator, and Marty Klein was enlisted as deputy political director. This group of young people comprised the core of Perdue for a New Georgia campaign team. No one other than Perdue and Poitevint was more than thirty-five years of age.

The main challenge for the Perdue team was to win a solid victory in the Republican primary, and preferably without a runoff. It was a tall order, as John Watson observes: "He [Perdue] was probably seen as the third place candidate. Linda Schrenko was a statewide success. She had been elected twice at that point statewide, was a female, and just given her name identification attributes, she was seen as number one. . . . You then had as number two Bill Byrne, who was a very successful CEO in essence, Cobb County Commissioner. Sonny was really seen as third in line."

To the surprise of many, Perdue and his team quickly overcame their long-shot positioning in the Republican primary, and on August 20 Perdue was able to win outright without an expensive and exhausting primary runoff election. Several members of the Perdue campaign team theorize how Perdue was able to come from behind to win the primary.

In John Watson's analysis, Bill Byrne and Linda Schrenko never connected with the Republican voters in spring and summer 2002. He reports, "Neither Schrenko nor Byrne was ever able to light a fire. Byrne was not a money raiser. While he had a fairly interesting bio in terms of work as a county commission chairman and former marine pilot, he was never able to marshal the resources that would get him any level of exposure through mail or television. Schrenko also never marshaled the resources." Paul Bennecke shares similar opinions about Linda Schrenko's and Bill Byrne's failures to connect sufficiently with the Republican primary voters: "Linda Schrenko had a lot of her powers stripped away by the governor [Barnes], so she wasn't able to really have a record of accomplishment as superintendent of education. She also wasn't able to raise money. . . . She didn't have the resources and she didn't have the organizational structure across the state. And you had a guy in Bill Byrne who felt that because he came from the most Republican county and as long as he carried high numbers in that county and he could tap into North Fulton and Gwinnett, that he could easily win the primary."

According to both Paul Bennecke and John Watson, Sonny Perdue's airplane was also a major factor in his success in the primary and in the general election. Bennecke comments, "An advantage we had over Bill Byrne and Linda Schrenko is the fact that Sonny Perdue is a pilot and has his own plane. Sonny was able to go to six, seven, eight events a day, while Bill Byrne and Linda Schrenko were driving around in a car, being able to do two or three events per day." Watson concurs: "His plane was a major factor in terms of tactically getting us around. In a state the size of Georgia, it is an unbelievable force multiplier to be able to be in multiple places." Watson also attributes campaign success to Perdue's work ethic. "The reality is it was Sonny's absolute dogged perseverance. The guy just won't be outworked."

Sonny Perdue was also much more effective in raising resources than either of his primary opponents. In their final campaign financial disclosures, Bill Byrne reported that he raised only $398,056 for his campaign, and the Schrenko campaign reported collecting $570,939. Both campaigns also reported spending all of their contributions, but Linda Schrenko's final report shows among her expenditures the repayment of a personal loan. By comparison, in the Perdue for a New Georgia campaign disclosure report dated July 3, 2002, fully six weeks before the primary vote, Perdue reported he had already raised $1,682,000, indicating that he had far more resources available to him than his opponents did on a combined basis. Perdue supported his campaign with a significant personal investment. His final 2001 required campaign disclosure reveals that he made sizeable contributions to the campaign on December 31, 2001, from each of several entities: Sonny Perdue personally, the Sonny Perdue for State Senate campaign fund, Houston Fertilizer and Grain Co., and AGrowStar each contributed $5,000 for the primary campaign and $5,000 to the general election campaign. In addition, he advanced $500,000 personally into the campaign account. He also reported more than $467,000 in contributions from others, including eighteen who contributed $5,000 or more, all of which he had raised in less than three months. So he began the election year with a relatively formidable war chest in comparison to his Republican opponents. John Watson comments on Perdue's fundraising for the primary election: "Through the process of just being dogged in pursuit, the governor was able to put some resources together. He also loaned his campaign resources that, thankfully, we were able to pay back."

In 2003 after the gubernatorial election, Georgians were astonished to learn that while she was running for governor and still serving as state school superintendent, Linda Schrenko had illegally appropriated several hundred thousand dollars in federal education grants to the State of Georgia and diverted some of those funds into her failed campaign. Schrenko was later criminally convicted and sentenced to serve a several-year term in a federal prison.

Although the Perdue campaign staff leaders all point to their targeted geographic strategies, the availability of air transportation, theirs and Perdue's hard work in campaigning, and their relative success in fundraising when compared to their Republican opponents' efforts, they also all agree that the infamous "King Roy rat video" was the *coup de grace* that catapulted the Perdue campaign to its primary victory. Rusty Paul reports that the Perdue campaign seemed to be in trouble in late spring 2002: "In the primary, Sonny's campaign was based in my office . . . and one day John Watson called us all in to show us some political polling data. . . . The poll numbers showed Linda Schrenko ahead, and Sonny in danger of falling into third place behind Bill Byrne." Watson relates that as a result of that disappointing polling data, the campaign staff determined that they needed to create a big splash for the campaign that would provide them free or "earned" media coverage. He explains, "Earned is what you get through news releases and what people report on you through newspapers radio and television—to counterbalance our deficit from a paid media standpoint. We focused on King Roy." Fred Davis and Dan McLagan were charged with creating the splash, and

McLagan describes the video titled "A New Day Dawning" that they developed to gain media attention.[7]

> It was a video that was mostly biographical about Sonny. We wanted to make a little bit of sensation so we tried to come up with something controversial that would get it launched in the media. It was Fred's idea to portray Roy Barnes as a giant rodent with a crown storming through downtown Atlanta. Actually that portion of the video was a very small portion. Most of it was biographical. Sonny went back and forth on it a lot. He finally decided to go ahead, and we spent $40,000 making the thing, which was a huge chunk of our campaign budget at the time. Then we had a party to air it at the Roxy in Buckhead. We invited all kinds of big donors to come down and see it. We told the media the day of it. The press kind of yawned and ho hummed, and I kept pushing it. Finally, I called Bill Nigut and a few others and said, "We are going to play this video that portrays the sitting governor as a giant rodent rampaging through downtown Atlanta." I remember Nigut was on his way to some opera, some artsy thing, and he said, "I will be there in five minutes." He came down, and a satellite truck met him, and it just exploded. What really made it carry further than that were a couple of things. First of all, the Barnes people fired back. They were mad. They fired back, and they generated controversy. Front page Metro—I have the front page story that has a picture of a rat in the Gold Dome. Not only that, the primary opponents sensed that we had gained some traction, and they attacked us. They said it was in bad taste and an insult to the governor. Well, in a Republican primary to become an apologist for Roy Barnes, it was a terrible move on their part, so we went on shooting back and forth with them. We never looked back after that. We sailed to victory.

John Watson also commentates on the benefit of the earned media from the rat video: "That really launched us in terms of Roy. Roy answered and tactically they should never have engaged us. Roy and his people were so aghast by that they actually started talking about us. As opposed to blowing us off, as they should have, they engaged us and really moved Sonny into the obvious opponent and really left Schrenko and Byrne in the dust. That moved us from number three to number one."

An *Atlanta Journal-Constitution* news article in the May 23, 2002, edition reports on the success of the video: "Perdue's campaign suddenly found itself swimming in attention. . . . His website jumped from its daily average of a few hundred hits to 89,000. That's where the campaign mounted a downloadable 10-minute video that combines a Perdue biography with footage of a computer-enhanced multistory rat stalking downtown Atlanta. The rat wears a crown and a necklace identifying it as King Roy." Soon the website hits climbed to 175,000 a week.[8]

Although the Perdue campaign did receive some criticism for the video, McLagan replied to the press that the video was "all in fun." Scott Rials offers his own justification: "That rat video would have never worked had not people already had the perception they did of Roy Barnes." Dick Pettys's observations about the video from a press perspective tend to support Rials's defense of their ploy:

> I think it [the video] was limited to the internet, but it certainly gave everybody an opportunity to look at this guy, Sonny Perdue. I think the first reaction we all had after seeing it was "this was really just way over the top, and obviously this guy is going to run as part of the lunatic fringe, so it would be safe to ignore." But the more we looked at it, the more important it seemed to become, because what it did was it gave kind of a face and a voice to the undercurrent that had been out there all along. "This guy has been a pretty dictatorial sort of governor," at least that's what some people thought.

Perdue supplies his own rationale for permitting the production of the controversial video: "We had to do something to distinguish ourselves in the primary. . . . This was directed at Republican voters, and it was directed to show people that I was willing to take on Governor Barnes and could be a competitor. He [Barnes] rather enjoyed sort of the political power, and he didn't shrink away from the 'King Roy label.' . . . I finally allowed it because strategically we realized we had to make a difference in the primary, and that was when we released it."

Unexpectedly, the Barnes campaign did retaliate late in the summer and ran several negative television ads against Sonny Perdue. Trey Childress reports that on the Friday before the August 20 primary election, Barnes supporters sponsored ads criticizing Perdue for writing several letters to the Pardons and Parole Board while he was a state senator, requesting that family members of his constituents be considered for either a pardon or an early parole from prison. In Childress's opinion, the ads just raised Perdue's name recognition without detrimental effect. Paul Bennecke concurs that the ads that were intended to be negative may have actually backfired on the Barnes team and aided Perdue in the primary: "You had Roy Barnes actually running negative ads against Sonny Perdue in the primary, which was unprecedented, and I think it gave Republican voters a question of why would an incumbent Democratic governor engage in a Republican primary against a particular candidate? There has to be a particular reason."

John Watson explains how another late primary campaign maneuver helped Perdue win the Republican primary without a runoff. The Perdue campaign developed a last minute mail-out disparaging Linda Schrenko's alleged improper use of state assets. "I am convinced that the reason we ran and won without a runoff actually was one last-minute flyer that we put out on Linda Schrenko. Linda had used the state jet a number of times to fly to D.C. She loved going to D.C. to cabal with all the educational bureaucrats. . . . It was a very effective direct mail piece that went into prime Republican households, and I am convinced it kept her numbers down and allowed us to get out without a runoff."

The Republican and Democratic primary elections were scheduled at an unusually late date in 2002—not until August 20. Astute political observers attribute this late date for a primary election to the desire of the Barnes administration to provide the winning Republican candidate with as little time as possible to mount a general election campaign against Barnes after a long and expensive primary contest. Michael Thurmond comments on this type of political maneuvering as being a potential danger to the party in power: "Let me tell you what started to happen. . . . The Democrats started playing with the election process. They started moving the dates around and just being one-half too smart."

When the Republican votes were counted, the results showed that Perdue had polled 259,966 votes representing 50.8 percent of the total, while Shrenko finished second with 28 percent and Byrne third with 21.2 percent of the votes. Perhaps the most impressive aspect of the Perdue victory is that he won the majority of votes cast in 147 of Georgia's 159 counties, losing only 11 counties, mostly in East Georgia, to Linda Shrenko, and only Bill Byrne's home county of Cobb to him by less than 5,000 votes. He also won a majority of votes in all but three of the 71 targeted rural counties. Almost 512,000 Georgia citizens voted in the Republican primary that year, compared to only 434,892 voting in the uncontested Democratic primary, making the 2002 election cycle the first in the state's history in which more Georgians voted in a Republican primary than in a Democratic primary election. Perdue's campaign chairman Alec Poitevint explains how important it was for the campaign to win the primary election without a costly runoff:

"With the money that Roy Barnes had, I really was worried about it....Looking back over it, there isn't any doubt about it that if we had been in a runoff in that primary with the resources that Roy had, we probably would not have won. We needed to win the primary." Chris Young shares Poitevint's opinion and adds that "the single most important factor of us winning the general election in November was him [Perdue] winning the primary without a runoff."

The 2002 General Election—Perdue v. Barnes

Once Perdue had won the Republican primary, he faced an even greater challenge in running against a powerful and extremely well-financed incumbent governor. Roy Barnes had served many years in the Georgia General Assembly in both the Senate and House and was regarded as a master politician and strategist. Many of Barnes's initiatives to improve education and relieve traffic congestion in Metro Atlanta were well regarded and popular with the state's business and civic leaders. However, in his zest to accomplish what he perceived as changes needed to move Georgia forward economically, Barnes apparently offended the sensibilities of several critical citizen groups. The Perdue campaign was able to attack Barnes on several of these issues and gain sufficient traction with some of these groups to overcome most all of Barnes's perceived campaign advantages.

Roy Barnes and his administration had focused much of their attention on a comprehensive A Plus Education Reform program to improve the quality of K–12 education in the state. In the late 1990s and the first years of the new millennium, the Barnes administration had ploughed several hundred million dollars in surplus state funds into new school construction. His reform legislation proposed to expand pre-kindergarten options and mandated lower class sizes but delayed the effective date until after the 2002 election cycle. Among other initiatives, the Barnes-sponsored legislation in HB 1187, passed in 2000, called for greater teacher accountability in improving student test scores and graduation rates. In addition, the Barnes administration talked about its support of merit pay for schoolteachers and principals, based on student achievement. Barnes also called for a more centralized approach to managing the educational delivery system in Georgia that purportedly would have given the State Department of Education greater influence over local schools. In an especially controversial move, the Barnes administration effectively eliminated tenure for newly-hired teachers by requiring renewable certificates of proficiency. Representative Bob

Holmes served on Governor Barnes's educational study commission and makes this observation about the tenure issue:

> I think he [Barnes] did a great job as governor. I thought he overreached because he tried to do too much. . . . I was on this blue ribbon task force that did this thing on K through 16. Then he came up with this notion that we had never even considered, and hell, we had been meeting for 18 months. . . . I said "Wait a minute, this thing hasn't been vetted—this certificate of continuous employment." In the university system it's tenure—why would you throw something out there like that in an election year?

Dick Pettys also comments on Roy Barnes's tendency to try to influence the outcomes of his education study commission: "He had these series of meetings. He had 50 or 60 people there. And if you went to the commission meetings, you would see that it was really—there wasn't any give and take—it was more Roy tossing out ideas and getting feedback from them. Roy was just having a big conversation with himself. And he was deciding on the results."

It turned out that many local educators strongly disagreed with what they perceived as Roy Barnes's fault-finding with the existing education system and current teaching methods. To many teachers it seemed like the Barnes administration was laying the blame at their feet for the defects in the educational system of Georgia, and many of them were resentful of what they considered to be Barnes's criticism.

Dick Pettys reports how he experienced this building resentment in the state's educational community:

> I was with Sonny on a campaign tour through Middle Georgia, and we ended up in Fitzgerald. . . . I think it was a teacher workday, and they were talking to him about how much they didn't like the Barnes education stuff. And then we ended up at a Friday night football game. And Sonny came in to the stands, and he stopped and talked to this teacher who was just raising all kinds of hell with Roy Barnes. He shook her hand and smiled and said "Help is on the way."

Perdue was able to take advantage of teacher dissatisfaction with Governor Barnes by campaigning on his promise to give a greater voice to parents, teachers, students, and local boards of education regarding the key decisions that affected their school systems. Dan McLagan describes how the teacher dissatisfaction with Barnes benefited the Perdue campaign:

> The teachers were mad. I mean Barnes, through tenure and some other things, just really "dissed" the teachers. He basically blamed them for failings in education; at least that was their perception of it. . . . This was probably the biggest bloc of votes that Barnes upset. . . . They should have been Barnes's base, being a Democrat. Teachers tend to be more Democratic in their unions. Their union that year did not endorse him that was seen as a huge slap in the face to Barnes. I think we got a pretty good chunk of those folks. . . . Teachers are not only individuals, but their families vote along with the interests of teachers.

Georgia has more than 200,000 active, retired, and former schoolteachers and school administrators, most of whom tend to be politically aware and active, and they constitute a large force of potential voters with which to reckon in any election campaign.

In the early years of his administration, Governor Barnes was successful in sponsoring and passing his legislation, partly because he was something of a master of legislative processes by virtue of his many years of experience in the state Senate and House and perhaps also because many of the legislative leaders were appreciative of his ability to counter the rising Republican tide and retain the governor's office for the Democratic Party for another term. In his first year as governor, Barnes was aggressive in developing new approaches to transportation and traffic congestion issues, especially in Metro Atlanta. In his first year in office, he sponsored and passed legislation through the General Assembly to create the Georgia Regional Transportation Authority with strong powers over regional transportation and large-scale commercial and residential real-estate development projects.[9] In addition, he increased the powers of the State Road and Tollway Authority and proposed an ambitious $8 billion GARVEE transportation bond program to build new roads. Both of these authorities, whose boards were either appointed or chaired by the governor, were regarded by the state transportation establishment embedded in the Georgia Department of Transportation (GDOT) as threats to their traditional power and influence over transportation decision making. Several members of GDOT's influential board, elected from each congressional district by members of the General Assembly, and some of the senior GDOT staff were somewhat resentful of the potential transfer of influence away from their bailiwick. There was a prevailing perception that

Roy Barnes was grabbing power away from the customary decision makers, and this belief provided the political fodder that inspired the Perdue campaign to produce the controversial rat video, portraying "King Roy" rampaging through the streets of Atlanta.

The Barnes administration was also considered to be the primary sponsor of a plan to build a "Northern Arc" limited-access superhighway through the largely pastoral exurbs of the north metro area, against the wishes of many of the residents in the Gwinnett, Forsyth, and Cherokee counties. Some real-estate developers with property interests in tracts of potentially developable land along the route of the proposed right-of-way of the Northern Arc highway were also reported among the financial contributors to Roy Barnes's reelection campaign, including developer Wayne Mason of Gwinnett County, who along with his wife contributed $20,000 to the Barnes reelection campaign in 2001.[10] The new roadway was to be financed by the GARVEE bonds that the Barnes administration planned to issue. The Perdue campaign capitalized on the opposition to this proposed new roadway.

Most of the residential neighborhood associations that were along the path of the proposed Northern Arc roadway were adamantly opposed to this addition to the state's transportation network and organized against the project. Business consultant Jeff Anderson of Forsyth County played a leading role in opposing the Northern Arc and invited Sonny Perdue to aid his efforts to stop the new road. According to campaign policy director Trey Childress, the Perdue for a New Georgia campaign set up a website to express its opposition to the Barnes-backed roadway. Dan McLagan relates how this issue played out:

> The Northern Arc was a big soft spot for him [Barnes]. We hit him so hard on it and so often on it, he actually temporarily withdrew the arc plan during the campaign, and he shelved it—I think with the intention of getting back to it after he got reelected. Talk about a group of riled-up, motivated people. They were just savage. It turned out that many of his buddies and campaign donors—road builder and developer types— had given him money. . . . We hit him pretty hard on that.

In the general election, voters in the three northern counties of Cherokee, Forsyth, and Gwinnett, along the proposed route for the Northern Arc, voted overwhelmingly for Perdue and against Barnes by an almost 2 to 1 margin. In fact, the Perdue votes from those three key counties accounted for slightly more than 20 percent of his total votes in that election.

The Perdue campaign also focused voter attention on another transportation and development-oriented issue involving the Barnes administration. The 6.2-mile Georgia 400 toll road that runs between I-285 on the north and I-85 on the south opened in the early 1990s under the management of the State Road and Tollway Authority (SRTA) and has been a huge success. The usage of the tollway was high enough in its early years that even with a low fifty cents toll, the revenues were sufficient for the tolling authority to accumulate several million dollars in reserve funds in their treasury. While he was board chair of SRTA, the board approved the purchase of a 6-acre tract of land adjacent to the new Atlantic Station development in midtown Atlanta from the project developer for a price in excess of $10 million, an amount that surpassed the later appraised value of the land. Some of the land was used to provide right-of-way for a new City of Atlanta street through the heart of the development, and the rest of the land purportedly was to be used at a later time for a transit terminal. However, there was some perception that the Barnes administration had misused its authority by diverting excess toll revenues to an unrelated development project and to the apparent benefit of the project developer, Jacoby Development Inc., that had contributed $10,000 in November 2001 to the Barnes reelection campaign for the primary and general elections. The Perdue team ran a campaign ad displaying stacks of toll quarters totaling $10 million and criticizing the land purchase as an abuse of power by Governor Barnes.

The manner in which the Barnes administration guided the adoption of a new state flag for Georgia also developed into a high-profile campaign issue. In 1956, at a time of heightened civil rights debates and following the 1954 United State Supreme Court decision of *Brown v. Board of Education*, the General Assembly of the state adopted a new state flag that featured the St. Andrews Cross, a battle emblem of the old Confederacy. Needless to say, this flag was a source of irritation to many African Americans in the state, and by the late 1990s it was also becoming a source of embarrassment to many business and civic leaders who were increasingly promoting tourism and economic development on a global basis, including Atlanta's hosting of the Centennial Olympic Games in 1996. Previous Democratic governor Zell Miller had proposed a flag change during his administration, but his plan met with so much resistance from legislators and citizens who advocated for retaining a flag that highlighted the Confederate heritage of the state that he withdrew his proposal. After his election to the governorship, Roy Barnes bravely took up the flag issue. When Cecil Alexander, a leading Atlanta architect, designed an alternative flag for Georgia that minimized the display of the Confederate battle emblem, Barnes seized upon the opportunity to adopt this new flag design as the official flag of the state. Alexander explained that Atlanta attorney Joe Beck helped him with the flag design that contained replicas of five flags that had flown over Georgia over the course of its history. Barnes urged the General Assembly to approve the proposed new flag, which they did rather rapidly. According to Trey Childress, the Barnes administration's House Bill 16, approving the new design for the state flag, moved rapidly through the General Assembly and passed both houses within five days of its being reported out of a House committee. This was a much-expedited process.

In fact, the flag vote in 2001 seemed to split across geographic boundaries as much as it did across political parties. Twenty-six rural white Democrats in the House voted against the flag change. In a much closer vote in the Senate, six Republicans from urban and suburban districts voted for the new flag, while four rural white Democrats voted against it, for a thirty-four to twenty-two final vote. Still, some detractors considered that Barnes's advocacy of the new flag was too heavy-handed, and their dramatic, Confederate flag-waving protest demonstrations around the state made the new Barnes flag a big campaign issue.[11]

The Perdue campaign promised Georgia voters an opportunity to select their choice of a flag by referendum and thereby provided a counterpoint to Barnes's flag position. During the campaign, the "flaggers," as those desiring to revive the 1956 flag came to be called, exacerbated this issue and provided constant visual reminders to Georgians that Governor Barnes had not allowed them a role in choosing their own state flag. According to Paul Bennecke, it appeared to the Perdue campaign team that in some more rural communities where Roy Barnes would go for fundraising events, he would seemingly eschew broad-based public appearances to avoid flagger demonstrations. "You didn't see Roy Barnes having real campaign events," Bennecke said, "going out and touching people, typically because of the protests and people that were demonstrating at the events. . . . Roy Barnes would go in the back door. Literally, they would pull their car up to the back door, go in and have their fundraiser and get back in their car and go to the airport."

Critics of the Perdue campaign accuse him of playing to racist bias in Georgia by resurrecting the flag debate. Criticism of the new state flag chosen by the Roy Barnes administration was seen by some as a throwback to the kind of race-baiting that was prevalent in Georgia politics in the 1950s and 1960s, and thereby, it was considered to be a racially divisive issue. Bob Holmes, an African-American veteran Democratic legislator, recognizes the potentially divisive nature of the flag issue but doesn't seem to believe the flag issue turned out to be particularly consequential in the 2002 election results:

> I think Governor Perdue saw it as something that would generate a lot of votes. He thought there was a latent sentiment against changing the flag and that by making it an issue it would bring these folks out. But by my calculations—and I could be wrong—but people's lives are not governed by symbolic things like that when the concern was what was going to be happening in this state in the future . . . tax cuts . . . the quality of educa-tion . . . SAT's. . . . The business community wasn't interested in that nonsense, and neither were the people who had moved to this state— people that moved here from Chicago and New York and everyplace else. Those people didn't give a damn about the flag. . . .The idea of it having a statewide impact was going to be inconsequential.

Michael Thurmond also comments on the race issue surrounding the flag debate: "It was a big issue. . . . I think it had a racial component to it, you can't deny that. . . . Were there some people that saw it as a symbol of white supremacy or black hatred? Yes. But I don't think everyone who supported the old flag was racist."

Journalist Dick Pettys picks up on the process issue on which Perdue was trying to focus the attention of the electorate, as opposed to just the racist symbolism of the 1956 flag, and also dismisses the flag issue as not being all that consequential in the 2002 election:

> I don't think that were that many votes out there to kill him [Barnes] on the flag change. . . . What I think is this—they didn't like the way it was done. It was sprung on the people; it was run through the House. In one day it came out of Rules and went to the House floor; he addressed the House; it passed the House. Over the weekend the Senate had time to think about it and they passed it, and within a week the flag was changed. And that's what people saw as Roy's arrogance. If he had said in the senate of the State "this is what I want to happen," you'd have the normal debate

... there'd be plenty of controversy, but there wouldn't have been this thing of "he shoved it down our throats."[12]

Sonny Perdue also criticized the Barnes administration for what he considered to be election-year overspending of state funds that had accumulated in the economic growth years of the late 1990s in the face of an economic downturn. And then, when the state experienced a decline in revenues in fiscal year 2002, the government was forced to use its revenue shortfall reserve to fund Medicaid and other programs that had been expanded by the legislature during the Barnes administration. Perdue also criticized the Barnes administration for replacing budgeted state cash funds for a massive new public school construction program with bond funds so that the previously appropriated cash funds could be diverted to other initiatives. Paul Bennecke summarizes Perdue's stance on state finances, "And you had someone in Sonny Perdue who consistently was a fiscal conservative who urged balancing the budget and not going into debt and living within our means, and just because it's an election year doesn't mean we can't make prudent cuts in state government. I think the deficit was an issue for fiscal conservatives, and the threat of possible tax increases because of the deficit." Perdue's positions on financial management quite likely appealed to fiscal conservatives around the state.

Continuing dissatisfaction over the 2001 reapportionment process was still a divisive issue during the 2002 gubernatorial campaign. The anguish over the split districts was particularly acute because 2002 was the first general election in which candidates had to run from the new districts. Because some of the new districts overlapped with the old ones, several incumbent legislators were forced to run against each other or not run at all. This situation was particularly prevalent in traditionally Republican districts, but even many Democrats resented the new district lines that divided counties and precincts that had previously been unified. John Watson comments on this campaign issue: "From a strategic level, reapportionment was an issue that people were reminded about constantly. It made them angry. What the Democrats had done was seen as a power grab. It was seen as not fundamentally fair."

Morgan Perry Cook, working on behalf of Senate candidates around the state in 2002, also sensed the citizens' concerns about reapportionment: "The biggest telltale signs were that you would go to South Georgia, and these people were angry with Roy Barnes. He had split up counties—and Georgia was the last state to leave the county unit system. Counties were important, and he had shown a blatant disregard for county lines and had been disrespectful of the political process." Senator George Hooks expressed his opinion about the significance of the redistricting issue when he said, "If I had to put my finger on one thing that turned it [the election], I think I would put it on reapportionment."

Even Barnes's support of laws against what many perceived as unsavory predatory lending practices earned him some opposition. Roy Barnes actively supported consumer groups that advocated for tighter restrictions on mortgage-lending practices to minimize the incidence of high interest rates, large fees, and other predatory lending activities. However, some business interests felt like the consumer protection laws passed under the Barnes administration had gone too far. The Federal National Mortgage Association even considered ceasing the purchase of mortgage loans originated in Georgia for fear that the penalties even for inadvertent error were too great to justify investment in Georgia-originated home mortgage loans. As Perdue's campaign aide Nick Ayers explains, "Bankers were treated like they couldn't be trusted to make loans without great regulation." Ayers expounds on how the Perdue campaign addressed a myriad of dissatisfactions with the Barnes administration:

> Sonny was out there talking about respecting the will of the people. He would always pull out a copy of the Declaration of Independence and give a really passionate speech about the importance of the power of the people versus the people of power. He really campaigned on returning respect to people whether it was on the flag or whether it was in education or banking. . . . Our website was really robust with what we were going to do in all of these different areas. It was like Roy had political diverticulitis. We were out saying how we were going to cure this pocket of dissatisfaction and this pocket of dissatisfaction.

Former Democratic House Speaker Larry Walker sums it up clearly: "Roy Barnes is the only governor in history that managed to make everyone mad at the same time...He was like the Confederate Army fighting on too many fronts at one time. I think the schoolteachers were upset with Roy, the flaggers were upset with Roy, the law enforcement people were upset with Roy, the sheriffs were upset with Roy. The Republican tide was running, and it was running strong."

Sonny Perdue also campaigned on a theme of what he labeled as "restoring trust in government." He called for ethics legislation that would limit what he called the revolving door from legislator to lobbyist or agency head to lobbyist, and he urged a ban on gifts from lobbyists and vendors to state officials and legislators. He also pledged to appoint an Inspector General to seek out and disclose fraud, waste, and abuse in state government practices.

In contrast to the Perdue campaign that was continually attacking Roy Barnes on various public positions that he had taken on a variety of issues, the Barnes campaign stayed focused primarily on promoting what they considered to be the virtues and accomplishments of the governor's first administration. The Barnes campaign largely ignored Perdue's candidacy and concentrated on a TV ad campaign extolling education reform, economic development, and tax relief from a "sales tax holiday" to state-paid increases in homestead exemptions. When Guy Millner had run against Roy Barnes in 1998, Millner pledged to repeal the property tax on automobiles for all Georgians. Later on, the Barnes administration had responded by introducing a program whereby homestead exemptions were gradually increased from $2,000 to $10,000 per household at the expense of the state government, which was required to reimburse local governments for the revenue lost as the result of higher homestead exemptions. He also sponsored legislation providing for "sales tax holiday" for Georgians buying school clothing and computers over a specified weekend, initially in March 2002.[13]

Only in the last weeks did the Barnes campaign really attack Sonny Perdue. Shortly before the election, the Barnes team ran television advertisements criticizing Perdue for voting against the state lottery in 1993 and for sponsoring natural gas deregulation legislation that resulted in some dislocations in the state's energy industry that became apparent during the economic downturn.

As the campaign progressed into the fall months, those staffers and volunteers who were continually traveling around the state with Perdue began to sense a victory, or at least they now dared to think it possible. The campaign team continued its focus on targeted rural counties, and Perdue was able to get his message across in farming communities especially by using the agricultural analogy that "It's time to rotate the crops in Atlanta." Paul Bennecke recollects, "There wasn't a county in the state where you didn't see Sonny Perdue signs. They were all over, and the difference is they weren't just on the side of the road. They were in people's yards . . . they were put in the windows of small businesses that were on the square in small towns."

Nick Ayers, who traveled constantly with Perdue, relates that he sensed the likelihood of winning fairly early in the general election campaign:

"Because he and I were really the ones out on the road, we realized we were going to win. . . . There was a hunger for change." Campaign Chair Alec Poitevint comments on his observations about the momentum of Perdue's campaign and that of Saxby Chambliss for the U.S. Senate that same year: "I knew we could win. . . . Saxby was running at the same time. There was a different energy in people for Sonny Perdue than there was for Saxby. There was not any doubt that they were for him [Saxby], but they were energized for Sonny Perdue. Sonny's campaign had the energy." Democrat Larry Walker also picked up on the momentum in the later days of the campaign: "Candidly, I didn't think he could win, but you heard so many people say 'Well, Sonny Perdue is not going to win, but I'm going to vote for him.' You heard a lot of that." Democrat Michael Thurmond also observed the growing support for Perdue and states, "I was out there running at the same time. So I was seeing the signs out there in rural Georgia, in the yards and on the byways and highways. He ran, literally, a grassroots effort—under funded compared to Barnes—but he tapped into something that ultimately made a difference."

Dan McLagan relates how Sonny Perdue's confidence grew as the campaign progressed: "Well, to be perfectly honest I think the only two people in the State of Georgia that knew that Sonny Perdue was going to win were Sonny and Mary Perdue. He was absolutely certain of it. He sensed it out there." Mary Perdue also felt the possibility of victory as she traveled the state. She and the wives of the other leading Republican statewide candidates, Julianne Chambliss and Cristal Stancil, traveled together on several occasions to different regions of the state primarily to attend women's events and ask for support for their husband's candidacies. Nick Ayers also reports on Perdue's optimism: "I think Sonny felt pretty confident that he was going to win in October and started talking about governing. He was getting ahead of the curve." Chris Young discloses that Perdue and some of Perdue's advisors began to discuss transition issues in late October: "About two weeks before the election, the governor said, "You know, we are going to have to govern,' and he and Morgan, and I and Bill Stephens—because Bill was to become the transition spokesperson—gathered, and we began to have really serious discussions about what a transition would look like. That's when I first heard him talk about having a CFO and COO and running it like a business. That's where names like Carl Swearingen and Hank Huckaby popped up." Hank Huckaby, Perdue's transition and first chief financial officer (loaned to the Perdue administration by the University of Georgia), and retired Bellsouth executive Carl Swearingen, who headed the Perdue transition team, acknowledge that Perdue contacted each of them a week or so before the election to secure commitments from them to assist him in the transition effort in preparation for taking office.

In the last weeks of the campaign, the Perdue team stepped up its polling activities. McLagan reveals that the polling numbers showed steady improvement as the campaign approached the date of the election, but Perdue was never ahead. "When I went out with Sonny, I would pick up on the energy of the crowds. There was something going on. People were fired up. We were also beginning to look at the poll numbers. We were polling particularly at the end, and we had a little surge, and we were getting pretty close, but we were never ahead of them, and it kind of tailed off."

Even though the polling numbers did not show Perdue ahead of Barnes, there was an indication that the Barnes campaign did not have a victory nailed down. John Watson explains how the campaign staff used tracking polls: "In politics you have what's called tracking polls. . . . Normal surveys are 500 to 700 to get statistical validity. What you do in tracking polls is you do a smaller sample, but you do it every third night. You pick up the newest data. We began to notice that Roy just simply could not get over 50 percent. After $20 million spent on his behalf, something was happening." Morgan Perry Cook summarizes her observations about the last few days of the campaign: "Roy Barnes's negatives kept rising. The undecideds stayed the same. Generally, when that happens, it's a good sign the undecideds are going to break your way. And the weekend before the election we had a bus tour, and we just had bigger and bigger crowds everywhere we went."

In the last few days, Paul Bennecke also began to sense that Sonny Perdue's support was strengthening. Perdue describes himself as a facts-based decision maker, and he and Bennecke were analyzing the polling results. Bennecke describes how they dissected the data:

> When you are in a non-presidential year, you always know turnout is going to be lower. . . . Now the question is the intensity of the people who are likely to vote in a low turnout year—the people who every time the polling place is open—turn out and vote. What is their intensity against or for a particular candidate? Even though Sonny Perdue was losing head-to-head among likely voters—among voters who were definitely voting, we were actually up. We knew that the intensity factor of those who wanted to kick Roy Barnes out or vote to elect someone new—those intensity numbers

were much higher for us than they were for Roy Barnes, which is an advantage in a low turnout year.

Scott Rials and Dan McLagan both think that many of the undecided voters rejected Barnes and were swayed toward Perdue because of a misstep by Barnes in a mid-October television debate between the candidates. When Barnes was asked about citizen concerns regarding the death of a child while in custody of the Georgia Department of Family and Children's Services, Barnes retorted to the effect that in a system as large as Georgia's child welfare agency where you have 20,000 kids, you could have a child die every day! The Perdue staff were stunned but seized the opportunity to spotlight Barnes's statement and profile him as not caring about children. Scott Rials relates, "We turned that around in twelve hours and had an ad up on TV."

Sensing the potential for electoral victory and commanding the resources to take advantage of the opportunity, however, are two different issues, and the Perdue campaign was at all times considerably out-funded by the Barnes campaign. Paul Bennecke discloses one of the tactics the Perdue team used to counter Barnes's extensive and expensive television ad strategy: "We didn't have the money to compete against Roy Barnes—the focus of our resources and our time were on little things—like having people pay for a newspaper ad in the county paper telling people why they were supporting Sonny Perdue. We literally had grass roots supporters all chipping in $5, $10, $15 to buy a $200 ad, signing their names endorsing Sonny."

The Barnes campaign raised much of its funding early in the campaign, as they had been fundraising the entire four years of Barnes's term as governor. As of the required campaign contribution disclosure date in April 2002, the Barnes campaign had already raised and reported total contributions of $11,318,920, of which only $316,440 had been expended on campaign activities. Several hundred of Barnes's donors had given the legal maximum of $5,000 for the election. The campaign had raised and retained such a substantial amount of funds that they had to pay federal income taxes of $58,256 on interest income earned on invested funds. At the same report date, the Perdue campaign had raised only $1,280,958 in contributions, of which almost half had been contributed or advanced by the candidate himself or his businesses. At that report date, he had only eighteen other contributions of $5,000 or more. Perdue's campaign had expended $288,649, almost as much as the Barnes campaign.[14] After the August primaries, in which Roy Barnes had won an uncontested election, the next reporting date was in early October. On October 7 the Barnes campaign reported having raised $17,832,767 and had spent $10,274,141, retaining a balance of over $7 1/2 million for the one remaining month of the campaign. More than 500 hundred different contributors had given $5,000 or more to Barnes's reelection effort by that date. As of October 6 the Perdue campaign reported raising $2,462,608, of which they had spent $2,011,229, retaining only $451,379 for the final month of campaigning. Perdue reported fewer than 50 contributions of $5,000 or more by that report date.

On the disclosure report dated November 2, 2002, the Barnes campaign reported cumulative contributions of $19,680,695, by which time they had expended almost all of it or $19,154,992. The Barnes campaign's largest expenditures were paid to LUC, Inc., of Marietta, Georgia, for media (over $8 million), to Strother, Duffy, Strother, LLC of Washington D.C. for political consulting, and to various printing and polling firms. In its October 25 disclosure report, the Perdue for a New Georgia campaign reported raising contributions of $3,192,515 and expenditures by that date of $2,788,307. Among the larger payees were National Media of Alexandria, Virginia (slightly more than $450,000), and Strategic Perceptions of Hollywood, California, which is Fred Davis's campaign strategy firm.

In the final analysis, Barnes raised and spent almost $20 million, compared to slightly more than $3 million raised and spent by Perdue before the November 5 election. The victor was outspent by his opponent by a margin of almost seven to one. Both the Barnes campaign and the Perdue campaign filed their required final disclosure reports in early January 2003. Barnes's reports revealed that his campaign raised a total of $20,086,299 and spent $20,045,587, including a post election contribution to the Democratic Party of Georgia of $88,000.

An analysis of Barnes's many contributors reveals the breadth of his team's fundraising ambition and prowess. Large contributors include many of the business leaders individually and the leading businesses of the state, including major banks, law firms or their partners, real-estate developers, and alcoholic beverage distributors. The Barnes campaign contributor lists also show generous donations by many businesses either doing business with the state or aspiring to do so, such as healthcare service providers, nursing homes, paving contractors, consultants, and lobbyists. A sizeable number of Democratic state legislators or their own campaign funds also gave generously to Roy Barnes's reelection efforts. Representative Bob Holmes is somewhat critical of the Barnes campaign for raising as much money as they did. "The amount of money he raised was almost obscene. And that sucked money out of what other people who were facing threats could do. . . . But I don't blame him, per se, because obviously your first thing is to protect yourself, but it seemed like overkill."

Not surprisingly, many businesses and individuals who had not given to the Perdue for a New Georgia campaign before the election gave immediately following Perdue's victory. On the Perdue campaign's final report, dated March 31, 2003, contributions by that time totaled $4,796,690, of which $3,655,202 had been expended. The Perdue campaign had more than a 50 percent increase in giving after his election as governor.

An analysis of the Perdue contributions given before the election reveals that most were smaller donations of less than $1,000 and were from individuals and mostly small businesses geographically distributed around the state. More than two dozen of Perdue's contributions were from fellow Republican legislators or their campaign funds. Only after the election did the Perdue campaign receive many contributions from companies and lobbyists doing business or seeking business with the state government.

John Watson comments on the political landscape in Georgia in 2002 and how difficult it was for Sonny Perdue to raise campaign funding before the election:

> It was not thought by the majority of those in the Party apparatus that Sonny had a chance. The race that the state party was focused on was Saxby against Max Cleland. That is what the White House wanted because ultimately they care about votes in the Congress more than they do about governors. The party apparatus and party resources were focused solely on Saxby. The only resources we got from the national party were very late. We got about a half million dollars from the RGA [Republican Governors Association] and RNC [Republican National Committee].

The November 25, 2002, Federal Elections Commission report for Chambliss for Senate shows that the Chambliss campaign had raised slightly over $6 million by the report date, or roughly twice what the Perdue campaign had been able to raise for the election.

Perdue also comments on his disappointment that his campaign did not receive substantial funding from the Republican Party: "We were not a priority at all for the state party or the national party. No one, just literally no one, thought that I would win. So it wasn't a priority. I finally got a little bit of money late in October from the Republican Governors Association because I had raised money from people who wanted to see me elected but were fearful of giving me money directly, and some of them gave to the RGA and we were able to get some of that money back."

Perdue's campaign chairman Alec Poitevint had been heavily involved in national Republican Party activities, having previously served as treasurer of the RNC, so he was influential in getting Perdue in front of the people in Washington that controlled party resources. Poitevint reports on his involvement in finally cutting loose some national party funding for Perdue:

> There were people at the national party level that did not believe Sonny Perdue was going to win. . . . I know for a fact that Jack Oliver did not believe Sonny could win early on. He, in essence, was running the Republican Party. He was deputy chairman at the national level . . . then in a very important meeting that occurred at the RNC in Washington in the fall before that election . . . [former senator] Mattingly was there. Eric Tanenblatt [a Republican fundraiser and later Perdue's first chief of staff] was there. Fred Cooper was there, I was there—I was national committeeman. At the end of all the presentation about why they ought to be helping Sonny Perdue, I said I never worked with anybody that I thought was as good or appropriate for leadership or had the skills that Sonny had. Then they began to look at Sonny, and he got a token amount from RGA.

In addition, President George W. Bush visited Georgia on two occasions to endorse and urge support of Sonny Perdue's and Saxby Chambliss's candidacies. The president came to a luncheon for Chambliss and Perdue on October 17 at the Marriott Marquis Hotel in downtown Atlanta. He returned to Georgia just before Election Day as a last-minute boost to the candidacies of Chambliss and Perdue.

Dan McLagan reports that party leaders Eric Tanenblatt and Fred Cooper helped in other ways also. Eric Tanenblatt, who is an attorney and a national party activist, escorted Perdue to a Republican Governors Association meeting in Florida and introduced him to several traditional donors to Republican candidates, who in turn made generous contributions to his campaign. Businessman Fred Cooper was also actively involved in Perdue's campaign fundraising efforts, both on behalf of Perdue himself and on behalf of the Georgia Republican Party. McLagan explains how Cooper raised funds for the party: "Fred Cooper was chairman of what we called Victory 02. Every year there is a victory committee. It is a special organization that spends money on what are called multi-candidate activities, like flyers, etc."

A few key Republican legislators also provided meaningful guidance and assistance to Perdue's campaign. Various members of the Perdue for a New Georgia team mentioned state senators Eric Johnson, Tom Price, Bill Stephens, and Tommie Williams and state representative Jerry Keen as being particularly supportive. Also, House members Glenn Richardson of Paulding and Larry O'Neal of Houston both served as county chairmen for Sonny Perdue. Larry O'Neal lived in and represented Houston County and knew Perdue through both business and personal relationships. Glenn Richardson is from Paulding County in West Georgia and explains why he supported Sonny Perdue and served as his Paulding County chairperson:

> I knew who Sonny Perdue was, but I didn't know him personally that well. . . . There were three candidates in the field—Linda Schrenko, Bill Byrne, and Sonny Perdue. . . . I didn't think she [Linda Schrenko] was electable, and Bill Byrne was the other choice, who is a very conservative guy—Cobb County Commission chairman—had great name ID, but I didn't think he had the personality to win the governor's race. So, I picked Sonny. . . . I called them [Perdue's campaign] up and told them I wanted to help. . . . I said I am going to do more than I've ever done to elect Sonny Perdue as governor. . . . There was a county-by-county vote total that had to be reached, and I was Paulding County.

Even though several Republican legislators and party leaders were very active in Perdue's election effort, some members of the Perdue campaign team were somewhat resentful that the state Republican Party was not as helpful to Perdue with respect to fundraising as they might have wished. When asked about the degree of state party support, Nick Ayers replied, "There just wasn't any. The Republican Party did almost nothing for Sonny. The things they did were forced onto them by our supporters calling and other party leaders demanding that they be helpful." Ayers and John Watson both acknowledge that the Republican Party of Georgia, under the chairmanship of former Christian Coalition director Ralph Reed, was being requested by presidential advisor Karl Rove and the national Republican Party to devote its resources primarily to Saxby Chambliss's campaign for the U.S. Senate. Ayers explains, "Karl Rove and the president had given Ralph a very clear order—defeat Max Cleland. To Ralph's credit, he put together a plan that was going to do that, and they were not going to deviate from it. So I don't blame them for that."

Rusty Paul was less complimentary of Ralph Reed's role in the Perdue campaign: "There were some in the party who were ambitious for their own future, who may have been undermining the campaign. I think Ralph was hoping he would be able to run for governor in four years, and if Sonny got elected, it would derail his plans." On the other hand, Senator Eric Johnson is complimentary of Ralph Reed's stewardship of party resources as it pertained to state Senate candidate races that year: "The party, Ralph Reed, said we will match every dollar you raise for the Senate. So, it was really an inspiration to us, and we had record fundraising. It was Ralph Reed frankly that helped us raise the money and helped us focus on the Senate. If we had won one or two seats less, we would nor have been able to flip the Senate with the governor."

Although both the national and state Republican parties eventually provided some financial and other assistance to the Perdue campaign, it was Sonny Perdue, Alex Poitevint, Leigh Ann Wood Gillis, and other members of their campaign team that ultimately raised most of the resources needed to pay the campaign costs. Perdue's campaign finance director, Leigh Ann Gillis, reported that Sonny Perdue and members of his staff had to work hard to get contributions. She explained that a number of business leaders simply refused to take their calls, and several of those who did return the calls declined to contribute to the Perdue campaign based on their ties to the Barnes administration and/or their existing business relationships with state government.[15]

Up to the last day before the election, most political analysts assumed Roy Barnes would be reelected as governor. Dick Pettys reports on his pre-election night analysis: "The night before—the Monday—I had been out to PDK. I wound up at a Barnes event when his fly-around ended there. . . . What I remember that night is asking Bobby [Kahn] and his pollster, off the record, to tell me what the race was really going to be. Don't forget that all this time we'd been seeing these AJC polls saying Barnes is going to win . . . so he tells me and his pollster says, 'yep, we've got a poll and we are going to win.'"

On Election Day, November 5, 2002, Sonny Perdue decidedly defeated Roy Barnes. Perdue polled 1,041,677 votes, or 51.4 percent of the total, to Barnes's 937,062 votes, or 46.3 percent of the total (with a Libertarian candidate receiving the remaining 2.3 percent of the votes). Barnes actually polled 4,014 fewer votes in 2002 in running against Perdue than he did in 1998 in running against Guy Millner, even though 233,052 more in total votes were cast in the 2002 gubernatorial election. Perdue won the majority of votes cast in 118 of 159 counties and tied Barnes in the number of votes in Dooly County.

The Team Perdue strategy of targeting seventy-one counties that they believed to contain swing voters proved to be beneficial to the success of the campaign. All these counties were largely rural in nature, and the majority of voters in those counties, who, like Perdue, were mostly born into the Democratic Party, undoubtedly could identify more closely with Sonny Perdue and his rural roots than they had with any Republican who had previously run for governor. Perdue won the majority of votes in sixty-six of these seventy-one counties and lost five of the counties by a total of less than a thousand votes.

By contrast, in the 1998 gubernatorial race between Roy Barnes and Guy Millner, Barnes won in seventy of these counties and Millner won only Madison County, but only by six votes. Perdue's victories in these seventy-one swing counties was a significant factor in his overall margin of victory, as Perdue won 221,836 votes to Barnes's 141,371 votes, a difference of 80,465. Perdue's overall statewide margin of victory over Roy Barnes was only 104,615 votes. Apparently, it took a Republican candidate with rural connectivity to overcome the Democratic bias of many of the voters in majority white rural Georgia, and Perdue was savvy enough to recognize and take advantage of this opportunity.

When asked what factors he thought contributed to his victory, Perdue replied, "I think probably my geography. I think frankly the fact that I had been a Democrat. I think all those things contributed to their trusting me. A vote is essentially about trust and who they trust to do right by them. I believe many people in Georgia were having the same thoughts that I had thought about the same internal conflict—that I was born a Democrat . . . but this is not a group that I feel I can identify with anymore."

In contrast, Roy Barnes carried all eighteen of the majority black counties in the state and either won or tied in all but three of the counties with the highest percentage black population. Perdue won in Greene County and Screven County and tied in Dooly County. However, black voter turnout in the 2002 general election was considerably lower than it had been in 1998. Only 50 percent of registered black females voted and 44 percent of registered black males voted. This contrasts with 55 percent of registered white females voting and a high 59 percent of registered white males voting in 1998.

In addition to winning the majority of votes in the seventy-one targeted rural counties, Perdue picked up the majority of votes in the highest-growth counties in the metropolitan Atlanta suburbs, which traditionally have been the strongest base for any Republican candidate running statewide. An analysis of the voting patterns in the governor's races of 1998 and 2002 in the thirteen suburban counties of Carroll, Cherokee, Cobb, Coweta, Douglas, Fayette, Forsyth, Gwinnett, Hall, Henry, Paulding, Rockdale, and Walton shows that Barnes earned 40.87% of the total votes in his 1998 contest against Guy Millner, and even though he received more votes from these counties in 2002, his share of the total shrank to 37.2 percent. The growth in votes in these thirteen counties was almost 120,000 over the four years, and Perdue, the Republican candidate, won 76.6 percent of the additional votes in those counties in the 2002 election. Perdue's total vote from these thirteen Metro Atlanta counties tallied 378,308, which was 36.3 percent of his total vote in the 2002 general election.

Various campaign staffers comment on how Election Night unfolded and describe the elation and excitement of the Perdue team victory. Political Director Paul Bennecke tracked the county-by-county voting results against their expectations, and fairly early in the reporting process, the numbers revealed that Perdue was tracking equal to or ahead of goal in a number of counties. Bennecke expounds on the team's response to the votes as they were reported: "We were tagging all of our goals—we had a goal for each county that we had given to each county chairman and to our county organizations. People were calling in excited. Some people were even crying, saying, 'We hit our goal; we exceeded our goal!' and these were in rural places a Republican had never won."

Campaign Communications Director Dan McLagan discusses the media's take on the voting patterns as they became apparent:

> Most of the A-list reporters were at the Barnes campaign. Well, the Barnes campaign was not happy. They knew what was happening too. At their party Bobby Kahn and other top people were disappearing from the party and going into some other room. . . . I started getting calls from the press saying, "What's going on here? These guys don't seem happy. Is it going to be closer than expected? Could this be? Might there have to be a runoff?"
> . . . They were talking on TV saying, "Stronger than expected showing by Sonny Perdue. This could actually be a long evening." They were absolutely perplexed that this could be happening. . . . As that feeling got out there, all the other candidates for all the other offices on the

Republican side started coming to our hotel—more and more people. We had to move one wall to expand into the second ballroom . . . the place was going nuts! It was packed to the gills, and people were ecstatic.

Dick Pettys of the Associated Press shares his recollections about election night:

So Tuesday night I go to the bureau, and you know, we get the returns, and at some point I'm looking at these things and I tell my boss. I said, "There's no way Barnes is going to win. He's lost this thing." And I remember calling up Dan McLagan after we called the race, and I said, "Well, Dan, you're right." And he keeps reminding me of that. . . . But I think we were all stunned. Because you know, for years we had been writing about "Republicans are eventually going to take over," but they never had, and all of the sudden it's here, so what does this mean? What's going to happen?

Campaign Chairman Alec Poitevint relates his remembrances of that evening: "Victory night was sweet! We were at the Grand Hyatt in Buckhead. We had a small war room. . . . It was a small group of people who had stuck with Sonny from the beginning. . . . The very first votes that came out showed Roy leading. There was some number like Roy had 80 votes ands Sonny had 59. The next time there was a report, Sonny was ahead, and he never was behind the entire night."   Among those in the war room with Alec Poitevint, Dan McLagan, Paul Bennecke, and Sonny Perdue were campaign manager Scott Rials, consultant John Watson, Chris Young, Trey Childress, former senator Mack Mattingly, former Georgia attorney general Mike Bowers, state senator Rusty Paul, Fred Cooper, and Nick Ayers, who had traveled the state with Perdue for most of 2002. According to McLagan, the first person to call and offer congratulations was President George W. Bush, because Karl Rove had already predicted that Perdue had won. McLagan retains a photo of the governor taking the call from the president. After the president's call, Governor Barnes called to concede the election. Scott Rials relates how the Perdue and Barnes campaign staffs had arranged to communicate with each other on election night:

Tim Phillips was Roy Barnes's campaign manager. At the debate the Sunday before the election, we exchanged phone numbers to call each other and congratulate the winner. He was kind of like, "Y'all call me. Call me on my cell. Here is my cell number." . . . Tim Phillips called me at probably eleven o'clock. Tim said, "Scott, the governor would like to talk to the governor elect." I was on my cell phone. It was a bad reception in there, and I said, "Tim, can I call you back on a land line?" He did not want to. It was like, "Can we just do this and get it over with?" I said, "Tim, you are breaking up. Let me call you back." So he gives me the number, and I still have the number written on a little card. So I called the hotel room back. Tim said, "Hold on. Here is the governor." So I stayed on the phone a second. Roy gets on the phone. I handed the phone to Sonny. They said nice words and went on about it.

Nick Ayers describes the atmosphere in the war room at the time Barnes called: "I remember the room. You could have heard a pin drop. The phone rang. Sonny answered. Scott and I were on each side of him, and I could hear Governor Barnes concede. Sonny put the phone down, and we all jumped."

Meanwhile, Perdue supporters were streaming into the hotel ballroom to support their candidate. Don Cole describes the scene:

People started flowing into the Grand Hyatt around 7:00 P.M. . . . There was an air of excitement in the room as Sonny came out to speak the first time. The room was set up with a large projector and laptop computer linked to the Secretary of State website. When the screen showed 88 percent of the returns in and Sonny holding a strong lead, the crowd started the familiar chant that has followed Sonny across this state, "Sonny, Sonny, Sonny."[16]

Scott Rials describes how Perdue and team moved from the war room to the ballroom to meet with his supporters: "We took Sonny down through the kitchen and brought him out. Alec got up and said, 'Ladies and Gentlemen, the next governor.' By that time the air walls were coming back as Sonny was walking out. The sea of people filled the empty space, and they just kept coming into the ballroom. By the time he finished his speech the whole place was full. I was thinking where have all these people been up until now?"

All in all, the Republican Party in Georgia had a successful night on November 5, winning several statewide races in addition to Perdue's victory. Former state legislator Kathy Cox of Fayette County defeated her Democratic opponent, Barbara Christmas, earning 54.2 percent of the votes, to become superintendent of education. Insurance Commissioner John Oxendine handily won reelection for his third term with over 64 percent of the votes, and Republicans Doug Everett and Angela Speir defeated

Democratic challengers to win both Public Service Commission seats that were open that year.

However, the GOP failed to win the lieutenant governorship, as former state representative Steve Stancil lost to incumbent Democrat Mark Taylor by approximately 125,000 votes and a margin of 45.6 percent to 51.9 percent. Stancil won the majority of votes in only fifty-six counties, with most of those being in located Stancil's home territory of North Georgia and in the suburbs of Metro Atlanta. He won few of the targeted, majority white, rural counties in Central and South Georgia that provided Sonny Perdue with his margin of victory. In addition, Mark Taylor raised and spent more than $6 million on his campaign, whereas Stancil raised and spent only a bit over $1 million. Moreover, Stancil had spent most of his funding in a three-person Republican primary contest and a close runoff election with former state senator, Mike Beatty, leaving him little in funding to mount a media campaign against the better-known Taylor.

Six incumbent Republicans retained their seats in the U.S. House of Representatives, and two new Republican representatives replaced Republicans Chambliss and Bob Barr in the House. However, the Democrats picked up the two new seats created by the 2001 reapportionment of congressional districts. The new partisan mix in the Georgia U.S. House delegation became eight Republicans and five Democrats.

To the great satisfaction of Georgia's Republican Party's leadership, popular congressman Saxby Chambliss defeated incumbent U.S. Senator Max Cleland by polling 1,071,153 votes for 52.8 percent of the total. Chambliss won the majority of votes handily in the traditional Republican-base counties in Metropolitan Atlanta, but like Perdue, he was also able to appeal to small-town and rural voters in swing counties. He won the majority of votes in sixty-three of Perdue's targeted rural counties.

Saxby Chambliss was significantly assisted in his campaign by the national Republican Party and by President George W. Bush himself, who actively campaigned in Georgia for Chambliss. However, when Bush came to Georgia on October 17, three weeks before the general election, he also provided support for Perdue. Rusty Paul describes the importance of the Bush visit:

> What saved the campaign in the end was the president of the United States, George Bush, coming in at a very crucial time. . . . Some of the party leaders were telling the president, 'You need to come down for Saxby, but nothing can be done to save Perdue.' To their credit, Alec Poitevint,

Eric Tanenblatt, and Fred Cooper all told Karl Rove in the White House that if the president was coming down for Saxby he should come down for Sonny too. It gave Sonny a lot of visibility at a crucial time.

Paul Bennecke comments on symbiosis between the Chambliss candidacy and the Perdue candidacy: "I think having Saxby Chambliss on the ballot the same year with the amount of finance that the Senate committee poured in against Max Cleland [helped Perdue]—no question it helped Metro Atlanta turnout. And Sonny was a candidate who could also appeal to those same people. . . . I think if you looked at Sonny's numbers in rural areas, he helped Saxby, and in the metro areas Saxby helped Sonny." Perdue concurs with Bennecke's assessment and observes,

> Let me tell you a little bit about synergy between Saxby's campaign and our campaign. Because I think Saxby had the money through the Senatorial Committee to get on television here, which gave the general Republican population in Atlanta the sense that there is a Republican Party here. And many of them came and voted for me, but not all of them. . . . But there was synergy. He had the ability to spend money on television here, which inured to my benefit, and my grassroots outreach around the state certainly inured to his benefit.

Perhaps as critical to the success of the GOP in Georgia as the victories of Perdue, Chambliss, and others were the losses in the 2002 general election of two of the most important and influential Democrats in the General Assembly, veteran House Speaker Tom Murphy and Senate majority leader Charles Walker. Dick Pettys describes it as a "bloodbath" for the Democratic Party. Murphy, who at the time was the longest-serving state House Speaker in the country with twenty-nine years in that leadership position and forty-two years of service in the Georgia House, was defeated in his home district of Haralson County by a relatively novice challenger. Bill Heath, an electrical engineer from Murphy's own town of Bremen, ran against Murphy previously in 2000 and lost that year by a relatively small margin. The next time around in 2002, Heath defeated Murphy decisively in a district somewhat altered as a result of the 2001 reapportionment. Heath relates how he happened to challenge the legendary Speaker of the Georgia House the first time:

> The first challenge was in 2000. I had gotten involved in the party and had been recruiting people to run against Murphy. I never really thought about

doing it myself. I had been recruiting I think five people who had shown some interest in running against him in 2000. The week before qualifying, I found out that the last of those five definitely was not going to take on that challenge. I was having lunch with some friends and made the mistake of asking if they thought there was any chance that I could pull that off, and that's how it started. It was close, roughly 48.5 percent to 51.5 percent. It was only five hundred and fifty people. I never quit running after 2000. I was a viable candidate. People in the community said, "You know what, he could actually do this." So that removed some of the fear of supporting me. . . . The district did get better. The legislature approved a new district that was known to be more Republican. Most folks didn't think Bill Heath was going to win.[17]

But Bill Heath did win the second race by a vote margin of 54 percent to 46 percent.

Charles Walker's state Senate district in Augusta was presumed to be safe for him. However, all during the campaign, Walker was under continuing investigation by the United States Department of Justice for a variety of alleged criminal activities. As a result of the investigation, Republican Augusta attorney Randy Hall surprisingly defeated Walker in Hall's first bid for the state legislature.

The Republicans in Georgia had hoped to win a sufficient number of new seats in the 2002 elections to gain control of the state Senate. After Sonny Perdue had resigned his Senate seat in 2001 to run for governor and been replaced by a Democrat, the GOP retained only twenty-three seats. Morgan Perry Cook's primary activity during the 2002 election cycle was to assist Republican candidates for the Senate. When the final votes were tallied on Election Night, partly as a result of the gerrymandered districts resulting from the 2001 reapportionment, they had picked up only three of the six seats needed to gain control of the Senate.

On Election Night, Senate leaders Eric Johnson and Tom Price were in Atlanta to participate in the activities and joined Perdue for his victory celebration. After the celebration, Perdue and his former fellow senators discussed a plan for the GOP to secure control of the Senate. They hoped to influence at least three recently reelected Democratic senators to switch parties. Morgan Perry Cook reports on the planning process: "That night after the grand hoopla, we were still counting numbers. The Senate had a suite, and the governor, after his last speech, he came to the Senate suite, and the rest of the night was focused on the Senate because we knew we were close.

When it looked like we hadn't gotten there—that we had come up short—we already had a list prepared that Sonny and Eric and I had already had a conversation about." At Perdue's and Johnson's direction, Morgan and Nick Ayers had developed a confidential notebook in which they had identified potential party switchers and the committee posts and other privileges those senators would likely hope to retain if they switched parties.

Perdue and his senior campaign staff invited Morgan Cook and Senators Eric Johnson and Tom Price, as the senior Republicans in the state Senate, to join them early the next morning for a continuation of their strategy session from the night before. Johnson describes his recollection of the meeting: "Sonny said come on down to the war room in the morning. We walked into his war room, and it had a white board on it with tasks to do, and the first one on it was 'Take the Senate.' He said, 'I am going to take the Senate before the Democrats know what happened.'"

Dan Lee of LaGrange was the first senator that Perdue contacted. Lee tells about his conversation with Perdue:

> After the election, that night I got a call about one o'clock in the morning. I was not at home. The governor called me and left me a message: "Dan, I appreciate your supporting me. I know you cast it on principle. Can you come to the Hyatt tomorrow at 7:30?" I got the message about 5:30. About 6:00 I left and went to the Hyatt, and we started a conversation about maybe getting the Senate. We started thinking about who might make a change. The discussion was along the lines of do we switch parties or do we just vote? The discussion became we have to switch parties because that's the open and direct thing to do.

According to Morgan Perry Cook, Lee had already committed to Perdue that he would support him in any way he could.

Dan Lee was certainly a likely person to support Perdue. Lee relates how Perdue had an early influence on his public service commitment:

> I ran for the state Senate in 1997–1998. When I made the decision to run, I could not decide what party to run with, so I just came here to the Capitol and told the guard I wanted to talk to the head Republican. He replied, "He's in that wing right there" and pointed right across the hall. I went in there, and there was not a soul over there. So I went back to the guard and said, "Where is the head Democrat?" He said "Well, that's probably the governor." So I said, "Is the head senator here?" The guard replied "Oh yeah. He's always here." I said, "Who is that?" The guard replied

Sonny Perdue. So I went to the third floor. I walked in and Sonny Perdue was sitting there. I introduced myself, and he said, "Sit down." Three and a half hours later he had convinced me to run as a Democrat. Well, I qualified and about two weeks after I qualified there was a phone call. My receptionist said, "This guy says he needs to speak to you. His name is Sonny Perdue." Sonny was on the phone, and he says, "I am going to announce Thursday that I am switching parties." I was just jokingly giving him grief, and I said, "I wish you had told me that eleven days ago."[18]

Lee was dissatisfied with what he considered to be Charles Walker's and Mark Taylor's lack of openness in Senate caucus meetings and with their heavy-handed style of managing Senate affairs. Furthermore, Lee had publicly declared his support for Sonny Perdue's candidacy in an address to the Carroll County Chamber of Commerce just before the general election. Lee announced to the audience that he was going to support Sonny Perdue for governor. Dan Lee was able to be more open about his support of Perdue because he was not opposed by a Republican challenger in the general election that year.

Jack Hill of Reidsville was the next Democratic senator that Perdue called and asked to convert to the Republican Party, but he was the last to make a public announcement. Hill had been especially close to Perdue and had been his Atlanta roommate for several terms of the General Assembly. Hill had experienced Republican opposition in his 2002 senatorial campaign and describes his frame of mind when Perdue won and as Perdue called him to urge him to become a Republican:

They spent a little bit of money trying to beat me. The Republicans did. That brought him from about 19 percent to 43 percent on Election Day. I was in a 55 percent Republican district. I even lost the big Republican county in my district [Effingham]. . . . There was plenty of incentive. . . . I was surprised I only got 56 percent of the vote when I had done everything right. . . . But they had done some pretty effective advertising. I was pretty sober about that. On the other hand, it flipped to elation when Sonny won because it's not every day when a person you consider at least as close a friend as anybody you know all of the sudden succeeds.

Hill reports on his first conversation with Sonny Perdue after the election:

The day after the election, I got up early and went to work like I do every morning. . . . The first call I got was from Sonny. It must have been about 7:30 in the morning. What I did not know was that Eric and Tom were in the room with him. He had it down. He said, "You are in a Republican district. I know where you are philosophically. . . . The press is saying I can't govern unless I have at least one of the two bodies." I said, "It will be tough for me, just running a hard campaign, to just flip parties." . . . That was on a Wednesday. We talked again a time or two. Dan Lee flipped. Don was next. So, all of a sudden, it was me. . . . I talked to a few supporters. I guess on the way back from Millen, on the phone that night, Sonny and I agreed what we wanted to do and kind of set the stage for the next few days. That was Thursday night.

Hill joined Governor-elect Perdue the next day in Savannah for a victory celebration, but did not at that time acknowledge that he intended to switch parties. He told the press that day that he had showed up to support Perdue. It was not until early the following week when Governor-Elect Perdue flew down to Statesboro in Jack Hill's district and met Hill at the airport there that Hill finally made his public announcement that he also was switching parties, even though he had made his agreement with Perdue and the Senate leadership the previous Thursday.

Eric Johnson relates his and Tom Price's involvement in the discussions with Jack Hill: "Sonny Perdue called Jack. Tom and I were with him the whole time. If Jack was being promised the Appropriations Committee, Tom and I had to say, 'Yes, we will keep that promise.' . . . The surprising thing was once we took the Senate all of the Republicans wanted to be Appropriations chair, but nobody really got upset with what we gave away."

Don Cheeks of Augusta was the second senator to announce he would switch parties. He too had supported Sonny Perdue in the governor's race. Cheeks admits that he even told Roy Barnes that he could not support him because of Barnes's close political connections to Charles Walker, of whom Cheeks did not approve. Cheeks reports on his conversation with Perdue the day after the election: "Sonny called me and he said Don, I need the Senate. I can't get the House. He said I know you don't vote Democratic, and I know that you have never voted except your beliefs and your constituents' wishes and mostly conservative. You ought to be a Republican. The Republican Party in the Senate had been inviting me every day, every week, every month to join them. Dan Lee had already committed that he would switch. After we had our conversation, it was about two days before I switched." Eric

Johnson and Tom Price, as the two Republican leaders in the Senate, also talked with Cheeks to assure him that they would honor any commitments made to him in exchange for switching parties. Eric Johnson relates his discussions with Cheeks: "We worked a little bit on Don. . . . He wanted to be in the Republican inner court. . . . We did not have a lot to promise. We agreed to give Cheeks Banking [a committee which he already chaired as a Democrat], and to keep him on Appropriations." Don Cheeks was also designated as one of the three Senate budget conferees for the 2003 and 2004 sessions of the General Assembly.

In a press interview in Augusta on Friday, November 8, when Don Cheeks announced he was switching parties, Cheeks acknowledged that he had also been assured by his new Republican colleagues in the Senate that they would continue to support funding for a cancer research center that had been proposed for the large Medical Center in Augusta that was connected with the Medical College of Georgia. When the governor-elect made his campaign victory stop in Augusta that day, Perdue did announce his support for the new cancer center in Augusta, according to press reports of that visit.[19] Also, both Dan Lee and Don Cheeks had been outspoken critics of the 2001 Democrat-driven reapportionment legislation, according to the Cook-Salzer press report that stated, "Lee and Cheeks were strong candidates for switching from the start. Both have been at odds with the state's Democratic leadership over the last few years, notably over redistricting. Cheeks was upset that his Augusta district was loaded with minority voters under the latest redrawing of political boundaries, and Lee complained bitterly about his West Georgia district being divided up in an effort to strengthen Democratic candidates elsewhere."[20]

Perdue arranged a four-city victory tour on Friday, November 8, to announce the conversions of Dan Lee and Don Cheeks and set up the expectation of additional party switching. By that time he also knew Jack Hill was committed to change parties, which would provide the Republicans with a majority in the state Senate. Tom Price and Eric Johnson joined Perdue in participating in the fly around with the first two stops being in LaGrange and Augusta. Later in the day, Jack Hill joined the senators in Savannah, and the victory tour concluded in Macon. Rooney Bowen was the third senator to publicly announce that he was switching parties on November 8. Bowen, an auto dealer and funeral director from Cordele, had served in the state Senate since 1980. According to the Cook and Salzer article, on the same day Dan Lee and Don Cheeks announced, Bowen reportedly "said in a press interview that he would leave the Democratic Party and join the Republicans in the Senate because it would be the best thing for his constituents."

Don Cheeks claims the credit for persuading Bowen to switch parties when he did: "The morning after the election I called Rooney and said, 'Rooney, I want to tell you up front I'm switching parties.' And he said, 'Well, I may change my mind and do it too.' Rooney called me back, and I said, 'I am going to switch when the governor gets to Augusta tomorrow. I am going to announce it.' He said then, 'I am switching!' Rooney swears to this day that he would not have switched if it wasn't for me." Perdue comments, "Rooney went ahead and announced it. Rooney kind of outed himself."

Nick Ayers reveals how he may also have helped induce Rooney Bowen to go ahead and announce his decision to switch parties:

> Rooney had gone back and forth, and I was dealing with Little Rooney, his son. They lived down in Cordele. They were in sort of a holding pattern of decision. I knew Sonny wanted it done. . . . I just went ahead and sent out the press release that Rooney switched. Little Rooney called me and said, "I think we are going to hold off another week." I said, "Rooney, we have a problem." He said, "What?" I said, "Well, I have already announced it." He said, "Okay."

According to Jack Hill, Rooney Bowen later denied he had made a press announcement about party switching, and perhaps he was referencing the Ayers press release in his denial. In any event, after Bowen switched parties, he retained his chairmanship of the Public Safety Committee in the Senate.

Jack Hill relates how he learned that Bowen had publicly disclosed his switch: " I had no contact with Rooney Bowen. I think Sonny made a call, but I don't think there was any negotiating going on. . . . It was a surprise. When he flipped that Friday morning, I was in the car with Sonny in Savannah. He said, 'Have you talked to Rooney?' I said, 'No, I haven't talked to him.' He said 'Well, the press is reporting he's flipped.'" Hill's comments reflect that a bit of disconnect may have occurred among the senators in the dispatch of organizing the party-switching announcements. Don Cheeks reveals that he did not know Jack Hill had decided to switch until the next week: "When I changed, Jack Hill and Rooney Bowen said they were not. . . . Rooney called me back and said I'm switching. But Jack Hill has not to this day said to me he was switching." Nevertheless, the new partisan mix in the state Senate became thirty Republicans to twenty-six Democrats. What the

GOP had strived to accomplish through the electoral process for the last several decades suddenly occurred in less than a week's time.

Dan McLagan describes the public relations effect of the "victory tour" fly-in: "We did a four city fly-around to welcome the new senators to our side, which completely stunned the Democratic establishment. They had lost one house of the legislature!" Dan Lee and Don Cheeks had not been opposed by Republican challengers in their legislative races that year, but Jack Hill and Rooney Bowen had been. Bowen experienced the closest race of any of the party switchers. His Republican opponent had garnered almost 48 percent of the total vote of the district. The Cook-Salzer press report of the fly around described Lt. Governor Mark Taylor's reaction as "angry." He was quoted as saying the party switchers should resign from their Senate seats and run for office again as Republicans. He was further quoted as saying, "The struggle is not over," and he would strive "to keep waffling Democrats in the fold."[21]

Morgan Perry Cook discloses that the Perdue team and Senate leadership carried on discussions with a few other Democratic senators over the days immediately following the election: "We tried Nathan Dean. We tried Peg Blitch.[22] We tried Tim Golden. Sonny Perdue really felt that Tim Golden was one of us. . . . I had gone to personally appeal to Tim Golden about switching parties, but he wouldn't do it, but he was real gentle about it and left the door open. . . . That frustrated the governor because he had recruited Tim Golden as a Democrat." Perdue had also suggested to Golden in 1998 that he should run for the state Senate as a Republican instead of a Democrat, but he had declined to do so at that time.

Nathan Dean, a long-serving senator from Rockmart in West Georgia, was another senator whom Perdue had urged to change parties. Nick Ayers comments on the 2002 approach to Dean, "Nathan was the one who sort of said yes and then said no and stayed no! He was sending mixed signals." Eric Johnson comments on the discussions with Nathan Dean.

> The last stop on the fly around was in Macon. We pulled the plane in and went into a back room. There was a call connection problem. Sonny basically said [to Dean], "It's now or never. We've got the majority. We want you to come over." Nathan kept sort of wanting to see what committees. Sonny said we aren't dealing—this is your last chance to come over and keep your seniority. You can keep your office. We can't tell you what you will get, but we will be grateful for it. Tom and I were there to confirm everything. Nathan basically said he could not do it.

Dean served the remainder of his Senate term to which he had just been elected as a Democrat and then retired from the legislature at the end of the 2004 session.

Veteran Democratic state senator George Hooks of Americus discloses that he also was approached by Sonny Perdue to change parties on November 6, 2002:

> I think I was the second person Sonny called, and he called me that morning. I was at my office. . . . My secretary came running in and said Sonny Perdue was on the phone. So I got on the phone a little after 9:00, and we chit-chatted, congratulated one another, and I told him I was proud of him and so forth. Then, he basically said, "Now I want you on my team." And I said, "I'll certainly be there, and I'll help you in every way that I can. . . . It went on, and he said "You don't understand, I really want you on my team." And I said, "Are you talking about changing parties?" And he said, "Yes." And I said, "Well, I have just been elected as a Democrat; the president of the United States just gave me a barbecue; I just won 67 percent of the vote. . . . I can't very well do that." And he said, "Well, I've got to have you." I said, "Who else have you called?" And he said, "You're the second person I called. Jack [Hill] was the first." Anyway, we chatted, and he said, "I'll give you until 5:00 this afternoon to make up your mind." And I said, "You've been up all night. . . . We need to talk about this another day." And that was the end of the conversation. Sonny and I never talked about that subject after that, never have.

Hooks further explained that his Senate district is and always has been majority Democratic in its leanings, and that he felt he owed too much to his Democratic Party to change. In addition, he stated that changing parties was "not anything I want to leave as a legacy," that being a Democrat is "just part of my heritage," and that it was not in his nature to change significant relationships in his life.

Former party chairman Rusty Paul comments on the difficulty of making the decision to switch: "I've never changed parties, but I've helped a lot of people through that process, and it is not an easy process. Very few people do it for political expediency. There are some, but most of them switch parties primarily because they reached some sort of political catharsis." As a case in point, state representative Vinson Wall of Gwinnett County served in the House for ten years as a Democrat and then switched parties in the early 1980s and served another twelve years as a Republican.

Alec Poitevint holds up Sonny Perdue's decision to change parties as a possible inspiration for others. "The party switching started with the election of Ronald Reagan in 1980, and it never stopped. So, it was always an ongoing process of us trying to figure out who it is that would be acceptable to our people. So certainly as soon as Sonny was elected, anyone who had ever thought about switching, who philosophically agreed with us, there was no reason for them not to."

While the Senate was converting from being Democratic controlled to majority Republican, the GOP actually lost ground in the Georgia House of Representatives on Election Day in 2002 under the recently drawn reapportionment maps that were less favorable to incumbent Republicans. The GOP lost 3 seats and retained only 72, compared to 108 seats for the Democrats. In addition, the Republicans in the House lost several members of their leadership team in this election cycle.

A few key Republican leaders had given up their seats in the General Assembly for various reasons. Mike Evans, caucus chair in the late 1990s, had declined to run again in 2000 in order to devote more time to his business. Former minority leaders Bob Irvin and Steve Stancil both chose to run for other offices that year. Irvin opposed Saxby Chambliss in the Republican primary for the U.S. Senate seat and lost, and Stancil ran and won in the Republican primary for lieutenant governor, but lost in the general election to incumbent Mark Taylor. 2002 Caucus Chair Garland Pinholster, who had served for several sessions as the primary recruiter for the GOP in the House, was essentially redistricted out of his seat and did not run for any office. Caucus Secretary Anne Mueller of Savannah, who had served in the House since 1983, was redistricted into a district with another incumbent Republican, Burke Day, who defeated her in the primary election. Kathy Cox of Fayette County ran for and won election as state school superintendent. Among the House Republican senior leadership team, only Minority Leader Lynn Westmoreland, Caucus Whip Earl Ehrhart and Caucus Vice Chair Sharon Cooper were reelected to the House that year. Westmoreland continued to serve as minority leader, but he was also beginning to focus on a future run for the U.S. House of Representative in 2004. Obviously, the significant loss of Republican leadership in the House in 2002 had a detrimental effect on the party's objective of gaining control of the House in that election cycle.

An Analysis of Victory

There are varied opinions as to why and how Sonny Perdue happened to be elected in 2002 as Georgia's first Republican governor since Reconstruction. The explanations range from his taking advantage of the state flag controversy, to the backlash against Roy Barnes's aggressive style of governance, to the superiority of Sonny Perdue's grass-roots campaign organization and his campaign strategies, to the particular qualities or sets of qualities of Perdue himself that appealed to a broader constituency of potential Republican voters than other GOP gubernatorial candidates had, to simply being in the right place at the right time as Georgia moved from being primarily a Democratic state to becoming primarily a Republican one. Probably all these factors contributed somewhat to his victory.

A few Democratic leaders, political observers, and analysts have opined that Perdue's blatant criticism of Roy Barnes's means of adopting a new state flag was a conscious attempt to polarize voters across racial lines that hearkened back to the race-baiting days of earlier Republicanism in Georgia when Senator Barry Goldwater won Georgia's electoral votes in his 1964 presidential campaign largely because of his opposition to civil rights legislation. Perdue's campaign promise was to allow Georgia voters the opportunity to vote on their state flag in a referendum rather than have it changed by legislative fiat. No doubt his stance appealed to a few diehard Confederate "flaggers" who advocated a return to a state flag with the controversial St. Andrews cross, but it is doubtful that the number of white "flaggers" whom Perdue attracted into his campaign in 2002 alone provided a significant enough voting bloc to swing the gubernatorial election to Perdue in 2002. Apparently, Saxby Chambliss also won most of the same votes that Perdue received without invoking the flag issue into his campaign against incumbent U.S. senator Max Cleland. Instead, it appears that the Republican Party was finally able to sway more rural and small-town voters away from the Democratic Party and into the folds of the GOP after many years of trying.

In fact, Sonny Perdue did put together a talented, hard-working, and dedicated, almost driven, campaign staff that generated considerable grass-roots support for Perdue's campaign. Sonny Perdue himself worked hard to see and meet many voters. In addition, Perdue certainly benefited from the growth of the state and the influx of new voters, many of whom came to Georgia with Republican leanings. Also, his strategies of targeting seventy-one swing vote counties and of running against Roy Barnes in his primary campaign, instead of his Republican opponents, contributed to the success of his campaigns.

In addition, Perdue and his team chose to focus on a few key campaign issues that differentiated his approach to governing from the voter perceptions of Roy Barnes' s approach. To a large extent, these strategies and approaches to the electorate allowed the Perdue campaign to compete effectively against Roy Barnes even though the Barnes campaign had vastly superior funding for getting its message out to voters. Perdue also had a benefit of geography on his side. Both Johnny Isakson, who lost in 1990, and Guy Millner, who lost twice in 1994 and 1998, were from Metro Atlanta. Perdue was the first Republican candidate for governor to run from a rural, agricultural Georgia base instead of a big city, business base. Nick Ayers offers an explanation of how this may have factored into Perdue's ability to build a broad coalition of support for his campaign:

> Sonny, with his agricultural background and his veterinary background, and with his University of Georgia background—just the people he knew—you know he had been involved in politics for twelve years, so he knew a lot of folks. When he would have people show up to see him, they were symbolic of the community. It was the guys who had the big farms. It was the guy who ran the local feed store who had heard of Sonny. I think the Republican connection helped him get the Atlanta votes where people vote for the R or the D, but his geographical background and the fact that he used to be Democrat helped him bring in the whole other coalition that made the difference.

Representative Mark Burkhalter observes how Perdue's Middle Georgia connectivity also may have helped him pull off the first Republican gubernatorial victory after the two previous Republican candidates for governor, Johnny Isakson and Guy Millner, who were both from the Metro Atlanta area, had not been able to win their races:

> Keep in mind that Georgia grew and changed. The Republican Party grew and changed. As we continued to have people come here from other parts, it wasn't just Metro Atlanta they were moving to; they were moving all over the state. But Sonny certainly, to his credit, took advantage of a couple of things. I think the new voters coming in, and some disenfranchised rural traditional Georgia Democrat voters. And the fact that he was a rural guy himself—it connected. . . . And Sonny, to his credit, was there to understand the baseline of opportunity is beyond the Metro Atlanta Republican voters. And he penetrated it, like nobody else.

Perdue's business background also may have provided an element of appeal to voters. A group of Citadel College political scientists have classified southern governors into the four classes of businessmen, populists, demagogues, and policy makers, and determined that the businessman category of governor was the most popular grouping in southern states.[23] So not only may Perdue's rural background and statewide business contacts have helped him, but the fact that he was an agribusiness man by background may have added to his appeal to a number of Georgia voters, particularly since Georgia was in the midst of a two-year recession and needed to cut back on the level of government spending.

Alec Poitevint suggests that Sonny Perdue's sense of integrity was also appealing to voters in that he inspired a sense of trust in most Georgians. John Watson offers that it may have been just the appearance of ordinariness and normalcy in the lives of the Perdues that made them so appealing to voters. He states, "I think the election was fundamentally about the fact that Georgians like Sonny and Mary Perdue. There is likeability about what they see in Sonny and Mary. He is anything but ordinary, but I think in the general public there is a sense of ordinary that gives them comfort. There is a sense of normalcy, familiarity, and comfort that is exhibited primarily because of his populist nature."

Perhaps another attribute of Sonny Perdue's that helped him cobble together a broad coalition of supporters was his faithfulness. He and Mary Perdue shared with many Georgians during the campaign how their faith had guided them toward the decision to run for the governorship. Perdue's willingness to talk openly about his religious beliefs no doubt appealed strongly to the more evangelical Republicans throughout Georgia.

Former House Speaker Terry Coleman, a Roy Barnes supporter in the 2002 election, perhaps oversimplifies it, but he opines that much of Perdue's success in that year's gubernatorial election was the result of Perdue just being an acceptable alternative to Barnes:

> I think Sonny played it right. As a matter of fact, it was almost an effortless thing for Sonny to do. The only thing he had to do was see people, campaign, say the right thing, and be the alternative of moderation, of family values, of conservative fiscal policy—he only had to show the difference between him and Roy—that Roy was more aggressive and much more liberal—and I guess Barnes had a negative with the flag—not so much the flag, but the fact that he brought it out and voted without much debate on it.

To a large extent, Morgan Perry Cook concurs with Coleman's assessment, asserting, "Sonny Perdue was a viable, respectable alternative. People felt safe going out on a limb with Sonny Perdue. And some of it might have been that he was a Democrat before he was a Republican."

The Speaker's Contest

Not only was Perdue's past working relationship with the Democratic leadership in the General Assembly likely a factor in his electability, but it was also a factor in positioning him to govern the state. Certainly his close ties with his former fellow Democrats in the Senate were a huge factor in equipping him to convince four key Democratic state senators to change parties within a week of his election. Perdue also had close ties with a few Democratic leaders in the state House of Representatives, notably Terry Coleman, House Appropriations chair, and Larry Walker, House majority leader. Perdue and Coleman worked together in their shared representation of Bleckley County, and Perdue and Walker shared representation of parts of Houston County. Walker reveals the depth of their longtime relationship: "He [Perdue] was my friend. . . . He had been my senator. His family and my family had been friends. His daddy did business with my daddy—my father was in the farm equipment business, and Mr. Erwin Perdue was a farmer—and we had kinfolks that were in each other's family." Quite likely Perdue's close relationship with Larry Walker convinced Sonny Perdue that he would probably be able to form a cooperative arrangement and perhaps even a sharing of power in the House if Walker could be elected Speaker to succeed the recently defeated Tom Murphy.

Still, it came as a surprise to most of the Perdue team when the governor-elect informed them that they were going to get involved in the Speaker's race between Larry Walker and Terry Coleman. Nick Ayers relates that Perdue's involvement in the Speaker race arose soon after his election: "What we turned to after we got the Senate was the House Speaker's race. I remember that's what we immediately switched to. It was a quick decision the governor made." Morgan Perry Cook discusses how the governor revealed to her his plan to form a coalition with Larry Walker and support him in a Speaker's race against Terry Colman: "The governor called me and said, 'I want to talk to you about a little project.' He said there is going to be a Speaker's race. I think the whole thing came as a really big shock to Terry Coleman because I think maybe Terry felt like Sonny had faith in him."

Given their key leadership roles in the House, both Terry Coleman, as Appropriations Committee chairman, and Larry Walker, as majority leader, had good reason to believe that they were the most likely candidates to succeed the defeated Tom Murphy. In addition, Jack Connell of Augusta, who had served under Tom Murphy as Speaker Pro-Tem from 1977 to 2002, had chosen not to seek reelection in 2002, ironically the same year in which Tom Murphy was defeated. So the Democrats in the House suffered a loss of some of their key leadership in the surprising 2002 elections, just as the Republicans had. Terry Coleman explains how he reached his decision to run: "I was up in Roy's room in the hotel over there, and it looked bad. We were watching Murphy's race, and somebody called me and said, 'Speaker Murphy's going to lose.' So, about fifteen or twenty minutes later I called him, and he said, 'Son, I believe I'm going to lose.' And he said, 'Now, I've asked y'all not to start running, but now I believe I'm gone, so you and Larry have at it.' And that's when I got busy running for Speaker." Walker relates what influenced his decision to run: "I had been led to believe that Mr. Murphy wanted me to be the Speaker when he left. Not that he was not close to Terry—he was."

Representative Bob Holmes comments on his observations about the contest for position of House Speaker in 2003:

Basically, I think everyone knew whenever the Speaker retired that these two guys were going to be the contenders. Many people said the Speaker has anointed Larry, because Larry, you remember, was going to run for governor at one time, and the Speaker apparently convinced him, "Hey, I'm going to be leaving soon, and you'll have an uncontested thing." But then the Speaker was gone and Terry as chairman of Appropriations Committee had been able to do an awful lot more favors for folks than had Larry. And Larry was also kind of unwilling to make commitments to people because several groups and individuals had asked him, "What are you going to do for me or what are you going to do for my district?" And the sense I got, personally as well as from talking to others, was that he was unwilling to do that.

There was another concern that was in the background. Could he be or would he try to maintain independence when the governor was his buddy, his neighbor, his fellow county member? Remember how the governor used to control who the Speaker was. . . . So many people had visions of, "Is this going to be another thing where the governor is going to be in charge," and they said "that's the last thing we need." . . . And that combination of factors, I think, gave Terry a clear majority.

Larry Walker explains why and how he aligned with Perdue in the Speaker's race: "I wasn't left with much of an alternative other than to form a coalition with the Republicans under the leadership of Governor Perdue. . . . I had been chair of the State Legislative Leaders Foundation and I knew this had been done in some other parts of the country successfully. And also I saw what was coming. I knew that the Democrats, in my opinion, were going to lose control of the legislative bodies. Frankly, it came two or four years before I thought it would come."

Scott Rials comments on how he thinks Perdue happened to involve himself in the Speaker's race: "I think it was as much Larry's idea as it was anybody else. He said, 'Okay, here I am. My world has shattered. Republicans have won—my friend Sonny.' They had the relationship. He knew that Terry Coleman was a strong candidate. I think he [Larry] knew the only way for him to win was to get Republican votes." John Watson describes how the political partnership between Walker and Perdue might have worked: "Larry was willing to deal. There would have been some Republican chairmen. There would have been a seat at the table through Appropriations. Larry, in essence, was willing to have a coalition government in the House."

On the other hand, Walker's willingness to align with Republicans to form a coalition was anathema to some House Democrats. Bob Holmes expounds on this concern: "The thing that happened thereafter was something that was unimaginable, frankly—the idea that Larry would try to form a coalition with his strong supporters and Republicans in order to be elected on the floor. . . . I mean Larry was *persona non grata* in the House. . . . Here is our leader, our majority leader, who's willing to sleep with the enemy, so to speak."

Governor-elect Perdue campaigned hard to help Larry Walker. Chris Young relates how Perdue was involved:

> Over the course of December, lots of phone calls were made. . . . There seemed to be days when we felt Larry was going to have the votes—then there seemed to be days where Terry had it sewn up. Then there seemed to be days where maybe one of them was going to switch parties. Then it became apparent it wasn't going to be a party-switching situation in the House; it was going to be Republicans plus a certain number of the Democratic caucus to elect a Speaker, but I remember the governor was involved making calls and going and visiting people.

Shortly before the General Assembly convened, Perdue hosted a reception at the Cherokee Town Club in Buckhead where Walker was given the opportunity to meet in a non-public location with several House members from whom he was seeking support. Representative Mark Burkhalter describes how House minority leader Lynn Westmoreland held the House Republican caucus together in support of Larry Walker's candidacy: "Lynn Westmoreland . . . consulted with us regularly and gave us the progress, how the dynamics were falling, who on the Democratic side were suspects or prospects for voting with Larry. So we met regularly with Lynn, and of course he was meeting regularly with Larry Walker and the governor. So we kind of knew who in the Democratic world was at least entertaining voting with Larry. . . . Lynn had us in lockstep, more so than any minority leader that I had ever served under." However, Burkhalter explains that he doubted that the Republican team would be successful at this effort due primarily to Terry Coleman's strong relationships within the Democratic Party. He states, "My impression was, I always felt like it was too good to be true. Terry Coleman is a good friend of mine, and I knew his savvy and about his years of being chairman of the House Appropriations Committee and how he's made a lot of friends . . . he was good at it. . . . So it was that style that I knew—that he had a touch that was ultimately going to probably allow him to beat Larry."[24]

In the end, Walker was never able to get a sufficient number of Democrats to join with the Republicans and elect him as Speaker. Walker discloses that he withdrew his candidacy just before a vote was taken. "We never voted. My opinion is that I had 87 votes [out of 91 needed]. I didn't have enough votes. The governor and I had told these people that were out on limb—Democrats that were going to vote for me—that unless we were absolutely sure we had the votes, we wouldn't pull the trigger on it. . . . We made a decision, I think early on the morning we were scheduled to vote— not to go through with it." Walker declined to identify which Democrats were supporting him or who was going to place his name in nomination. In retrospect, Sonny Perdue admits, "In thinking back, I probably just should have stayed out, but I chose to do that and worked really hard to try to get it done."

John Watson offers his analysis of Coleman's election: "Terry Coleman's relationship with the Democrats at that time as Appropriations Chair was too much to overcome. Terry just swamped him [Walker]." Some observers of the process have stated that Terry Coleman had to make many promises to fellow Democrats about the influence they might have in the House if they supported his candidacy for Speaker, and that the promises he made and kept somewhat hamstrung his ability to keep several rural whites in the Democratic fold over the next two years. Larry Walker also comments on how Coleman won the contest: "Terry got elected with urban Democrats and conservative rural Democrats. It was difficult for him, but he did a good job as Speaker. That was a difficult thing to try to hold together." In fact, the fragile coalition of generally more liberal urban black and white Democrats with conservative rural Democrats did prove impossible to hold together, and it fractured in 2004 when a number of South Georgia Democrats either switched parties or lost their elections to Republican challengers.

CHAPTER 6

Governing Georgia and
Taking Control of the House

In addition to the Speaker's race, two other significant developments occurred during the first week of the 2003 legislative session. As the new Republican governor, Sonny Perdue, along with his advisors, presented to the General Assembly the first set of budget recommendations developed by a Republican administration since 1872. Somewhat unfortunately for the GOP, the economy was in recession, and there were only limited opportunities to effect policy changes through the budget that year. Secondly, as the Senate convened to adopt its rules after the GOP had become the majority party as a result of four Democrats converting to the Republican Party, by a strict party-line vote, Republicans stripped the Democratic lieutenant governor of most of his powers to manage and influence Senate business, with the exception of his constitutional right to preside over Senate sessions. Senator Eric Johnson reports on how this was accomplished:

> Tom (Price) was basically in charge [as the new majority leader]. He basically took charge of the rules. He was the brains behind finding every darn rule he could find, including taking the Parliamentarian position away from the lieutenant governor and giving it to the Speaker pro tem. That was when Taylor got the maddest. The constitution said that the lieutenant governor was the presiding officer of the Senate. His duties were assigned by the rules, but we could not take the podium away from him, but we could take everything else away. We had the budget. We cut his staff.

The other major initiative that the Georgia Republican Party undertook early in 2003 was to file a lawsuit challenging the constitutionality of the 2001 Democrat-driven reapportionment maps and legislation. Governor Perdue persuaded his campaign chairman Alec Poitevint to run for a third term as Republican Party chairman to replace Ralph Reed; and after being elected, one of Poitevint's first actions was to decide to attack the 2001 reapportionment plan on the basis that it defied the one man-one vote rule of constitutional law. Poitevint comments on his decision: "After I became chairman, I redirected the resources of the Republican Party to one man-one vote. . . . The truth of the matter is that my first year as chairman, all of the money we raised and every effort went into paying bills and doing redistricting." Glenn Richardson reports on his role in helping to raise funds to sustain the lawsuit: "I had been pressing that lawsuit since before 2002. I was on that; I kept pressing and pressing, and nobody wanted to do anything. And we couldn't get the money. We came very close to letting that lawsuit go. . . . And I started calling representatives before I was floor leader. And each committed to give like $500 or something like that to pay for legal fees, and it wound up being only 40 or 50 of us that did it. But we got enough for the legal fees."

Republican attorney Frank Strickland filed the lawsuit of *Sara Larios et al. v. Cathy Cox* (Georgia's Secretary of State) in the United States District Court of the Northern District of Georgia in March 2003. According to Strickland, because the lawsuit involved a voting rights issue of one person-one vote, the case was automatically assigned to a three-judge federal district court panel. The judges on the panel were Stanley Marcus of Miami who served on the Eleventh Circuit Court of Appeals and Northern District Court of Georgia judges Charles Pannell and Bill O'Kelley, the latter of whom had extensive experience in redistricting cases. Eric Johnson reports that it would have been doubtful the party could have managed to pursue the lawsuit if the Republicans had not secured the governor's office and the Senate. "If he had not have won the governor's race and flipped the Senate, we would not have been able to raise the money to pay for the attorney to keep that suit going."

While the Republicans were consolidating power in the statehouse and suing to set aside the gerrymandered legislative districts, the party was also beginning an organized effort to convert the Georgia House of Representatives to a Republican majority in the next election cycle. Nick Ayers became Sonny Perdue's primary political operative in a position outside of state government. He worked out of the Perdue for a New Georgia campaign office, which was co-located with the state Republican Party headquarters in the Prado Shopping Center in Sandy Springs, just inside of I-285. Ayers relates how Perdue directed him to work with the party leadership in scheduling his participation in their efforts to gain a majority of seats in the state House of Representatives: "Sonny asked that I be the one to organize all of his 2004 legislative efforts and put together a plan of whom we target in the House and the Senate. Jay Walker was the guy actually running those campaigns, so Jay and I closely coordinated how to use the governor from an earned media and from a fundraising standpoint."

While Ayers was representing Perdue's political interests in trying to win Republican gains in the 2004 General Assembly elections, he also was beginning to organize for Perdue's 2006 reelection bid. In 2003, Ayers had helped engineer the victory of Karen Handel, one of Perdue's former deputy chiefs of staff, in her race for the chairmanship of the Fulton County Commission. At age twenty-three he was already sufficiently experienced in Georgia politics to win Perdue's confidence to manage his next gubernatorial campaign.

At the same time, the state Republican Party organization was working hand in glove with Perdue and Ayers to focus on winning a majority of the seats in the state House of Representatives in the upcoming 2004 elections. Alex Poitevint appointed Perdue's former campaign manager Scott Rials as executive director of the party, and Rials chose his former College Republican ally Paul Bennecke to be the senior political director of the party. They then selected Jay Walker as party political director to coordinate House races and Tony Simon as party political director for the Senate contests. Bennecke explains how the team concentrated on winning the House: "We had to do candidate recruitment—have a real system put in place for recruitment—based on population centers, quality of candidates, finances, the ability to raise money, and credibility among the business community—all of the different aspects. The Republican Party never had that sophisticated of a system in candidate recruitment."

Scott Rials recounts how the political team interacted with Governor Perdue, his political team, and the legislative leadership: "We had weekly phone calls, and the governor was on them. We had one for the House and one for the Senate. By the end, it was one call. We had Sonny and John [Watson], Nick and Paul and Jay and Tony Simon and myself and Alec, Eric [Johnson], and Lynn Westmoreland. When Westmoreland left to go run for

Congress, Glenn [Richardson] kind of stepped in as 'going-to-be' minority leader."

According to Dick Pettys, "Westmoreland was very active in recruitment, and frankly I think he laid the groundwork for the takeover that occurred in 2004." Westmoreland resigned as House minority leader in October 2003 in order to devote more time to running for Congress. At that time, Glenn Richardson was elected by House Republicans to succeed Westmoreland as minority leader.

Richardson's rise to power within the House GOP caucus was rather rapid. He had served as Paulding County attorney and had only been elected to the House seven years before, in 1996. However, Sonny Perdue had chosen Richardson, who had been a county chair in the Perdue gubernatorial campaign, to be his first floor leader in the House after his election as governor.

Glenn Richardson describes, from his perspective, the steps that occurred in fall 2003 that allowed him to emerge as the leading candidate for minority leader:

> After we got through the 2003 session . . . Westmoreland announced he was running for Congress. . . . He called me up one night and said he was going to resign and run. Jerry Keen was very interested. He beat Earl [Ehrhart] for whip. He was the whip, and he was very interested. And within thirty minutes of him (Westmoreland) calling, I called Jerry Keen and told him I wanted to meet with him. And he said, "Well, I'll be up in Atlanta in the next couple of weeks." And I said, "No, I want to meet with you. I'll be on the plane tomorrow morning on the first flight into St. Simons." This was in the afternoon. And I flew there, met with him personally, told him I was running, asked for his support—and he was contemplating running. . . . I guess the next day he called me and told me he would support me. And who else ran? Tom Rice ran and Representative Jeff Brown from LaGrange ran. I worked hard and got the votes. I still have that piece of paper that I carried around with me all the way. . . . We had one ballot. I got elected and thought this was going to be easy!

Popular Republican representative Mark Burkhalter, who also had ambitions of becoming House minority leader, actually ended up nominating Richardson for the position. Burkhalter explains how he determined not to oppose Richardson and ended up supporting him instead:

When Lynn Westmoreland decided he was going to run for Congress, he stepped down, I made it abundantly clear I was interested in running for minority leader, and I was out there going through the motions. I talked to a lot of my friends and felt very confident about where I stood. And then Governor Perdue asked me if I would be one of his floor leaders. . . . I think at the time he only had two—Glenn Richardson and Larry O'Neal. And so I did it, kind of with the attitude that this was a unique opportunity. . . . And I'd have to wait for an unknown date that Westmoreland might step down. . . . So after I did that then Westmoreland steps down, and then Glenn runs for minority leader. And I had just gotten settled in, not even a month or two in the job, and I had made a commitment to the governor, and I felt like it was the right thing to do. . . . I may have short-sighted myself a little bit and sort of abandoned the minority leader idea, but I knew [floor leader] was a job I could engage in right away. . . . I was surprised to some degree that Glenn asked me to nominate him in the caucus; I really didn't know him all that well. But I knew his capabilities, and I took it as an honor, and I nominated him. And I think it helped him, because I had a group of Republican legislators that didn't know about him.

Richardson tells a somewhat humorous and ironic story about the first session in which he served as minority leader in the House: "On the Friday before the session began in 2004, I was driving to the Capitol, and my secretary called me from Dallas and said, 'The *Atlanta Journal* is calling. A representative has switched parties.' And I went, 'Oh man, all right! I'm going to go up a member, and we're going to go in with some momentum. I'm going from 72 to 73.' She said, 'No, they sounded like a Republican switched to a Democrat.' And I went, 'What? I know all I've got. No way!' Well, it turned out it was true. Scott Dix switched from Republican to Democrat just before the 2004 session began."

While the party and Perdue's campaign office were strategizing about how to elect more Republicans to the General Assembly, Perdue's legislative affairs team was focusing on building relationships with Democratic House leaders both to coordinate the processes of government with them and to lay some groundwork for potential party switching in the future. Morgan Perry Cook details the efforts she and legislative affairs coordinator Hunter Towns made in 2003 to build these relationships: "The legislative session of 2003 was really rocky. None of us had our sea legs under us. . . .The governor dispatched Hunter Towns and me to cover the state. I spent that entire late spring and summer and fall traveling, getting to know these rural

Democrats. He [Perdue] said I want you to get to know them. I want you to get as close to Terry Coleman as you can. . . . And you know, I began to make friends with all of his friends. . . . We had a core group of people who were willing to change parties if Terry did. They were loyal to Terry; they were going to hang in there with Terry."

While serving in his second year as House Speaker in 2004, Terry Coleman must have had one of the most challenging years in his long political life. Coleman was the focus of many competing political interests. Many of the Democratic House members who had supported Coleman's candidacy for Speaker were urging him to protect Democratic programs that Governor Perdue had recommended as budget cuts in the amended 2004 and new 2005 state budgets, years in which the state was still facing an uncertain economic future after the 2001 recession and sizeable reductions in state tax revenues in fiscal years 2002 and 2003. Also, the potential of an adverse judgment on the lawsuit filed by the Republican Party of Georgia, challenging the 2001 reapportionment maps, was looming overhead. In addition, he and his closest political allies among the rural Georgia Democrats were being actively solicited by Governor Perdue and other Republican leaders to consider changing political parties or at least forming an alliance with the House Republicans to share power with them by sharing leadership positions within the House committee hierarchy.

The most critical issue with which the Democrats had to deal arose early in the 2004 legislative session. The redistricting case of (*Sara) Larios v. (Cathy) Cox* was heard from January 6 to 9, 2004, and on February 10 the three-judge panel unanimously ruled that the state legislative redistricting maps of 2001 were unconstitutional on one person-one vote grounds. The order stated:

> We conclude that Georgia's state legislative reapportionment plans plainly violate the one person, one vote principle embodied in the Equal Protection clause because each deviates from population equality by a total of 9.98 percent of the ideal district population, and there are no legislative consistently applied state policies which justify these population deviations. Instead, the plans arbitrarily and discriminately dilute and debase the weight of certain citizens' votes by intentionally and systematically underpopulating districts in rural South Georgia and inner-city Atlanta, correspondingly overpopulating the districts in suburban areas surrounding Atlanta and under-populating the district held by incumbent Democrats.[1]

The court then invited the Georgia General Assembly, which was still in session, to submit new maps that would not violate the one person-one vote principle. According to new minority leader Glenn Richardson, "What dominated the session was what we were going to do about a map. . . .The court had ruled the maps needed to be redrawn." The Senate easily passed a redistricting plan that should comply with the court order; however, the Georgia House of Representatives experienced substantial difficulty in trying to build consensus around a particular map, and the negotiations among all the parties became quite intriguing. Frank Strickland recounts, "A lot of people came out of the woodwork to comment on the maps: the Democratic Caucus, the Black Caucus, the Democratic Party, and others." Terry Coleman comments from his perspective on the political difficulty in building consensus around a new redistricting map in the 2004 session of the General Assembly: "We had the Democratic Party fooling with it. The Black Caucus had their own plan, and then we had the House plan. . . . We could never get our folks together." Bob Holmes reports on how the map discussions progressed and how the members of the Legislative Black Caucus were involved in the process:

> They [the Democrats] could not reach a consensus. The issue came back to "who's going to be sacrificed?" To be blunt, that's what it really was. And many people felt, in the caucus, that these folks were more about saving themselves in the leadership and saving their buddies than they were in maintaining or perhaps increasing, but the idea was to maintain caucus members because the likelihood was that some Democrats were going to go. . . . You had all kinds of maps being drawn up—we had the folks over at the American Civil Liberties Union—the southern region office—helping us—but there were never enough votes to be able to effect anything.

Morgan Perry Cook reveals that she and fellow legislative aide Hunter Towns worked with a group of rural Democrats to try to draw a map that would appeal to a majority of the Democratic House leadership and the governor:

> The governor said, "Get those men [rural Democratic leaders] into a room and draw a map. Hunter Towns and I worked with a core group of those conservative Democrats on drawing a map. Terry Coleman knew about it. . . . He didn't stop us. . . . This was a source of tense blood sometimes between Westmoreland [the former Republican House minority leader] and the governor. . . . So we worked on this map, and we had enough votes

to get it on the floor. . . . All Terry Coleman had to do was pull the trigger. But in pulling the trigger, it meant he turned his back on all the Black Caucus. It meant he turned his back on some of the white Democrats who had stood by him during the Speaker's race. And when push came to shove, he wouldn't do it.

At the same time the reapportionment maps were being debated, Governor Perdue was trying to convince Speaker Coleman to switch to the Republican Party eventually and to agree on a redistricting map that would allow Coleman and his closest associates to protect their seats in the House, form a governance coalition with the House Republicans, and later, after the fall elections, switch parties. Hunter Towns confirms that Terry Coleman might have continued as House Speaker for at least another term if he had been willing to change parties and other rural Democrats would have switched with him. But that was not to be. Coleman acknowledges that he and Governor Perdue discussed both party switching as well as forming a coalition of Democrats and Republicans of like-mindedness, but no agreement was reached. Representative Mark Burkhalter reveals his role in these discussions:

> As floor leader I was very engaged. The governor knew of my relationship with Terry. . . . Once I became floor leader, the governor was engaged in trying to get Terry Coleman to become a Republican and get some more to come with him. And he solicited my help, and I was sort of a go-between in a lot of conversations. . . . I went as far as facilitating off-campus meetings with the governor and Terry Coleman to have some of these conversations. I knew they couldn't have them in the Capitol, and I even set up one at my condo (near Centennial Park). I tried to help, but in the end Speaker Coleman did not switch.

Republican Senator Bill Jackson of Columbia County, who first served in the House in 1979 as a Democrat, and later came back as a Republican House member and still later as a Republican state senator, served in 2003 and 2004 as an advisor to House Speaker Terry Coleman while Jackson was out of elected office. Jackson related that he also talked with both Governor Perdue and Speaker Coleman about the possibility of Coleman switching parties, but Coleman could not do it. He reportedly felt that he would be turning his back on all the Democrats who had supported him for Speaker when Larry Walker challenged him.[2] Perhaps even more importantly, Coleman believed that the House would continue to stay under Democratic control for at least two more years, according to Senator Jackson. Mark Burkhalter confirms Senator Jackson's assessment: "Terry Coleman didn't think he was going to lose. The Democrats didn't expect that."

Glenn Richardson provides an in-depth account of the tense discussions occurring among the governor's office, the House Republicans, and the Democratic leadership in the House, from his perspective, and how he may have complicated the process:

> We had a Republican Senate and a Republican governor, but the House couldn't get the votes. And of all the things I've done in my career to advance a majority and stay in the majority, I believe that session is when I think I outmaneuvered the Democrats. . . . Every single day they would come, and they were getting close to a redistricting plan. And I would always tell them that I had a different plan. I couldn't ever make their committee vote it out, but I had an amendment drawn. But we had a hodgepodge of Democrats that wanted to be with us. As I recall, we had eighteen, and there were seventy-one Republicans. I had taken the seventy-one Republicans, and we had gotten into a back room over there, and I made everybody be there. It was an unusual set of events, and I wrote up this pledge. And I got it before them, and it said, "We pledge to stick together on a vote of the caucus. . . . I knew we had seventy-one votes. And everyone signed it. . . . And what happened is that the governor was trying to get Terry and them to switch, so we started having conversations. And the conversations were centered around pulling out a map that we all agreed to and a switch. But the switch was not something I ever liked because it had Terry and nineteen of his friends switching to make twenty plus our seventy-one to make it a ninety-one majority. Yet, whenever it got down to brass tacks, it wasn't about them switching until after the '04 cycle. . . . The deal that was trying to be brokered was that Terry would remain Speaker, and I would be majority leader. And we had this very extensive written agreement that we were signing that would let Terry pick certain chairs—I would pick certain chairs—it was shared power. When we got close to the signatures, Terry didn't know for sure what Democrats I had. I had eighteen that gave us eighty-nine votes. I had all these maps drawn up . . . and I kept threatening that if they called their map to the floor that I had an amendment and that I had the votes to beat them on the floor . . . so they never would call the vote. So we got down to the last few days, and I was supposed to go talk to Terry. So I went and we had it all written out. And he goes through it all, checked it, . . . and he said, "This says we'll switch after the 2004 elections, and I will be elected Speaker in 2005—What happens after the 2006 election?" . . . And I

looked at him, and I said, "I'm running for Speaker." And he sat there for a minute, he folded the piece of paper and shoved it back across the desk, and he said "No deal!" I believed the judges would draw a set of maps that we could win by. And thank goodness that saved the day, Because the rest is kind of history.

Mark Burkhalter comments on Richardson's assessment of the difference in approach between Glenn Richardson and Governor Perdue: "Well, I remember specifically Glenn Richardson sort of put his foot down and said, 'I'm not trying to get a sitting Speaker to switch. I want his job instead.' And it was viewed as a little bold and presumptuous that we were going to get the majority. But the governor was trying to deal with what was in front of him at the time, and he had good relationships with these guys. He spent many years representing Middle Georgia [with the Democratic leaders]."

Morgan Perry Cook essentially confirms Richardson's and Burkhalter's recollections of the negotiations: "We had a strategy laid out. Terry Coleman would have remained Speaker for a defined period of time. It would have been a power share almost like what they did for a period in North Carolina. . . . And there would have been a period of transition during which it was worked out who was going to keep what, and those conservative Democrats would have ultimately become Republicans, which they did anyway."

Richardson's and Burkhalter's comments reveal a certain tension between the governor's team and a few of the Republican leaders (notably Richardson and Westmoreland) over the proposed "shared power" model of House governance. Some of the House Republicans were not particularly favorable toward the possibility of a shared governance model in which the GOP members in the House would agree to support the reelection of Terry Coleman as Speaker and the continuation of some of his allies as committee chairmen while they continued to be Democrats with no iron-clad assurance and no set timetable about party switching. Sonny Perdue acknowledges that Richardson may "have scared Terry away" and describes how he proposed to assemble a governing coalition in the House in 2004: "We had the package put together in the House, like what I had done in the Senate. We had the package put together that people signed on. Morgan Perry had the commitments. All it took was Terry agreeing to go and he could have been Speaker. It would have been a majority there."

Perdue was open to a shared governance model for a limited period of time because he was concerned that the Republican Party had never governed Georgia and that the new GOP legislative leadership could learn from conservative Democrats who might be willing to share power and eventually change parties. As the new chief executive officer of the state in a period of economic distress, he was somewhat anxious because the new Republican leadership in the House had never chaired committees or been primarily responsible for drawing up state budgets, and he considered that the state might benefit from a smoother transition of power from Democratic to Republican over time. From his vantage point, a transition over a year or two must have appeared workable. Perdue explains his position: "I definitely thought our crowd needed training. . . . They had never had any responsibility whatsoever. I thought Georgia would have been a lot better off if they had sat under the tutelage of a Butch Parrish, a Terry Coleman, a Larry Walker—those conservative Democratic chairs. I thought they could have taught them a lot. . . . I absolutely believe the young Republican caucus could have learned a lot from those guys, just over process."

However, Perdue now seems to understand that he may have been somewhat idealistic in thinking and hoping that a shared power model could have worked. From the perspective of looking back, he observes, "The shared government probably would have crumbled over a lack of trust or probably 'too-soon' ambition. It's the way politics happens. Kind of like some of the same things they said about me. 'I've always been a Republican. I'm a real Republican, and what's this guy doing over here? We're in charge.' So I think it probably would have crumbled."

Chris Young comments on Sonny Perdue's willingness to be more flexible on the issues of shared power and the timing of party changes: "It was Sonny Perdue, the old Democrat, versus the new breed of Republican. There were some who got so frustrated and said, 'They need to switch now, they need to do it yesterday!' and Sonny said, 'Look, these people have been running for thirty years as Democrats. Let them do it on their own terms. They are going to do it—these people have given me their word.' But there were some impatient sorts." When the two parties in the House failed to adopt any shared power arrangement and thereby could not agree on a redistricting map, the Georgia General Assembly adjourned without approving any new reapportionment plan.

As a result of the state legislature's failure to agree on a new plan, the Federal District Court developed and approved its own plan of new districts that did not violate the one person-one vote principle with a map that largely maintained the integrity of county lines. It turned out to be a map that allowed the Georgia GOP perhaps its first ever opportunity to win a majority of House seats. Glenn Richardson describes how important he feels the court-drawn maps were to the Republican Party's success in taking control of the Georgia House of Representatives: "I still think the greatest accomplishment I've ever made legislatively was preventing a map from being drawn and letting the court draw the map."

Then, on June 30, 2004, the last day of that term of the Supreme Court of the United States, the high court affirmed the opinion of the U.S. District Court, voiding the 2001 legislative maps and upholding the new court-drawn maps. The Court cited two bases for voiding the 2001 maps: "The first was a deliberate systematic policy favoring rural and inner-city interests at the expense of suburban areas north, east, and west of Atlanta. The second is an intentional effort to allow incumbent Democrats to maintain or increase their delegation by overpopulation of Republican districts." The ruling also stated which "the creators of the state plans did not consider such traditional redistricting criteria as district compactness, contiguity, protecting communities of interest and keeping counties in tact."[3] Essentially all the arguments advanced by Republicans against the Democratic maps drawn during the 2001 special session of the General Assembly, in the end, were supported by the United States District Court and the Supreme Court of the United States in their decisions.

After the new court-drawn districts were determined in spring 2004, there was relatively little time for the Republicans or the Democrats to organize and execute recruitment and campaign plans based on the new districts. Party Chair Alec Poitevint comments on the challenge: "Once we prevailed we had a very narrow window to recruit everybody. You have this residency rule, I think it's twelve months. The great decision was we formed this war room. We put up the maps; we put up the people, and we were all engaged in recruiting and phoning people. Glenn Richardson was the minority leader, and between him and Jay Walker, they were engaged. The governor was personally engaged. We knew what the districts were, and we tried to recruit the people." Paul Bennecke describes Governor Perdue's active role in the process: "The governor was on the road constantly doing events for targeted candidates, we had a list of tiered campaigns that we felt we could win—there were about thirty in the House, and there were four or five, or maybe six in the Senate—that drove the governor's [campaign] schedule."

Glenn Richardson describes how the legislative leadership and the state party leadership came together in this undertaking in a more cooperative arrangement than had previously existed:

> There was a distrust between Republican elected officials and the state Republican Party. I remember vividly Lynn Westmoreland telling me, "All right, now Bubba, don't give them your money because if you give them your money, they'll go spend it on federal races, and you'll be left with nothing." Well, the key to winning was us pooling money and making decisions. It was not us trying to keep it all for ourselves. I went out there, and I had a meeting with Alec and Jay Walker, and I said "Listen! I am going to raise a bunch of money. And every penny I raise, I am going to get House members to commit to give money to the party, but I need to have input, and I need the final say on what elections we do or don't participate in. And I committed to do it, and they committed to let me have it. And Alec Poitevint, to his credit, helped make decisions, but we raised a lot of money and spent money perfectly on the right seats.

Paul Bennecke expands on Perdue's and Glenn Richardson's roles in raising the funding for the Republican takeover of the House: "The governor raised most of the money. Glenn was a part of that team. He began a process of trying to get [House] members on a plan to contribute to the party and to the candidates as much as they could, particularly if they were unopposed and had a budget."

Scott Rials attributes Richardson's skills as a trial attorney as a significant factor in persuading candidates to run for the House and getting GOP donors to support them. Richardson recounts how he set up the fundraising: "I would go to people and ask them to write ten $1,000 checks . . . to ten names of candidates who are running, and I want you to write a $1,000 check to each of them and send the checks back to me . . . and I'll send them to them [to the candidates]. That was the money we spent for the party." In addition to funds Richardson raised for the party coffers, he created his own political action fund called MMV Alliance. The 2004 disclosure reports indicate he had contributions of $66,000, from which he spent funds for public relations, technology consulting, and computer equipment.

Scott Rials also explains a mentoring program designed to aid in the recruitment effort: "We kind of had this mentorship program. . . . If we had a Republican in South Georgia or North Georgia or wherever, we'd find the nearest Republican to say, 'You can trust this party; they helped me in 2002. They know what they are talking about.'" Glenn Richardson elaborates on the mentoring program he organized for the 2004 House elections: "I divided seventy-one into seven groups of ten. And to each group of ten, I assigned a set of races. They had a captain and beneath that each race had at least two people assigned to them. They were supposed to get called two or three times per week. I would get the seven chairs and we would meet once every two weeks and go through the races." Republican House leaders Jerry Keen and Mark Burkhalter frequently joined Richardson and Jay Walker in the recruiting efforts. John Watson comments on the campaigning done by Governor Perdue in partnership with the Republican leadership of the House and the party leaders and staff:

> The governor was in some thirty districts, traveling like crazy. . . . I think there was also a good level of coordination at the House level. We were working with Glenn and Jerry and with Mark Burkhalter, who had a number of relationships with Democrats from his days of working closely with those folks. . . . You have to give a lot of credit to Glenn Richardson. Glenn traveled the state and worked his tail off on the House races. At the staff level you had Jay Walker, Nick, and others. It was really a team environment. This was really a sweep that was all about "Send me to Atlanta to help Sonny." That was the campaign.

Mark Burkhalter also relates how arduously he and Glenn Richardson campaigned for their candidates that year:

> We sacrificed a lot that year. I'll never forget driving down I-75 wondering, "What is this for? Is it even going to matter?" And I knew that if we got the majority that regardless of where we fell, it was going to matter. It was going to be a better and different day. I gave up a lot of income, and so did he [Richardson]. . . . And we were close enough. We knew those judge-drawn maps were probably our best crack at it. But yeah, there was a lot of sacrifice. Just when you thought you couldn't go to another fundraiser or get in the car again, you were in the car the next day. But it was the best thing that ever happened to us. We were able to forge a friendship and working relationship from that.

Governor Perdue is also credited with raising much of the funding that the Georgia Republican Party needed to finance a large number of competitive House races in 2004. Dan McLagan elaborates on the fundraising: "Really Sonny Perdue was the linchpin. He got the governor's office, and suddenly you can raise a bunch of money."

When Paul Bennecke was asked how much money the party and the Republican elected leadership raised for the 2004 legislative races, he replied, "'I want to say we spent a million and a half, maybe two million, on the Senate and maybe two and a half million on the House. If you were in a targeted House seat, we were probably spending about $100,0000 to $150,000 just through the party, on top of whatever they were spending in their individual campaign." Bennecke reveals how the ads for Republican legislative candidates were combined with ads for a Republican Public Service commissioner's reelection: "Everything the party spent on behalf of a candidate was multi-candidate. Because in 2004 we had Bobby Baker running for Public Service Commission, every piece of communication also had Bobby Baker's name on it."

The coordinated and cooperative efforts of the state's Republican leadership at that time paid huge dividends for the party. In the general election on November 2, Republican candidates won ninety-six seats. A few incumbent Republicans did not run that year, but fifty-eight incumbent Republicans were reelected, four Democrats changed parties before the election and ran as Republicans for the first time, and thirty-four new Republicans were elected, three of whom had previously served in the House. After the election, three more Democrats changed parties to provide the GOP with a strong majority of ninety-nine in the House, compared to only eighty-one Democrats. Representative Tommy Smith, who had chaired the House Reapportionment Committee in 2001, was one of the Democrats who filed that year as a Republican after examining the makeup of his new court-drawn district. He explained that in the court-drawn redistricting he kept his home county of Bacon, but the rest of the district was new to him, and it was mostly Republican-leaning. He also disclosed that he had met with Governor Perdue to discuss changing parties and received some assurances that the Republican Party would not solicit a candidate to oppose him if he chose to run as Republican that year. In addition, Smith relates that he had considered switching parties for more than a year and had prayed for guidance because he was concerned about the Democratic Party's more liberal positions on some social issues as well as the changing demographics of his district. He said the decision to change was not easy, particularly because he "hated to part company with Terry Coleman."

John Watson comments on the party-switching activity in 2004: "The governor primarily gets credit for convincing people to change parties, in a number of one-on-one meetings with them in his office and elsewhere."

Former House Republican leader Bob Irvin comments on the sudden success of the GOP in taking control of both houses of the General Assembly: "I said to people for years that I thought if we ever became kind of a 51 percent Republican state that we would become a 60 percent Republican state overnight because voters would switch and elected officials would switch." Irvin's prognostication proved to be correct.

Bob Holmes provides his Democratic perspective on the 2004 party switching by former Democrats in the House: "I think after the 2002 election people began to say, 'Well, it's kind of happened.' I think that was the tipping point. Then the governor persuaded four of the Democrats in the Senate to change parties. So again they saw the wave coming, and they wanted to get ahead of the wave. So, they changed parties—some of them after the election and some of them when they were running for reelection."

The Republican Party also picked up four additional seats in the state Senate elections that year, growing their majority from thirty to thirty-four members. Eric Johnson attributes winning the four additional seats to the 2004 redistricting. One anomaly in the state Senate elections that year was the defeat of two of the party switchers, Don Cheeks and Dan Lee. Cheeks had been redistricted by the court-drawn plan and ironically was thrown into the same district as his old nemesis, Charles Walker, and Walker managed to defeat Cheeks even though there were 127 federal indictments pending against Walker during the campaign. The criminal charges included mail fraud conspiracy, falsifying tax returns, diversion of charitable funds for personal purposes, and various other fraud and conspiracy schemes.

Don Cheeks explains how the 2004 redistricting worked against him, even though it helped many other Republicans: "Charles Walker beat the hell out of me because he had a 79 percent black district after reapportionment." Former governor Roy Barnes even made a campaign visit to Augusta to boost Walker's candidacy. Later, Charles Walker and his daughter were convicted on many of the charges, and he was no longer permitted to serve in the Senate. Dan Lee was drawn into a pairing in the same district as another incumbent Republican senator, Seth Harp, and the new district favored Harp more than Lee. Of the four state senators who switched parties in 2002, only Senator Jack Hill was reelected in 2004. Senator Rooney Bowen chose not to seek reelection that year.

In another 2004 victory for the Georgia Republican Party, Johnny Isakson, who had worked for more than thirty years in various elective offices to advance Republicanism in Georgia, won the open United States Senate seat with 58 percent of the vote, following Zell Miller's retirement from office. For the first time since a brief period during Reconstruction, both U.S. senators from Georgia were Republicans. Bobby Baker also easily won reelection to the only Public Service Commission post up for a vote that year. In U.S. House races in 2004, following redistricting, all Republican incumbents who ran—Jack Kingston, John Linder, Charlie Norwood, Nathan Deal, and Phil Gingrey—handily won reelection, and former state Senate and House leaders Tom Price and Lynn Westmoreland won the two open Georgia seats in Congress. However, the Democratic Party did reclaim one seat, changing the mix of the Georgia House delegation to seven Republicans and six Democrats.

AJC reporter Nancy Badertscher describes the drama of the 2004 elections when she wrote, "Republicans completed their shocking two-year takeover of state government Tuesday when they seized control of the House of Representatives for the first time in 134 years." She quotes Glenn Richardson as saying, "It took 134 years, but we did it." Badertscher also reports that Richardson attributed much of the party's electoral success to Sonny Perdue.[4]

In addition, Badertscher reports that the Democrats blamed their historic defeat in part on the strong showing at the top of the ballot of President George W. Bush and Johnny Isakson.[5] And the Democratic point of view is certainly understandable since both President Bush and Johnny Isakson captured approximately 58 percent of the total votes cast in Georgia. Political writer Jack Bass describes the significance of the Bush victory in the South for the GOP: "In the Republican sweep of 2004, George W. Bush painted the region solid bright red, receiving a higher percentage of the vote in every southern state than his national average. . . . His coattails proved sufficiently long to sweep in five U.S. Senate seats in the South left open by retiring Democrats, catapulting Republicans from a 13-9 lead in the Senate to an 18-4 dominance. Republicans held a 7-4 edge among governors."[6]

Former Georgia governor Zell Miller, who had just retired from his U.S. Senate seat, stated in his analysis of the early twenty-first-century political landscape in America that "Southerners believe the national Democratic Party does not share their values. They do not trust the national party with their money or the security of the country."[7] He further emphasizes the disaffection of many southerners from the Democratic Party by quoting pollster Mark Penn who reported in 2003, "The Democratic Party is hurt by current perceptions that Democrats stand for big government, want to raise taxes too high, and are too liberal and are beholden to special interest groups."[8] Miller's and Penn's comments, however, seem to pertain most appropriately to white Democrats in the South. According to Earl and Merle Black's exit poll vote analysis of the 2004 elections, most African Americans nationwide continued to vote overwhelmingly Democratic, as did non-Christian whites and many new ethnic minorities, while Republican voters were more likely to be non-evangelical white Protestant men, evangelical white Protestants of both sexes, and Catholic men. Non-evangelical and Catholic white women tended to be the swing voters.[9] Earl and Merle Black also report that in the 2004 elections, 55 percent of southern white voters aligned with the Republican Party, and only 24 percent still thought of themselves as Democrats, while 80 percent of African Americans voted as Democrats.[10] University of Georgia political scientist Charles Bullock III observes, "Among voters, Georgia had the second greatest party shift in Republican Party identification, after Alabama, between 2000 and 2004."[11]

North Carolina State political scientist Andrew Taylor comments on how the national Republican Party's organizational efforts helped achieve electoral victories in southern states: "In 2004 the GOP established extensive and sophisticated organizations at the state, county, and precinct levels in critical swing states or marginal districts across the country. Much of the GOP voter mobilization effort is dizzyingly high-tech direct mail, like Richard Viguerie's RNC data base called 'voter vault.' . . . Underneath the national party organization are similarly effective mature and sophisticated state and local parties that complement the RNC."[12]

The overall high voter turnout in 2004, particularly among white voters in Georgia, certainly helped the GOP secure a majority of seats in the House that year. Dan McLagan offers his explanation as to why the Democrats lost control of the state House in Georgia in the 2002 to 2004 timeframe: "You know the Democrats had never really had to run campaigns. The one-sidedness of the state basically created a situation where the Democrats were no good at running because there was no professional talent base here. There weren't any real consultants. The Democrats just thought you raise a whole bunch of money because the governor helps you raise a bunch of money, and you spend it on some ads." John Watson concurs: "The Democrats never had television ads run for or against them. They never had direct mail." With particular respect to the 2004 legislative races, former party executive director Jay Morgan observes, "The Democrats were overconfident. They had it wrapped up, and they sat there on the election day and still had a million dollars in the bank that they did not spend, a combination of what Coleman had, the party had, and what was in the campaign accounts of some of the committee chairmen. They probably could have maintained control of the House maybe another cycle if they had spent that correctly, but they did not. They got blown away."

A review of the final 2004 campaign financial disclosure report of the Democratic Party of Georgia and those of several House leaders reveals that the party and its elected leadership actually raised substantial funding and contributed considerable sums to support Democratic House candidates in 2004. The Democratic Party of Georgia reported receiving contributions of $4,084,000 and paying out campaign expenses and donations to candidates of $4,319,000 for 2004, with a remaining fund balance of slightly less than $200,000. The party and Terry Coleman both reported him as contributing $175,000 to the party from his own campaign account, and he also made donations ranging from $500 to $1,000 to essentially every Democratic House candidate who had electoral opposition. The balance remaining in his campaign account was reported to be only $87,000. House Democratic Majority Leader Jimmy Skipper, who retired from the state legislature that year, had only $21,589 remaining in his campaign account, according to campaign disclosure reports. Roy Barnes contributed $50,000 to the party, Columbus representative and caucus chair Calvin Smyre also contributed $50,000, and Mark Taylor donated $500,000. Taylor retained a large balance in his campaign account, but he was anticipating a future run for governor. These spending reports suggest that the Democratic Party and leadership did spend fairly generously for their candidates, but apparently the funds were not expended effectively enough for the Democrats to maintain control of the House.

Moreover, the Democratic leaders all seemed to believe that they would win a sufficient number of seats in the House to continue their control of it for the next two to four years. Representative Mark Burkhalter comments on their level of confidence: "Right before the election, in October on a Saturday or a Sunday, I had a chance to spend some time with Terry [Coleman], a group of us—some of his friends—Butch Parrish and some of those guys. We literally spent the better part of two days, and we never talked about the obvious—that's how convinced they were that things were going to rock right along—they assumed they were going to win. . . . Coleman didn't think he was going to lose. The Democrats didn't expect that."

African-American Democrat Bob Holmes reports he was more pessimistic about the Democrats retaining control of the House in 2004 when asked his reaction to the turnover of enough House seats to shift control from the Democrats to the Republicans. He replied, "I thought they would. I was surprised at the margin. There were more than I had anticipated. I had thought that this would probably be enough to push the Republicans into a majority, but I thought that we would still be in a position that we might be able to block some things, but with that margin it was clear that they didn't need us at all."

On January 10, 2005, history was made when Glenn Richardson was elected and sworn in as the first Republican Speaker of the Georgia House of Representatives since Reconstruction. However, both Mark Burkhalter and Glen Richardson disclose that they both had aspired to win the office of Speaker. Burkhalter describes the competition over summer and fall 2004:

> We were raising money and giving it away and trying to win races and trying not to radiate our intentions of running for Speaker. We didn't have a majority. We thought we might get it, but we weren't convinced of it. But you knew you were going to be close enough to where you had to start planning for "What if?" to some degree. . . . It's funny. Glenn was raising money and was giving it away to our candidates. I was raising money and giving it away to candidates. So we weren't hurtful of the cause. We were respectful of the end game. But make no mistake about it; we wanted the same job. So it created some tension, to say the least. We had meetings. I remember one specifically where we met. John Watson was assigned the job—lucky him—to sit down with Glenn and me to sort of say, "This has gotten to a point where you may be hurting our cause, the two of you, by even suggesting that you are interested in being Speaker, if we get a majority." We were at the Georgian Club one day, and Glenn got a little upset because he wanted me to commit in advance that if we got the majority that I would not accept any Democratic votes for Speaker if I were a candidate for Speaker. And I said, "I am not going to commit to anything. We have got to win the majority, and let's see the dynamic." And he was very frustrated by that.
>
> It got to the point where we saw each other so much that I thought, "Let's be adults about this." So I called him up one day to get lunch. . . . I think our first lunch was at Houston's down on West Paces Ferry, and it was uncomfortable. . . . But it was those forced lunches and conversations that calmed him down enough where we made it work. It culminated at a dinner at Morton's, Jerry [Keen] was there, and for lack of a better descrip-

tion, a deal was brokered, with some conditions. He acknowledged that in a very close situation or if we were only a vote or two away or a tie—a 90-90 scenario—that I was probably more of a broker than he was. But he [stated], "I am the minority leader and the credit, in large part, should go to me if we get the majority. And we agreed to that. . . . And from there we have honored that agreement.

Richardson gives a supporting but more abbreviated account of their competition for the Speakership:

After getting through the 2004 legislative session and knowing I had held the Republicans [together], I was a little surprised at the challenge. But Mark [Burkhalter] was going around trying to raise money, and he was challenging me—a lot of mumbling that if we came up short that he could get the Democrats to go with him. The governor wouldn't weigh in. I asked him to, but he stayed out of it. . . . Two weeks before the election I got Mark and Jerry in a restaurant . . . and I made them an offer. I said if you support me for Speaker, I'll support you [Mark] for Speaker Pro Tem and Jerry for majority leader. He [Mark] accepted that night and Jerry accepted. We walked out of that restaurant and had a press release the next morning. . . . On election night, we were saying, "Oh my God, we've done it!" It makes you almost tear up that you did something that big, and it's really a good feeling to have accomplished something like that.

Just as the Republicans in the state Senate changed their rules in 2003 after winning control of the chamber, House Republicans had to reorganize their chamber in late 2004 and early 2005. Mark Burkhalter relates the challenge they faced: "The work that was done from the day we got the majority to the day we were sworn in was major. . . . You are rewriting the rules. You're trying to come up with this matrix game of 180 members and committee assignments for Republicans and Democrats and chairmen. We interviewed people in our caucus for chairmanships. They had to come in and make their case to the committee on assignments—seven minutes we gave them. . . . We did it over the holidays. And I chaired the committee to rewrite the rules." Once they were organized, the new Republican leadership lost little time in assuming the reins of power in the House and introducing and passing legislation on issues that their party had endorsed for several years.

Certainly, there had been several critical social and political issues that had galvanized conservative Republicans and challenged the fragile Democratic Party coalition in Georgia over the previous two decades.

Political scientist David Lublin elaborates on the types of issues that tended to divide the Democratic Party in the South and advance the cause of Republicans: "The rise of social issues like abortion, gay rights, and gun control in the 1980s increasingly attracted religious and social conservatives to the banner of the GOP. The rising liberalism among Democrats on social issues combined with the staunch conservatism of Republicans on the same questions allowed for partisan change centered on social issues to occur. The increased funneling of white conservatives by both issues and institutions into the GOP eventually broke the back of Democratic dominance."[13]

State Senator Bill Jackson opined that the gay marriage issue was one of the factors that accelerated the Republican takeover of the Georgia House of Representatives in the 2004 elections. It's his view that Terry Coleman's decision to allow the Georgia House of Representatives to vote on and pass a resolution allowing a Georgia constitutional amendment vote on same-sex marriages in 2004 resulted in a larger than usual voter turnout in the general election among Christian conservatives who tended to support Republican candidates on the ballot while voting against gay marriages. The 2004 general election in Georgia voter turnout and vote results seem to support Senator Jackson's opinion. In a high 77 percent voter turnout, 76.2 percent of the voters cast their ballots in support of a state ban on same-sex marriages.

No doubt this controversial issue influenced greater participation by conservative voters. Conservative Georgians also tend to support national defense and the United States military to a greater extent than in other regions of the country. Georgia experienced a significant buildup of military bases in the state during World War II and in the decades following the war. Georgia was fortunate to have several senior senators and representatives, mostly Democrats, who chaired or served on important national defense committees in Congress, supported the location of military bases in the state, and then protected these bases from closure. As a consequence, Georgians have traditionally valued both the economic and patriotic dimensions of the United States maintaining a strong role for the its military around the world. Therefore, as some national Democrats became more vocal in opposition to United States military involvement in world affairs, Republicans picked up the backing of more Georgians. The Bush administration's quick response to the September 11, 2001, airplane attacks on New York City and Washington, D.C., by terrorists and its subsequent declaration of war on Iraq further shifted public opinion in Georgia toward the GOP.[14]

The gradual shift in the political leanings of many white southerners from Democrat to Republican from the mid-1960s to the first decade of the twenty-first century can be largely explained by the difference in how the Republican Party responded to contemporary social and political issues compared to how the Democratic Party responded. This analysis doesn't necessarily explain why Georgians were slower than other southern states to shift their political allegiances at the state House level. State Senator Jack Hill, who converted from Democrat to Republican in 2002, opines that the Democratic Party leadership in Georgia was as conservative as the national Republicans, and therefore there was not much need to change.

> I am thinking, in all fairness to the Democratic Party, that the state had a history of conservative leadership. . . . When it came time to do something important for the state; the leadership stepped forward and did it. . . . When Zell Miller went in, he was only elected by just the thinnest of margins. But you know, he came out of that election as a conservative. I can remember the first meeting that was held, the Democrats were talking about cutting the welfare rolls and two strikes and you're out. I mean there were several super conservative things that did not sit well with the some of the Democrats.

Longtime Democrat leader Larry Walker concurs with Hill's assessment: "The job was being done—fiscally conservative balanced budgets—the state was running well. It was a well-oiled machine, and I think that's why Democratic dominance lasted as long as it did in Georgia." Michael Thurmond expounds the "well-oiled machine' concept: "Tom Murphy held the Democratic coalition together long past the time when it should have been in place—primarily between conservatives, some say rural whites and urban blacks, and he was a political genius. And just through his electioneering skills and his ability to use the levels of government, he was able to hold a coalition. But the coalition was fraying."

Undoubtedly, the court-drawn redistricting maps also aided the Republican Party in finally winning a majority of seats in the General Assembly. Perhaps the GOP might have captured more seats sooner in one house or the other, had it not been for the Democrats' tight control over reapportionment. In addition, the fact that Georgia has 159 counties, more than any other state in the nation except for Texas, may have contributed to the longtime hold on the legislature by the party in power. Much of the political machinery of the state is organized at county level, and when a single party dominates local government, as the Democrats did for so long in Georgia, it is arguably difficult to build coalitions for effective partisan change at the state level. However, the 2001 redistricting may have pushed some of the county political organizations away from their historic Democratic ties. Michael Thurmond sums up the consequences of that reapportionment process on the Democratic Party in Georgia: "The Democrats started playing with the election process. . . . Whenever you see people in power start playing with election machinery, it's just a matter of time before their power collapses."

In the 2006 election cycle, Republicans won even greater influence over the state's political affairs. Sonny Perdue stood for reelection and soundly defeated Democratic challenger Lieutenant Governor Mark Taylor. Taylor had been challenged in the Democratic primary by two-term Democratic Secretary of State Cathy Cox in a close contest that somewhat rifted the party, and Democratic support for Taylor was fragmented. Bob Holmes describes their primary contest as a "blood-letting" that "sunk the possibility" of a Taylor/Democratic victory. However, the Perdue team did not take his reelection for granted and worked hard to secure his reelection. According to Nick Ayers, Perdue's campaign director, the governor had charged the campaign team to run aggressively and "be driven by a campaign plan that no matter what the poll numbers say, we will campaign every day as if we are ten points down."

In the November 7 general election, Perdue trounced Taylor by winning 1,229,724 votes or 57.9 percent of the total to 811,049 votes for Taylor or 38.3 percent, with a Libertarian candidate winning 3.8 percent. In this election, Perdue carried 130 of Georgia's 159 counties, compared to 118 he won in 2002. Perdue also won the majority of votes in ten-county Metro Atlanta, which neither he nor Saxby Chambliss had accomplished in the 2002 election. Perdue picked up 91,326 more votes from the Metro Atlanta region and garnered 39.68 percent of his total votes there in 2006, versus only 38 percent four years earlier. Perdue also picked up a higher percentage of black Georgia votes in 2006 than he had before. Although Mark Taylor won the vast majority of African-American votes and outpolled Perdue in fourteen of the eighteen counties with the highest black population, Perdue won in the other four counties, all of which he had lost to Roy Barnes in the 2002 election. 2006 was a relatively low voter turnout year with only 42.8 percent of registered blacks voting, compared to 52.5 percent of registered whites voting. Mark Taylor won the lowest percentage of the total votes cast of any

Democratic gubernatorial candidate since Reconstruction and a lower percentage of the total votes than any Republican gubernatorial challenger had won since Republican Guy Davis's race against incumbent governor Joe Frank Harris in 1986.

Republican state senator Casey Cagle from Gainesville surprised many political observers by beating former state GOP chairman Ralph Reed in a hotly contested primary battle for lieutenant governor. Reed was well known in Republican circles as the former head of the Christian Coalition, a traditional GOP power base, but Cagle successfully associated Ralph Reed with Jack Abramoff, an influential Washington lobbyist who in early 2006 was convicted of defrauding American Indian tribes and corrupting public officials. Cagle won 56 percent of the votes in the Republican primary in July 2006. In the November general election, he defeated long-serving Democratic representative Jim Martin of Atlanta by winning 1,134,517 votes, or 54.1 percent of the total, to become the first Republican lieutenant governor in the history of the state. Cagle had widespread support and carried 127 of 159 the counties in the election.

In other statewide races in the 2006 election, Fulton County Commission Chairperson Karen Handel captured 54.1 percent of the vote to defeat convincingly a Democratic opponent in an open seat race to become the first Republican secretary of state since Reconstruction. Republicans Kathy Cox and John Oxendine were the top Republican vote getters in statewide races to win their reelections as superintendent of education and insurance commissioner, respectively. GOP member Stan Wise also won reelection to the Public Service Commission, and Republican newcomer Chuck Eaton also won a PSC seat in a runoff vote. However, the three incumbent Democratic constitutional officers, Attorney General Thurbert Baker, Labor Commissioner Michael Thurmond, and Agricultural Commissioner Tommy Irvin also won their contested reelections by ten-point margins or better. Michael Thurmond characterizes their wins that year: "People were betting against it when you had a very popular Sonny Perdue running for reelection, and the Republican leaders had said that their goal was to take every office. All things being equal, we were up against it because you had unlimited money and a popular governor with what appeared to be a strong ticket. The fact that I, Thurbert, and Tommy were able to hold them off was a huge win, maybe even an unexpected one."

The GOP held onto its thirty-four seats in the state Senate and picked up a net addition of seven seats in the state House of Representatives. Before the 2006 qualifying date, four leading Democratic representatives announced they were switching parties and registered and ran for the first time as Republicans. These former Democratic stalwarts were Butch Parrish of Swainsboro, Mickey Channell of Greensboro, Richard Royal of Camilla, and Johnny Floyd of Cordele, all of whom had previously chaired important committees of the House. They also were among the Democratic Party allies of Terry Coleman that Morgan Perry Cook and Hunter Towns had engaged in party-switching discussions in summer and fall 2003. No doubt their decision to switch parties was made easier by Terry Coleman's decision not to seek another term in the state legislature in 2006 after serving thirty-four years in the House. From one Democrat's perspective, Michael Thurmond expresses how he understands these representatives' decisions to change parties after serving so long in the state House as Democrats:

> The people who were left out in the cold as a result of the 1990 reapportionment in a very sharp and significant way were white rural Democrats, because they paid the price when they bleached the districts. They felt it made their election possibilities much slimmer as Democrats. And so part of it was—when you look at Butch Parrish and Richard Royal—they were switching because they felt the earth shattering. . . . They saw what the result was. Once the Republicans took power, everybody lost their chairmanships. It wasn't just the white Democrats, but the black Democrats lost their committee chairmanships; they lost their influence over the budget; they lost in every way. They lost their parking spaces; they lost their offices, they lost all the patronage and everything you could have associated with being in power.

In recognition of their knowledge and experience in the state legislature and in appreciation for their conversion to the GOP, party switchers Butch Parrish, Mickey Channell, Richard Royal, and Johnny Floyd were all given positions of influence in the House committee structure by the Republican House leaders when the House organized for a new term in 2007.

In addition to picking up party switchers, the Republican leadership in the House again organized their membership into reelection campaign teams, just as they had in 2004, to help members in contested seats win their reelections and to assist Republican candidates running for the first time. Representative Edward Lindsey, an attorney from Buckhead in North Atlanta first elected in 2004, explained that his race was uncontested in 2006, so he was assigned to help five other candidates that year. He helped them in generating publicity for their campaigns and in getting out the Republican votes in their districts. He reported that four of them won their races, and only one lost. When all the votes were tallied that year, the Republicans picked up seven more seats and now outnumbered Democrats in the House 106 to 74, an almost exact reversal of the partisan mix of the state House in 2001. Soon after the election, Democrat Mike Jacobs of North DeKalb County switched parties to become a Republican, giving the GOP 107 seats in the House. If there was ever any lingering doubt that the Republican victories in 2002 and 2004 were not some sort of anomalies, the 2006 election in Georgia dispelled any doubts that the Democrats had now lost control of the state House in Georgia. In the congressional races of 2006, all incumbent Republicans won reelection, maintaining the partisan balance in the Georgia delegation at seven R's and six D's. However, at the national level, the Democrats defeated a large number of Republicans, netting thirty-three new seats, to retake the majority in the United States House of Representatives. Once again, Georgia lagged the national trend by not losing any of its Republican representation in Congress and in picking up even more dominance in the state House. Georgia Speaker Pro Tem Mark Burkhalter comments on the GOP wins in Georgia that year: "We have our legislative leaders and speakers conferences that you go and get to talk to your counterparts. And one thing that's been fun—you almost get to brag about being from Georgia—is what we've been able to do in our short term in the majority. And in 2006 when Republicans took a bath—not just in Congress, but in many state legislatures—we had gains. Cumulatively, seventeen GOP seats were gained in all fifty state legislatures in 2006, and about half of them were in Georgia."

After being the last state in the South to elect Republicans to statehouse leadership, in just the four years between 2002 and 2006, Georgia voters finally elected and then reelected a Republican governor, chose their first Republican lieutenant governor, and gained control of both houses of the state legislature after many years of trying. The looming question then becomes, what finally happened to break the longtime Democratic lock on the Georgia state House? Since the Republican takeover started with the gubernatorial victory of Sonny Perdue, analysis should first focus on that election. Sonny Perdue possessed several attributes that aided him in becoming the first Republican governor of Georgia since Reconstruction. Most notably, he was able to leverage his rural roots and former Democratic alliances to win a majority of votes in rural Georgia while holding on to the

Republican base in Metro Atlanta, something no other Republican guberna-torial candidate had ever done. This expanded voter base enabled him to win the 2002 Republican primary without a runoff as well as the general elec-tion. In addition, his business background and connections seem to have appealed to a broad constituency of Georgians. Finally, he was successful in first seeing and then capitalizing on the dissatisfaction of several voting blocs with some of Roy Barnes's policies and practices, most notably his educa-tional policy changes and recommendations, the 2001 redistricting plan, and the process of changing the state flag without a referendum. And then imme-diately following his election, Perdue and his colleagues in state Senate leadership moved rapidly to convince four Democratic senators to switch parties within a week of his gubernatorial victory, a feat that undoubtedly would have been difficult to pull off had not Perdue worked collaboratively with the converts as a fellow Democrat before he switched parties. Also, Perdue forged a strong alliance with other Republican leaders in the Senate after he switched parties in 1998, so that they were able to work effectively as a team in turning the Senate.

Once he became governor, Perdue was able to raise sufficient funds from business and political interests to enable the Republican Party to afford and sustain the lawsuit challenging the constitutionality of the 2001 Democratic redistricting plan. Eric Johnson explains the importance of a Republican winning the governor's office in order eventually to win the House: "We won the [redistricting] case which then gave us good maps. I don't think we would have been able to raise the money to pay the attorneys to keep the suit going if we hadn't won the governor's race." Also, the hard work and dogged tenacity Sonny Perdue, Glenn Richardson, and several others was a critical factor for the GOP finally to be able to win the majority of seats in the state House of Representatives in 2004, after the court-drawn reapportionment plan provided more favorable districts. Once the Georgia Republican Party had won the opportunity to streamline the operations of state government and design the framework for what Perdue called a New Georgia, their big challenge became how to govern the state in a manner that would continue to generate the confidence and support of the state's citizenry for the Republican Party.

U.S. senators Saxby Chambliss and Johnny Isakson with State Representative Jay Roberts. Isakson's election in 2004 marked the first time in Georgia's history that both of the state's U.S. Senate seats had been held by Republicans. Credit: Georgia House Photographer/Kelly Blackmon.

2003 photo of recently-elected Governor Perdue in the second week of January giving his first State of the State and budget address to a joint meeting of the Georgia General Assembly. He is being welcomed at the podium by Lt. Governor Mark Taylor and Speaker of the House Terry Coleman. Credit: Georgia House photographer/Kelli Musselman.

Sonny Perdue and Larry Walker, who Perdue backed for House Speaker against
Terry Coleman in January 2003. The photo shows the long time close connection
between them that spurred the unusual action of a newly-elected governor
getting involved in a Speaker election. Credit: Larry Walker.

Morgan Perry Cook and Hunter Towns, who were Gov. Perdue's legislative affairs coordinators in 2003-04 and worked to form a coalition with Democratic House members and help convinced some to change parties in the 2004 elections. Credit: Governor's office photographer/Kelli Musselman.

State senator Jack Hill, one of the party-switching senators, at his seat in the Senate in 2005. Credit: Georgia Senate photographer/Tyna Duckett.

Current "Dean of the Senate" Democrat George Hooks, who declined to change parties. Credit: Georgia Senate photographer/Tyna Duckett.

State senators Tommie Williams, Eric Johnson, and Jack Hill on a plane together during the 2006 campaign. Credit: Georgia State Photographer/Tuna Duckett

Gubernatorial candidate Sonny Perdue runs onto the field with the Fitzgerald High School football team prior to their game with Cairo High School in October 2002. Credit: AP Photo/*Atlanta Journal-Constitution*/Rich Addicks.

Former state Senate Majority Leader Bill Stephens in a 2006 press conference.
Credit: Georgia Senate Photographer/Tyna Duckett.

January 2007 inauguration of Gov. Perdue for his second term and the inauguration
of Casey Cagle (with Mrs. Cagle) as Georgia's first Republican Lt. Governor and
Karen Handel as Republican Secretary of State (with husband Steve Handel).
Credit: Governor's office photographer/ Kelli Musselman.

State senator Bill Heath in the well of the Senate in 2007. Heath defeated long-serving House Speaker Tom Murphy in 2002. Credit: Georgia Senate photographer/Tyna Duckett.

"Sine die" with newly-elected Republican Lt. Gov. Casey Cagle on the phone with Speaker Glenn Richardson, agreeing to adjourn the 2007 legislative session. Credit: Georgia Senate photographer/ Tyna Duckett.

Lt. Gov. Casey Cagle and House Speaker Glenn Richardson at the rostrum in a joint meeting of both houses of the General Assembly in 2008. Credit: Georgia Senate photographer/ Tyna Duckett.

Speaker Pro-Tem Mark Burkhalter, House Republican Majority Leader Jerry Keen, and Speaker Glenn Richardson at the House rostrum. Credit: Georgia House Photographer/Elizabeth Erikson.

Jerry Keen and Glenn Richardson in spirited debate on the House floor.
Credit: Georgia House photographer/ Elizabeth Erikson

Gov. Sonny Perdue with former governor and senator Zell Miller, taken July 1, 2009,
in Atlanta at swearing in of new Chief Justice. Credit: Ashley G. Stollar.

Republican leaders Governor Sonny Perdue, House Speaker Glenn Richardson
and Lieutenant Governor Casey Cagle in 2007 fly around Georgia.
Credit: Georgia House Photographer/Elizabeth Erikson.

CHAPTER 7

Future Challenges
for the Georgia GOP

After winning control of the governor's office and the state Senate in 2002 and later the House in 2004, Governor Perdue focused much of his attention of creating his vision of a New Georgia that would operate with increased efficiency, effectiveness, and accountability, and the majority of Republicans in the state legislature supported his initiatives, especially in the early years of his administration. As he promised, one of his first actions was to draft and adopt a policy that laid out a code of ethical conduct governing all of his appointees to the staff of the governor's office and all agency heads. Among other provisions, his Code of Ethics prescribed a $25 limit on the value of any gifts or meals or other entertainment that could be accepted, and he declared that none of his appointees, including agency and authority executives, would be allowed to lobby state government on behalf of any client until at least one year after the appointee had left state employment. Also as planned, he appointed three new senior-level positions of inspector general, chief operating officer, and chief financial officer to work in partnership with the traditional governor's office positions of chief of staff and executive counsel. In addition, Perdue appointed deputy chiefs of staff for external affairs, administration, and policy, and he created and staffed the Policy Office as a separate entity from the Governor's Office of Planning and Budget based on his deeply held conviction that policy should drive budget decisions, as opposed to the budget driving policy.

As governor, Perdue enlisted a blue-ribbon commission of twenty-two leading CEOs of major Georgia businesses and institutions to study and recommend initiatives to him and his management team designed to improve the efficiency and effectiveness of state government. Since its inception in 2003, the commission has organized 23 separate task forces comprised of more than 350 volunteer citizen members and several top flight business consultants that have provided their professional services on a pro bono basis in order to formulate more than 85 actionable recommendations. Perdue appointed Lonice Barrett, the respected and long-serving head of the Department of Natural Resources, and a small team of associates to lead the implementation of the vast majority of these recommendations. Operating improvements have run the gamut from the consolidation of state construction and property management services, to improvement in financial management practices, to enhanced workforce development, to the establishment of a statewide customer service program and the attainment of considerable cost savings in procurement practices and better asset management. In addition, the Perdue administration and Republican legislative leaders were successful in passing meaningful tort reform legislation in 2005.

During the legislative sessions of 2007 and 2008, the lack of effective teamwork and clear policy consensus, and even some competitiveness among the governor's office and Senate and House leadership, indicates that the Georgia Republican Party needs to improve its collaboration on major policy initiatives in order to continue to govern the state effectively. Former state Republican Party chairman, Alec Poitevint, comments on the challenge ahead for the Georgia GOP to sustain these changes in state government: "We have to keep steady to those goals to create a new Georgia—it's honest government, it's treating taxpayer money as though it is your own. It's for making government work. . . . We have to keep on recruiting strong candidates that can have enough guts to be for things that are sometimes controversial."

Eric Johnson also speaks to the challenge from his perspective in the state Senate: "The first two years, even in the recession, it was almost easier, from my perspective, because we were so aligned with the governor. We were all on the same side fighting the Democrats. . . . When we took the House, the learning curve over the next two years was how do you deal now that we are in control of everything, and it began to get a little bit tougher. . . . All right, now you are in charge, and everything isn't black and white. . . . We are still learning to be the majority party and learning what the responsibility is and the give and take that comes with it."

Johnson's observations are particularly salient if the Georgia GOP is to learn from the difficulties recently encountered by the Republican Party in the United States Congress. The lack of sustained moral and principled leadership and the fractiousness that existed within the Republican majority in the United States House of Representatives in recent years caused the national party to lose its control of the House to the Democratic Party in the 2006 election cycle, and in the 2008 elections Democrats also won a clear majority of the seats in the United States Senate.

The Democratic Party also won back the presidency in 2008 with the 51 percent to 48 percent victory of former Illinois senator Barack Obama over Arizona senator John McCain. In Georgia, McCain outpolled Obama 2,048,744 votes, or 52.2 percent of the total, to 1,844,137 votes for Obama, or 47 percent of the total. However, McCain's percentage of the total votes cast in Georgia for the United States presidency was lower than the 55 percent and 58 percent vote tallies won by George W. Bush in the 2000 and 2004 elections. Obama also cut into Bush's Solid South vote by winning the electoral votes of Florida, North Carolina, and Virginia.

In Georgia, Barack Obama received a majority of the votes in thirty-four counties and won a strong 58 percent of the votes cast in Metro Atlanta. Of particular note, he won the largest number of votes in three metro-area counties that had a long history of supporting Republican presidential candidates—Douglas, Newton, and Rockdale counties. Voter turnout was 76 percent overall in Georgia in the 2008 election, with a higher than usual 75.8 percent participation among black registered voters, compared to a 77.4 percent turnout among white voters.

Republican Saxby Chambliss experienced a close call in his reelection bid for the United States Senate in 2008. Democratic challenger, former state representative Jim Martin, and a Libertarian Party candidate held Chambliss to 49.8 percent of the votes in the general election, forcing a runoff race. Forty-three percent fewer voters participated in the runoff, and Chambliss won 57.4 percent of the votes cast to defeat Martin, showing once again that Georgia Republicans are usually more successful than the Democrats in getting their supporters out for runoff votes. Republican Public Service Commission candidate Lauren "Bubba" McDonald won in a runoff against a Democratic candidate who outpolled him in the general election but failed to get a majority. Republican Doug Everett handily won reelection in another PSC race by receiving two-thirds of the votes cast. All incumbent representatives to the U.S. House from Georgia were reelected in

2008, maintaining a delegation of seven Republicans and six Democrats. Republican Paul Broun had replaced Charlie Norwood in a special election in 2007 after Norwood died while in office, but Broun managed to hold the seat for the GOP in 2008.

In the state legislature, the Senate continued to have a mix of 34 Republicans and 22 Democrats, but the House Republicans lost a net of two seats, changing the mix to 105 Republicans and 75 Democrats. Three incumbent Republican representatives were defeated, and in turn two incumbent Democrats were defeated, but the Democrats won an open seat previously held by a Republican. The Democratic Party might have won more seats in the 2008 elections if they had challenged more Republican incumbents. In the state Senate races, Democrats challenged only 13 of 34 seats held by Republicans, and in the House the Democrats put up challengers in only 23 seats held by Republicans. In total, only 39 of 180 House seats were contested by candidates of the other party in the 2008 election cycle.

In addition to the gains made by the Democratic Party of Georgia in the 2008 presidential election, the Republicans should have some concern about the voting patterns in the 2008 party primaries. Only 21 percent of registered Republicans voted in their primary, in comparison to 24 percent of Democratic eligible voters participating in their primary process, with a strong 50 percent turnout among black Democrats. Perhaps more significant than the percentage of participation is the total number of voters participating. 1,056,251 Georgians voted in the Democratic primary in contrast to only 958,293 Georgians voting in the Republican primary. It was the first time in six years that more Georgians voted in the Democratic primary than the Republican one.[1]

Conclusion

The quick transition from many decades of a Democratically solid statehouse in Georgia to the modern-day Republican era has been truly remarkable. To quote historians Earl and Merle Black, "The Republican advance among southern whites is the most spectacular example of partisan realignment in modern American history."[2] However, the Blacks also point out that the Republican sway over the South is not nearly as strong a rule as the Democrats enjoyed during their single-party era of the late nineteenth and early twentieth centuries: "The southern transformation, however, has not resulted in enormous Republican surpluses comparable to those produced by southern Democrats in the one-party era. The modern South is far too diverse to produce a Solid Republican South similar in magnitude to the Solid Democratic South."[3] A couple of recent 2008 congressional elections in Alabama and Louisiana have shown that formerly Republican-leaning districts can still be won by conservative Democratic candidates. Journalist Greg Hitt commented on the Democratic strategy to engage Republicans more aggressively in the South in the 2008 election cycle:

> Spurred by the souring economy and a newfound willingness to embrace conservative candidates, the Democratic Party is running its most competitive campaigns across the South in 4 years, fielding potential winners along a rib of states stretching from Louisiana to Virginia, the heart of the Old Confederacy. . . . The party's rising prospects point toward a once unthinkable goal: a reversal of the "Great Reversal," the switch in political loyalty in the 1960s that made the South a solid Republican stronghold.[4]

Georgia Democratic congressmen Jim Marshall and John Barrow, who were reelected in 2008, are good examples of the trend of conservative southern Democrats winning in recent years in swing districts.

So, even though the Republican Party in Georgia has essentially taken control of state government after 130 years of Democratic Party dominance, the Democratic Party in Georgia will quite likely try to improve its organizational effectiveness in the coming years and provide greater competition to the Georgia GOP.

Analysis of the votes in the recent presidential election reveals that what some political observers call "the bluing of the suburbs" is already taking place in Georgia, like Barack Obama winning the largest share of the vote in the formerly Republican-leaning counties of Douglas, Newton, and Rockdale in Metro Atlanta. An influx of Democratic newcomers to the South and the relocation of minority voters to the suburbs are the causes of these partisan shifts. Hence, it may be incumbent on the Republicans in Georgia and the rest of the South to begin to broaden the GOP base to include more upper and upper middle-income African Americans and more of the new minorities of Latinos and Asians relocating here. Earl and Merle Black's studies of voting patterns in the South show that few African Americans have tended to vote for white Republican candidates in recent years, and, consequently, they conclude that "Republicans need to secure about three-fifths of the much bigger white vote in order to win elections."[5] Since Georgia is one of the states with the highest percentage of black populations, 28.7 percent according to the 2000 U.S. Census, it may be even more important for the Georgia GOP to make inroads into the African-American voting bloc. Zell Miller observed in his recent 2003 exposition of the Democratic Party that Republicans were beginning to benefit from outreach efforts to African-American voters at the expense of the Democratic Party:

> For many years now in the South, the magic formula for the Democratic nominee to win in a general election against a Republican is to get 40 percent of the white vote and 90 percent of the African-American vote. Increasingly over the years it has been easier to get 90 percent of the African-American vote than 40 percent of the white vote. I believe that the margin of African-American votes for the Democrats is going to change soon. It only has to change a fraction in the South to make a huge difference. . . . Virginia voters figured out some time ago that they were not going to get many more white votes, so what did they do? They started quietly going after African-American support.[6]

Sonny Perdue attracted a larger percentage of African-American voters in his reelection campaign than he did in his first race for governor. Perdue's former deputy chief of staff for external affairs, Dylan Glenn, an African American, unsuccessfully challenged Lynn Westmoreland in the Republican primary for a congressional seat in 2004, but made a respectable showing, finishing second in a four-person race and winning 44.5 percent of the vote in a runoff election. Also, since Perdue has been in office, two African Americans have been elected to the House of Representatives in Georgia: Willie Talton of the governor's home county of Houston, and Melvin Everson of Gwinnett County. David Casas, also from Gwinnett County, is a Republican who is Hispanic. So some limited progress has been made by the Georgia GOP in becoming more diverse in its appeal to Georgia's changing electorate.

However, Representative Bob Holmes explains that Georgia Republicans are going to have be considerably more outreaching to increase their electoral appeal to African Americans: "What I've always said is that people, for the most part, do vote their own interest. And when you have the reputation that the Republican Party has . . . that there is no major outreach effort on policy issues and things of that nature, you say, 'What are you doing to attract African Americans?' It's a very simple thing. You've got your different wings of the party, and if the right wing is in control, you're not going to have them. If you have the more moderate wing of the party come in, then you can probably attract them." One hopeful sign for the Republican Party's possible outreach to African Americans is the recent selection of an African American, Michael Steele, the lieutenant governor of Maryland, as the new chair of the Republican National Committee.

If the Republican Party chooses not to reach out to African Americans on policy issues, then it will become even more important for the party to develop a greater appeal to Latinos and Asian voters who are a growing element in the Georgia electorate. In 2008, whites comprised only 62.28 percent of all registered voters, having decreased from 72.4 percent of registrants in 2000. Over the same period, African Americans increased from 25.4 percent to 30 percent of registered voters, and although Latinos were only 1.4 percent and Asians 1.2 percent in 2008, their share of the registered electorate more than doubled over the previous eight years.[7] Journalist Jay Bookman quotes political science professor Charles Bullock III, who comments on the changing electorate in Georgia as it may affect the Republican Party:

> Bullock points out that in the '08 election, the dominance of the Republican Party in Georgia began showing some pretty large cracks. The party's success has been built on drawing overwhelming support among white voters, he says, but that demographic group is shrinking pretty quickly, at least in relative terms. According to Bullock, "The consequences of whites constituting less of the electorate are obvious. Georgia will turn blue again. Have Republican leaders begun to ponder how to frame issues either to attract a larger share of the black vote or to become the preferred option for the state's growing number of Latino and Asian voters?" he asks. "They need to devise a strategy to succeed in 2010 but the clock is ticking."[8]

Futurist writers Morley Winograd and Michael Hals support Bookman's opinions about the challenges to the GOP on a national level. In spring 2009, they editorialized,

> If the Republican Party thinks it has problems now, just wait. The party's poor performance among young voters in the 2008 election raises questions about the long-term competitiveness of the GOP. The "millennials"—the generation of Americans born between 1982 and 2003—now identify as Democrats by a ratio of 2-to-1. They are the first in four generations to contain more self-perceived liberals than conservatives.

. . . Only 9 percent of millennials expressed a favorable opinion of the Republican Party. . . . By contrast, 65 percent of millennials had a favorable opinion of the Democratic Party. . . . Republicans will need to find a new message and much better messengers if they want to truly connect with today's young voters.[9]

On the other hand, the Democratic Party in Georgia has two issues with which it has to deal before it can effectively become the party of power in Georgia again. First, the national Democratic Party needs to guard against swinging too far toward the left if it is to attract southern moderates back into the ranks of its voters; that may be challenging because white southerners are no longer an influential bloc within the national Democratic Party. Earl and Merle Black observe and comment on the implications of this change: "Conservative southern Democrats no longer constitute a significant wing within the Democratic Party in the House or the Senate. Their absence frees the Democratic Party leadership to speak more authoritatively as an aggressively liberal force."[10] The recent selection of Barack Obama as the Democratic presidential candidate seems to indicate that this shift is beginning to take place. Michael Thurmond comments on the possible effect of the Obama presidency on the Democratic Party's future success in Georgia:

Well, it depends on how he does. If he does well and kind of reshapes what some people see as Democrats—particularly national Democrats—I think an African American has a greater probability of reshaping that image and attitude than even a white Democrat because people see African Americans as liberals and taxers and all that negative stuff. So now they're watching him. So he can redefine how people see all Democrats. Because if he is not a fire-breathing left-winger, but is a moderate who makes good solid decisions on taxes and war and peace and so forth, then that is going to reshape how people see the broader number of Democrats.

In order for the Democrats to win a majority of votes in Georgia and most other southern states, their party is going to have to develop a more favorable and coherent political appeal to voters. Drew Westen, an Emory University clinical psychologist and professor, has recently written a book, *The Political Brain,* which analyzes the messaging of each of the national political parties. He concludes that the political brain is an emotional brain that responds more favorably to emotional appeals, such as those employed by Republicans, than it does to "ideas" more often promulgated by the

Democrats. Westen observes that Republicans have been able to identify their party as "conservative," a word that has positive political connotations, while Democrats have been labeled as "liberals" with its less favorable connotations. He reports, "Everyone knows exactly what someone who calls himself or herself a conservative purportedly values: military strength, tax cuts, minimal government, fiscal restraint, traditional values, patriotism, and religious faith. This clear message starts conservative candidates with 35 to 60 percent of the vote before opening their mouths, depending or the state or district. . . . We don't even know what to call people on the left."[11] Westen concludes that the Democratic Party needs to be more pronounced and emotional about issues of importance to their constituency, if their party is to be more successful in the future.

Second, the Democratic Party in Georgia does not yet seem to have reorganized and reenergized sufficiently to overcome the Republican dominance in the near future. Longtime Democratic representative Bob Holmes expresses his disappointment that his party has not recently adopted a clear and concise platform for their candidates to use in trying to achieve statehouse victories: "I have mentioned to the minority leader and the caucus chairman that we have not done the things, I think, that are needed to position ourselves to be able to make a strong effort in 2010. I said, 'Can you tell me what our platform was in the legislature?' The minority leader appointed nine committees. . . . Only three of them made reports . . . so we didn't even have an agenda. So what I'm saying is that I haven't seen the organizational effort, the enthusiasm, the fundraising."

It seems apparent that the Democratic Party in Georgia still has some organizational work to do before they become an imminent threat to the Republican control over statehouse politics in Georgia again. Also, the political alliance between rural and suburban whites in the Georgia Republican Party is much closer than the looser coalition of African Americans and urban and rural whites in the Democratic Party ever was. Former Democratic statehouse majority leader Larry Walker comments on this situation: "The Republican Party has always been better organized than the Democratic Party, in my view. . . . The Democratic Party was a coalition that worked a long time, but it was a strained coalition at times. The philosophical difference in the most conservative Republican and the most liberal Republican is an inch wide, but the philosophical difference in the most conservative Democrat and the most liberal Democrat is a mile wide." Citadel College political scientist Robert Steed seems to concur: "Of the two grassroots southern political parties, the Republicans are considerably more homogenous."[12] That consideration should bode well for the GOP and its chances to continue to be the controlling political party in Georgia's statehouse for the foreseeable future.

Bibliography

P R I M A R Y   S O U R C E S

Publications

Atlanta Journal-Constitution

Georgia Legislative Review. The Southern Center for Studies in Public Policy, Clark Atlanta University. Atlanta. 2003–2004.

Georgia's Official Statistical Registers. State of Georgia Archives. Morrow GA.

Georgia's Official Statistical Registers. General Library. Georgia State University. Atlanta.

Georgia Trend

Journal of the House, State of Georgia.

Journal of the Senate, State of Georgia.

"Members of the General Assembly of Georgia—Senate and House of Representatives." Handbook published annually by the Office of the Secretary of the Senate and the Clerk's Office of the House. Atlanta: 1970–2009.

"New Day Dawning." Video at http://www.youtube.com/watch?v=Qvq1LT9yon4. Perdue for a New Georgia Campaign. May 2002.

"ORVIS: A Targeting project by the Republican Party of Georgia—A Special Project Prepared for the State Chairman and the Executive Committee." 25 July 1987. From the personal archives of Jay Morgan, Atlanta.

Wall Street Journal

"91 in Y2K." From the personal archives of Garland Pinholster, Ball Ground GA.

Databases

Georgia Official and Statistical Register, 1923–1990. http://dlg.galileo.usg.edu/statregister.

http:// pundits.thehill.com/2008.

Campaign Contribution Disclosure Reports & Candidate Financial Disclosure Statements. http://sos.georgia.gov/cgi-bin/disclosureindex.asp.

http://www.barnesgovernor.org/issues

http://www.cnn.com/ALL Politics/stories/1998.

http://www.ethics.ga.gov/campaign Campaign Reports 2006-2008

Campaign Finance Reports and Data, 2002. http://www.fec.gov.

http://www.gagop.org/history

Georgia Statistics System. http://www.georgiastats.uga.edu.

Georgia General Assembly, 1996–2008. http://www.legis.ga.gov/legis.

Candidate Information/Campaign Disclosure Information, 1998–2008. http://www.sos.ga.gov/elections.

Voter Registration Statistics, 1962–2008. http://www.sos.ga.gov/elections—Results and Statistics/.

Historic Voter Turnout by Demographics, 1996–2008. http://www.sos.ga.gov/elections—Results and Statistics/.

Court Decisions
Baker v. Carr, 369 U.S. 186 (1962).

Gray v. Sanders, 372 U.S. 386 (1963).

Wesberry v. Sanders, 376 U.S. 1 (1964).

Reynolds v. Sims, 377 U.S. 533 (1964).

Larios v. Cox, 300 F.Supp.2d 1320 (N.D.Ga. 10 Feb 2004).

Cox v. Larios, 542 U.S. 947 (30 June 2004).

U.S. v. Charles Walker, 490 F. 3d 1282 (6 July 2007).

Interviews by Others
Coverdell, Paul. Interview by Dr. Cliff Kuhn. 4 and 10 May 1989. Georgia Government Documentation Project, Special Collections and Archives, Georgia State University Library, Atlanta. Folders 2 and 3, box B-2.

Felton, Dorothy. Interview by Diane Fowlkes. 25 March 1988. Georgia Government Documentation Project, Special Collections and Archives, Georgia State University Library, Atlanta. Folder 3, box C-1.

Isakson, Johnny. Interview by Thomas A. Scott. 22 May 1992. Georgia Government Documentation Project, Special Collections and Archives, Georgia State University Library, Atlanta. Folder 5, box B-3.

Lawrence, Thomas E. Interview by Cliff Kuhn and Gretchen MacLachlan. 16 April 1993. Georgia Government Documentation Project, Special Collections and Archives, Georgia State University Library, Atlanta. Folder 1, box N-1.

Savage, John. Interview by Sally Flocks. 1 May 1987. Georgia Government Documentation Project, Special Collections and Archives, Georgia State University Library, Atlanta. Folder 3, box B-8.

Tuttle, Judge Elbert P. Interview by Clifford Kuhn. 21 September 1992. Georgia Government Documentation Project, Special Collections and Archives, Georgia State University Library, Atlanta. Folder 2, box B-9.

Interviews by Author
Ayers, Nick. 16 March 2007. Digital recording. Atlanta.

Bennecke, Paul. 2 July 2008. Digital recording. Atlanta.

Burkhalter, Mark. 9 September 2008. Digital recording. Atlanta.

Cheeks, Don. 14 April 2008. Digital recording by telephone to Augusta GA.

Childress, Trey. April 2008. Atlanta.

Coleman, Terry. 8 January 2008. Digital recording. Atlanta.

Cook, Morgan Perry. 21 December 2007. Digital recording by telephone to Mountain Brook AL.

Gillis, Lee Ann Wood. May 2008. By telephone. Atlanta.

Golden, Tim. 17 March 2008. Atlanta.

Heath, Bill. 10 January 2008. Digital recording. Atlanta.

Hill, Jack. 15 March 2007. Digital recording. Atlanta.

Holmes, Bob, 29 December 2008. Digital recording. Atlanta.

Hooks, George. 7 October 2008. Digital recording. Atlanta.

Irvin, Bob. 26 March 2007. Digital recording. Atlanta.

Jackson, Bill. 26 March 2008. Atlanta.

Johnson, Eric. 1 March 2007. Digital recording by telephone to Central Georgia.

Lee, Dan. 12 February 2007. Digital recording. Atlanta.

Levison, Jarvin. 2 May 2008. Atlanta.

Lindsey, Edward. 15 May 2008. Atlanta.

McLagan, Dan. 14 March 2007. Digital recording Atlanta

Millner, Guy. 23 May 2007. Digital recording. Atlanta.

Morgan, Jay. 6 February 2007. Digital recording. Atlanta.

Paul. Rusty. 12 January 2007. Digital recording. Atlanta.

Perdue, Sonny. 15 January 2009. Digital recording. Atlanta.

Pettys, Dick. 1 October 2008. Digital recording. Atlanta.

Pinholster, Garland. 27 July 2007. Atlanta.

Poitevint, Alec. 20 March 2007. Digital recording. Atlanta.

Ralston, David. 1 April 2008. Atlanta.

Rials, Scott. 5 April 2007. Digital recording. Atlanta.

Richardson, Glenn. 12 May 2008. Digital recording. Atlanta.

Smith, Tommy. 30 July 2008. Telephone to Nicholls GA.

Stancil, Steve. 27 July 2007 and 11 March 2008. Atlanta.

Strickland, Frank. 1 May 2007. Digital recording. Atlanta.

Thurmond, Michael. 10 December 2008. Digital recording. Atlanta.

Walker, Larry. 16 January 2008. Digital recording. Atlanta.

Watson, John. 27 December 2006. Digital recording. Atlanta.

Young, Chris. 7 July 2008. Digital recording. Atlanta.

SECONDARY SOURCES

Badertscher, Nancy. "Election Coverage." *Atlanta Journal-Constitution.* November 2004.

Barnes, Roy, "What Works: Georgia's Regional Authority." *Blueprint Magazine.* 1 September 2000. http://www.ndol.org/print.cfm?contentid=2121.

Bass, Jack. "Introduction." *Writing Southern Politics: Contemporary Interpretations and Future Directions.* Edited by Robert P. Steed and Laurence W. Moreland. Lexington: The University of Kentucky Press, 2006.

Bartley, Numan V. *The Creation of Modern Georgia.* Second edition. Athens: The University of Georgia Press, 1990.

————. *The New South 1945–1980: The Story of the South's Modernization.* Baton Rouge: Louisiana State University Press, 1995.

————. *From Thurmond to Wallace: Political Tendencies in Georgia 1948–1968.* Baltimore: The Johns Hopkins University Press, 1970.

Bartley, Numan V., and Hugh D. Graham. *Southern Politics and the Second Reconstruction.* Baltimore: The Johns Hopkins University Press, 1975.

Binford, Michael, Tom Baxter, and David E. Sturrock. "Georgia: Democratic Bastion No Longer." *Southern Politics in the 1990s.* Edited by Alexander P. Lamis. Baton Rouge: Louisiana State University Press, 1999.

Black, Earl, and Merle Black. *Divided America.* New York: Simon and Schuster. 2007.

————. *Politics and Society in the South.* Cambridge: Harvard University Press, 1987.

————. *The Rise of Southern Republicans.* Cambridge: The Belknap Press of Harvard University, 2002.

Bookman. Jay. "More Than Personal Political Fortunes at Stake in '09." *Atlanta Journal-Constitution.* 12 January 2009.

Bullock, Charles S. III, "Introduction" and "Georgia, the GOP Finally Takes Over." *The New Politics of the Old South: An Introduction to Southern Politics.* Edited by Charles S Bullock III and Mark J. Rozell. Third edition. Lanham MD: Rowman and Littlefield, Publishers, Inc., 2007.

————. "Republican Office Holding at the Local Level in Georgia." *The 2000 Presidential Election in the South: Partisanship and Southern Party Systems in the 21st Century.* Edited by Robert P. Steed and Laurence W. Moreland. Westport CT: Praeger Publishers, 2000.

Bullock, Charles S. III, and David J. Shafer. "Party Targeting and Electoral Success." *Legislative Studies Quarterly* 22/4. November 1997.

Cole, Donald E. *Grassroots: Leading Others to Accomplish the Impossible.* Self-published, 2003.

Coleman, Kenneth (general editor), Numan Bartley, William F. Holmes. F. N. Boney, Phinizy Spalding, and Charles E. Wynes. *A History of Georgia.* Second edition. Athens: The University of Georgia Press, 1991.

Cook, Rhonda, and James Salzer. "Switchers put GOP in Control—Georgia Senate: 3 Democrats cross aisle to give Perdue sway over half of Legislature." *Atlanta Journal-Constitution.* 9 November 2002.

Cooper, William J. *Liberty and Slavery: Southern Politics to 1860*. Columbia: University of South Carolina Press, 1983.

Coulter, E. Merton. *Georgia: A Short History*. Chapel Hill. Third edition. Chapel Hill: The University of North Carolina Press, 1960.

Douthat, Ross Sr., and Reihan Salam, *Grand New Party: How Republicans Can Win the Working Class and Save the American Dream*. New York: Doubleday, 2008.

Foner, Eric. *A Short History of Reconstruction 1863–1877*. New York: Harper and Row, Publishers, 1990.

Garrett, Franklin M. *Atlanta and Environs: A Chronicle of Its People and Events*. Volume 1. New York: Lewis Publishing Company, Inc., 1954.

Gould, Lewis L. *Grand Old Party: A History of the Republicans*. New York: Random House, 2003.

Hitt, Greg. "The New Southern Strategy—Democrats Run Conservative Candidates in GOP Bastions." *Wall Street Journal* vol. CCLII. August 2008.

Hulbary, William C., and Lewis Bowman. "Recruiting Activists." *Party Organization and Activism in the American South*. Edited by Robert P. Steed, John A. Clark, Lewis Bowman, and Charles D. Hadley. Tuscaloosa: The University of Alabama Press, 1998.

Hyatt, Richard. *Zell: The Governor Who Gave Georgia HOPE*. Macon GA: Mercer University Press, 1997.

Kapeluck, Branwell Dubose, Robert P. Steed, and Laurence W. Moreland. "Southern Governors and Legislatures." *Writing Southern Politics: Contemporary Interpretations and Future Directions*. Edited by Robert P. Steed and Laurence W. Moreland. Lexington. The University of Kentucky Press, 2006.

Lublin, David. *The Republican South: Democratization and Partisan Change*. Princeton NJ: Princeton University Press, 2004.

Miller, Zell. *A National Party No More: The Conscience of a Conservative Democrat*. Atlanta: Stroud and Hall Publishers, 2003.

Morgan, James L. "Post-Election Analysis." 18 November 1986. From the personal archives of the author.

———. "1990 Election Analysis." Undated. From the personal archives of the author.

Pomerantz, Gary M. *Where Sweet Auburn Metes Peachtree: A Saga of Race and Family*. New York: Penguin Books, 1996.

Rogers, William Warren, Jr. *A Scalawag in Georgia: Richard Whiteley and the Politics of Reconstruction*. Urbana: University of Illinois Press, 2007.

Shadgett, Olive Hall. *The Republican Party in Georgia: From Reconstruction through 1900*. Athens: University of Georgia Press, 1964.

Steed, Robert P. "Conclusion." *Party Organization and Activism in the American South*. Edited by Robert P. Steed, John A. Clark, Lewis Bowman, and Charles D. Hadley. Tuscaloosa: The University of Alabama Press., 1998.

Sturrock, David E. "Out of Phone Booths—Republican Politics on the Deep South." *Writing Southern Politics: Contemporary Interpretations and Future Directions*. Edited by Robert P. Steed and Laurence W. Moreland. Lexington: The University of Kentucky Press, 2006

Taylor, Andrew J. *Elephant's Edge: The Republicans as a Ruling Party.* Westport CT: Praeger Publishers, 2005.

Towery, Matt. "Georgia Power." *James Magazine.* Atlanta. January 2007.

Westen, Drew. *The Political Mind: The Role of Emotion in Deciding the Fate of the Nation.* New York: BBS Public Affairs, 2007.

Notes

CHAPTER 1

1. Lewis L. Gould, *Grand Old Party: A History of the Republicans* (New York: Random House, 2003) 10.

2. Ibid., 14.

3. William J. Cooper, Jr., *Liberty and Slavery: Southern Politics to 1860* (Columbia: University of South Carolina Press, 1983) 255.

4. Eric Foner, *A Short History of Reconstruction* 1863–1877 (New York: Harper and Row, Publishers, 1990) 104–105.

5. Ibid., 114.

6. Olive Hall Shadgett, *The Republican Party in Georgia: From Reconstruction through 1900* (Athens: University of Georgia Press, 1964) 76.

7. Ibid., 48.

8. Foner, *A Short History*, 217.

9. Ibid., 244.

10. Gould, *Grand Old Party*, 119.

11. Ibid., 152.

12. Ibid., 31.

13. Earl Black and Merle Black, *Politics and Society in the South* (Cambridge MA: Harvard University Press, 1987) 233.

14. Numan V. Bartley and Hugh D. Graham, *Southern Politics and the Second Reconstruction* (Baltimore: The Johns Hopkins University Press, 1975) 90.

15. Earl Black and Merle Black, *The Rise of Southern Republicans* (Cambridge MA: The Belknap Press of Harvard University, 2002) 45.

16. Bartley and Graham, *Southern Politics*, 52.

17. Ross Douthat and Reihan Salam, *Grand New Party: How Republicans Can Win the Working Class and Save the American Dream* (New York City: Doubleday, 2008) 35.

18. Gould, *Grand Old Party*, 357.

19. Numan V. Bartley, *The Creation of Modern Georgia* (1983; 2nd ed., Athens: The University of Georgia Press, 1990) 225.

20. Bartley and Graham, *Southern Politics*, 187.

21. Douthat and Salam, *Grand New Party*, 46.

22. Black and Black, *The Rise of Southern Republicans*, 210.

23. William C. Hulbary and Lewis Bowman, "Recruiting Activists," *Party Organization and Activism in the American South*, ed. Robert P. Steed, John A. Clark, Lewis Bowman, and Charles D. Hadley (Tuscaloosa: University of Alabama Press, 1998) 14.

24. David Lublin, *The Republican South: Democratization and Partisan Change* (Princeton: Princeton University Press, 2004) 209.

25. Black and Black, *The Rise of Southern Republicans*, 212.

26. Ibid., 25.

27. Gould, *Grand Old Party*, 434–35.

28. Black and Black, *The Rise of Southern Republicans*, 5.

29. Andrew J. Taylor, *Elephant's Edge: The Republicans as a Ruling Party* (Westport CT.: Praeger Publishers, 2005) 48.

30. Jack Bass, introduction, *Writing Southern Politics: Contemporary Interpretations and Future Directions*, ed. Robert P. Steed and Laurence W. Moreland (Lexington: University Press of Kentucky, 2006) ix.

31. Charles S. Bulloch III, *The New Politics of the Old South: An Introduction to Southern Politics*, ed. Charles S. Bullock III and Mark J. Rozell (3rd ed.; Lanham MD: Rowman and Littlefield Publishers, Inc., 2007) 3.

32. Bulloch, "Georgia, The GOP Finally Takes Over," in *The New Politics of the Old South*, 53.

C H A P T E R   2

1. Olive Hall Shadgett, *The Republican Party in Georgia: From Reconstruction through 1900* (Athens: University of Georgia Press, 1964) vii.

2. Eric Foner, *A Short History of Reconstruction* 1863–1877 (New York: Harper and Row, Publishers, 1990) 87.

3. Numan V. Bartley, *The Creation of Modern Georgia* (1983; 2nd ed., Athens: The University of Georgia Press, 1990) 44.

4. Foner, *A Short History*, 133.

5. Franklin M. Garrett, *Atlanta and Environs: A Chronicle of Its People and Events*, vol. 1 (New York: Lewis Historical Publishing Company, Inc., 1954) 771.

6. Foner, *A Short History*, 129–30.

7. Bartley, *The Creation of Modern Georgia*, 59.

8. E. Merton Coulter, *Georgia: A Short History* (1933; 3rd ed., Chapel Hill: The University of North Carolina Press, 1960) 370.

9. Kenneth Coleman et al., eds., *A History of Georgia* (2nd ed.; Athens: University of Georgia Press, 1991) 213.

10. Foner, *A Short History*, 150–52.

11. Franklin Garrett, *Atlanta and Its Environs*, 1:777.

12. William Rogers Warren, Jr., *A Scalawag in Georgia: Richard Whiteley and the Politics of Reconstruction* (Urbana: University of Illinois Press, 2007) 211.

13. Foner, *A Short History*, 165–68.

14. Bartley, *The Creation of Modern Georgia*, 81.

15. Shadgett, *The Republican Party in Georgia*, vii.

16. Ibid., 90.

17. Numan Bartley, *From Thurmond to Wallace: Political Tendencies in Georgia, 1948–1968* (Baltimore: John Hopkins University Press, 1970) 3.

18. See http://dlg.galileo.usg.edu/statregister. Republicans Will Richards of Jasper and Henry M. Stanley of Due, Georgia, served in the General Assembly in the 1920s, and Robert Tillman Hampton from Mineral Bluff, Hayden Hampton from Ellijay, Cecil Hartness and Rufus Stiles from Blue Ridge, and Thomas Chastain from Table Rock were among the Republicans who served in the General Assembly in the 1930s.

19. Georgia Official Register 1959–1960, State of Georgia, Department of Archives and History, http://dlg.galileo.usg.edu/statregister, p. 411.

20. David Ralston, interview by author, Atlanta GA, 1 April 2008.

21. Elbert P. Tuttle, interview by Clifford Kuhn, 21 September 1992, Georgia Government Documentation Project, Special Collections and Archives, Georgia State University Library, Atlanta, box B-9, folder 2.

22. Kiliaen Townsend obituary, *Atlanta Journal-Constitution*, 27 March 2008, D9.

23. John Savage, interview by Sally Flocks, 1 May 1987, Georgia Government Documentation Project, Special Collections and Archives, Georgia State University Library, Atlanta, box B-8, folder 3, folder 2, p. 4.

24. Gary M. Pomerantz, *Where Peachtree Street Meets Sweet Auburn: A Saga of Race and Family* (New York: Penguin Books, 1996) 83.

25. Bartley, *From Thurmond to Wallace*, 51.

26. Jarvin Levison, interview by author, 2 May 2008, Atlanta.

27. 369 US 186 (1962).

28. 372 US 368 (1963).

29. 376 US 1 (1964).

30. 377 US 533 (1964).

CHAPTER 3

1. Johnny Isakson, interview by Thomas A. Scott, 22 May 1992, Georgia Government Documentation Project, Special Collections and Archives, Georgia State University Library, Atlanta, box 3, folder 5, p. 34.

2. Dorothy Felton, interview by Diane Fowlkes, 25 March 1988, Georgia Government Documentation Project, Special Collections and Archives, Georgia State University Library, Atlanta, box C-1, folder C-3, p. 18.

3. Rusty Paul, interview by author, 12 January 2007, Atlanta.

4. Professor Numan Bartley defines the "Black Belt" in Georgia as "the southern part of the state (that) arches through the center (and) includes 54 counties containing a non-white

population of 40 percent or more" (Numan Bartley, *From Thurmond to Wallace: Political Tendencies in Georgia, 1948–1968* [Baltimore: John Hopkins University Press, 1970] 16).

5. Ibid., 43.

6. Ibid., 61.

7. Ibid., 77.

8. Charles Weltner was later elected to serve as a Georgia Supreme Court justice.

9. Bartley, *From Thurmond to Wallace*, 93.

10. Numan V. Bartley and Hugh D. Graham, *Southern Politics and the Second Reconstruction* (Baltimore: The Johns Hopkins University Press, 1975) 149.

11. Dick Pettys, interview by author, 1 October 2008, Atlanta, 2.

12. Johnny Isakson, interview by Thomas A. Scott, 39.

13. Bob Irvin, interview by author, 26 March 2007, Atlanta.

14. Dorothy W. Felton, obituary, *Atlanta Journal and Constitution*, 22 February 2008, D-8.

15. Bob Irvin, interview by author.

16. Paul Coverdell, interview by Dr. Cliff Kuhn, 4 March 1989, Georgia Government Documentation Project, Special Collections and Archives, Georgia State University, Atlanta, box B-2, folder 2, pp. 27–28.

17. Ibid., 28.

18. Jack Bass, foreword, *Writing Southern Politics: Contemporary Interpretations and Future Directions*, ed. Robert P. Steed and Laurence W. Moreland (Lexington: University Press of Kentucky, 2006) viii–ix.

19. Alec Poitevint, interview by author, 20 March 2007, Atlanta.

20. Jay Morgan, interview by author, 6 February 2007, Atlanta.

21. Earl Black and Merle Black, *The Rise of Southern Republicans* (Cambridge MA: The Belknap Press of Harvard University, 2002) 122.

22. Charles S. Bulloch III, *The New Politics of the Old South: An Introduction to Southern Politics*, ed. Charles S. Bullock III and Mark J. Rozell (3rd ed.; Lanham MD: Rowman and Littlefield Publishers, Inc., 2007) 52.

23. John Savage, interview by Sally Flocks, 1 May 1987, Georgia Government Documentation Project, Special Collections and Archives, Georgia State University Library, Atlanta, box B-8, folder 3, folder 2, p. 59.

24. Earl and Merle Black, *The Rise of Southern Republicanism*, 136.

25. Frank Strickland, interview by author, 1 May 2007, Atlanta.

26. Earl and Merle Black, *The Rise of Southern Republicanism*, 125.

27. Ibid., 360–61.

28. Johnny Isakson, interview by Thomas A. Scott, 42.

29. Earl Black and Merle Black, *Politics and Society in the South* (Cambridge: Harvard University Press, 1987) 179.

30. http://sos.georgia.gov/elections/voter_registration_history.pc.

31. Terry Coleman, interview by author, 8 January 2008, Atlanta.

32. Larry Walker, interview by author, 16 January 2008.Atlanta, 7.

33. Paul Coverdell, interview by Cliff Kuhn, 30.

34. "ORVIS: A Targeting Project by the Georgia Republican Party—A Special Project Prepared for the State Chairman and the Executive Committee," from the personal archives of Jay Morgan, 25 July 1987.

35. Charles S. Bullock III and David J. Shafer, "Party Targeting and Electoral Success," *Legislative Studies Quarterly* 22/4 (November 1997): 573.

36. Johnny Isakson, interview by Thomas A. Scott, 43.

37. Thomas E. Lawrence, interview by Cliff Kuhn and Gretchen MacLachlan, 16 April 1993, Georgia Government Documentation Project, Special Collections and Archives, Georgia State University, Atlanta, box N-1, folder 1, p. 3.

38. Michael Thurmond, interview by author, 10 December 2008, Atlanta, 2. Besides being the first African American in Georgia elected to represent a majority-white district, Thurmond believes he was also the first black elected in the whole South since Reconstruction to represent a majority-white district.

39. Bob Holmes, interview by author, 29 December 2008, Atlanta.

40. David Lublin, *The Republican South: Democratization and Partisan Change* (Princeton: Princeton University Press, 2004) xvi.

41. Lublin, ibid., 66.

42. Charles S. Bullock III, "Republican Office Holding at the Local Level in Georgia," *The 2000 Presidential Election in the South: Partisanship and Southern Party Systems in the 21st Century*, ed. Robert P, Steed and Laurence W. Moreland (Westport CT: Praeger, 2000) 119–20.

CHAPTER 4

1. Pierre Howard's father, Pierre, Sr., served in the state senate, and his grandfather, Schley Howard, served in the United States House of Representatives.

2. James L. (Jay) Morgan, 1990 Election Analysis, from the author's personal archives.

3. Michael Binford, Tom Baxter, and David E. Sturrock, "Georgia: Democratic Bastion No Longer," in *Southern Politics in the 1990's*, ed. Alexander P. Lamis (Baton Rouge: Louisiana State University Press, 1999) 114.

4. Charles S. Bulloch III, *The New Politics of the Old South: An Introduction to Southern Politics*, ed. Charles S. Bullock III and Mark J. Rozell (3rd ed.; Lanham MD: Rowman and Littlefield Publishers, Inc., 2007) 55.

5. Rusty Paul, interview by author, 12 January 2007, Atlanta, p. 6.

6. Earl Black and Merle Black, *The Rise of Southern Republicans* (Cambridge MA: The Belknap Press of Harvard University, 2002) 205–206.

7. Steve Stancil, interview by author, 11 March 2008, Atlanta.

8. John K. Watson, interview by author, 27 December 2006, Atlanta, 4.

9. Guy Millner interview by author, 23 May 2007, Atlanta, 1.

10. Richard Hyatt, *Zell: The Governor who Gave Georgia HOPE* (Macon GA: Mercer University Press, 1997) 331.

11. Zell Miller, *A National Party No More—The Conscience of a Conservative Democrat* (Atlanta: Stroud and Hall Publishers, 2003) 50.

12. Jack Hill, interview by author, 15 March 2007, Atlanta, 8–9.

13. Hyatt, *Zell: The Governor who Gave Georgia HOPE*, 372–73.

14. Binford, Baxter, and Sturrock, "Georgia: Democratic Bastion No Longer," 119.

15. Eric Johnson, interview by author, 1 March 2007, Atlanta, 5.

16. Binford, Baxter, and Sturrock, "Georgia: Democratic Bastion No Longer," 125.

17. Garland Pinholster interview by author, 27 July 2007, Capital City Club, Atlanta.

18. Glenn Richardson, interview by author, 12 May 2008, Atlanta, 1–2.

19. Ibid., 3.

20. David E. Sturrock, "Out of Phone Booths: Republican Politics in the Deep South," in *Writing Southern Politics: Contemporary Interpretations and Future Directions*, ed. Robert P. Steed and Laurence W. Moreland (Lexington: University Press of Kentucky, 2006) 108.

21. Bullock, *New Politics of the Old South*, 57.

22. See http://www.cnn.com/ALLPOLITICS/stories/1998/11/03/elections/governors/georgia/.

23. See http://pundits.thehill.com/2008/04/14/.

24. Bullock, *New Politics of the Old South*, 57.

25. Black and Black, *The Rise of Southern Republicans*, 316–17.

26. See http://www.legis.state.ga.us/legis/1999_00/gass18.htm

27. George Hooks, interview by author, 7 October 2008, Atlanta. Hooks was first elected to the state House in 1980 and then was elected to the Senate in 1990. He chaired the Senate Appropriations Committee from 1993 through 2002. Pierre Howard served as the Democratic lieutenant governor of Georgia from January 1991 to January 1999.

28. Sonny Perdue, interview by author, 5 January 2009, Atlanta.

29. David Lublin, *The Republican South: Democratization and Partisan Change* (Princeton: Princeton University Press, 2004) 29.

30. Morgan Perry Cook, interview by author, 21 December 2007, by telephone to Mountain Brook, Alabama.

31. Chris Young, interview by author, 7 July 2008, Atlanta.

32. Alec Poitevint, interview by author. In the 1980 U.S. Senate election, a majority of Houston County voted for Republican Mack Mattingly over Democrat Herman Talmadge, and it was the only mostly rural county in Georgia won by the Republican candidate. However, the majority of Houston County voters supported Democrats Zell Miller for governor in 1990 and 1994 and Max Cleland for U.S. senator in 1996, but the county generally voted for the Republican candidate for United States presidency.

33. Tim Golden, interview by author, 17 March 2008, Atlanta.

34. Don Cheeks, interview by author, 11 April 2008, by telephone to Augusta GA.

35. Scott Rial,s interview by author, 5 April 2007, Atlanta, p. 6.

36. Bullock, *New Politics of the Old South*, 65.

37. Ibid., 67.

38. Bob Irvin, interview by author, 26 March 2007, Atlanta, 7.

39. Larios v. Cox, 300 F. Supp.2d 1320 (N. D. Ga. Feb. 10, 2004), 15.

40. Ibid., 6.

41. Tommy Smith, interview by author, by telephone to Nicholls, Georgia, 30 July 2008.

42. Matt Towery, "Georgia Power," *James Magazine* (Atlanta GA), January 2007, 16. Dick Pettys, now a journalist with the publishing company that prints *James Magazine*, reports that popular representative Bill Cummings of Rockmart, who served in the House for twenty-six years, was one of the legislators that Speaker Murphy was helping to protect from the plan to provide Murphy with a safer legislative district.

C H A P T E R   5

1. In a special election held early the following January, Democrat Michael J. Moore was elected to take Perdue's eighteenth district seat in the state Senate. Moore took office just as the legislature was convening for the new 2002 session.

2. Dan McLagan, interview by author, 14 March 2007, Atlanta, 12.

3. Paul Bennecke, interview by author, 2 July 2008, Atlanta, 2.

4. Nick Ayers, interview by author, 16 March 2007, Atlanta.

5. For several months, the Perdue campaign rented office space from Epps Air Service at Peachtree DeKalb airport for $2,900 a month, according to campaign finance disclosure reports on file with state government.

6. Donald E. Cole, *Grassroots: Leading Others to Accomplish the Impossible* (self-published in 2003) 35–36, 38.

7. http://www.youtube.com/watch?v=Qvq1L.T9yon4.

8. Cole, *Grassroots*, 67.

9. See http://www.ndol.org/print.cfm?contentid=2121.

10. See http://sos/georgia.gov/cgi-bin/disclosureindex.asp. See also http://en.wikipedia.org/Roy_Barnes/04/25/2008, 3.

11. Jeffrey Williams and Nykia Greene, "Other Issues," *Georgia Legislative Review* (Atlanta: Southern Center for Studies in Public Policy, Clark Atlanta University, 2001) 86.

12. In March 2003, Roy Barnes was recognized for his leadership in changing the controversial Georgia flag by being awarded a President John F. Kennedy Profile in Courage Award by the Kennedy Presidential Library in Boston.

13. See http://www.barnesgovernor.org/issues/tax_relief.html.

14. http://sos.georgia.gov/disclosure/2002/gov.

15. Lee Ann Wood Gillis, interview by author by telephone in Atlanta, May 2008.

16. Cole, *Grassroots*, 177.

17. Bill Heath, interview by author, 10 January 2008, Atlanta.

18. Dan Lee, interview by author, 12 February 2007, Atlanta.

19. Rhonda Cook and James Salzer, "Switchers Put GOP in Control Georgia Senate," *Atlanta Journal-Constitution*, 9 November 2002, A1.

20. Ibid.

21. Ibid.

22. Ibid., In the November 9 AJC article, Senator Peg Blitch was quoted as saying "she was sticking with the Democrats, despite pressures from Republicans."

23. Branwell Dubose Kapeluck, Robert P. Steed, and Lawrence W. Moreland, "Southern Governors and Legislatures," *Writing Southern Politics: Contemporary Interpretations and Future Directions*, ed. Robert P Steed and Laurence W. Moreland (Lexington: University of Kentucky Press, 2006) 285.

24. Mark Burkhalter, interview by author, 9 September 2008, Atlanta.

C H A P T E R   6

1. *Cox v. Larios*, 542 U.S. 947, p. 3.

2. Bill Jackson, interview with author, 26 March 2008, Atlanta.

3. *Larios v. Cox*, 542 U.S. 947, p. 1.

4. Nancy Badertscher, "Election Coverage," *Atlanta Journal-Constitution*, 3 November 2004, EX12.

5. Ibid.

6. Jack Bass, foreword, *Writing Southern Politics: Contemporary Interpretations and Future Directions*, ed. Robert P. Steed and Laurence W. Moreland (Lexington: University of Kentucky Press, 2006) ix–x.

7. Zell Miller, *A National Party No More—The Conscience of a Conservative Democrat* (Atlanta: Stroud and Hall, Publishers, 2003) 15.

8. Ibid., 230.

9. Earl Black and Merle Black, *Divided America*, 25–26.

10. Ibid., 79.

11. Charles Bullock, *The New Politics of the Old South*, 13.

12. Andrew J. Taylor, *Elephant's Edge: The Republicans as a Ruling Party* (Westport CT: Praeger Publishers, 2005) 162, 167.

13. David Lublin, preface, xvii.

14. Taylor, *Elephant's Edge*, 109.

C H A P T E R   7

1. http://sos.geeorgia.gov/elections/voter_registration.

2. Earl and Merle Black, *Divided America*, 35.

3. Ibid., 189.

4. Greg Hitt, "The New Southern Strategy: Democrats Run Conservative Candidates in GOP Bastions," Wall Street Journal 252/32 (7 August 2008): 1.

5. Earl Black and Merle Black, *The Rise of Southern Republicans* (Cambridge MA: The Belknap Press of Harvard University, 2002) 378.

6. Zell Miller, *A National Party No More—The Conscience of a Conservative Democrat* (Atlanta: Stroud and Hall Publishers, 2003) 17.

7. http://www.sos.ga.gov/elections results and statistics/voter registration statistics.

8. Jay Bookman, "More Than Personal Political Fortunes at Stake in '09," *The Atlanta Journal-Constitution*, 12 January 2009, A8.

9. Morley Winograd and Michael D. Hals, "GOP Tone-Deaf to Generation That Will Shape Politics," Atlanta Journal-Constitution, 14 May 2009, A13.

10. Black and Black., *The Rise of Southern Republicans*, 36.

11. Drew Westen, *The Political Brain: The Role of Emotion in Deciding the Fate of the Nation* (New York City: Public Affairs, Perseus Books Group, 2008) 158.

12. Robert P. Steed, "Conclusion," *Party Organization and Activism in the American South*, ed. Robert P. Steed, John A. Clark, Lewis Bowman, and Charles D. Hadley (Tuscaloosa: University of Alabama Press, 1998) 220.

Index

91 inY2K, 65, 66, 67

A

A New Day Dawning, 114
A Plus Education Reform, 115
Abramoff, Jack, 183
AGrowStar, 113
Alexander, Cecil, 122
Allen, Ivan, Jr., 25
Allen, Nora, 41
American Independent Party, 9, 39
Amerson, Amos, 68
Amos, Bill, 41
Anderson, Jeff, 120
Arnall, Ellis, 21, 22, 36
Ashe, Kathy, 86
Atkins, James, 19, 20
Augusta Ring, 16
Ayers, Nick, 95-99, 104-107, 125, 133,
    137-138, 142, 146-147, 151, 153,
    160-161, 182
Ayers, Whit, 57, 110, 127

B

Badertscher, Nancy, 81, 175
Bailey, Patsy, 82
Baker v. Carr, 25
Baker, Bobby, 58, 130, 173, 175
Baker, Thurbert, 72, 183
Balfour, Don, 69
Bannister, Charles, 48
Barnes, Roy
    introduction, xiii
    1998 election, 71-73
    Miller appointment, 84
    2001 reapportionment, 86-89, 92
    2002 election, 96, 101-102, 106-108
    114-131, 134-136, 144, 150-152
    2006 elections, 174, 177
Barr, Bob, 58, 139
Barrett, Lonice, 198

Barrow, John, 201
Bartley, Numan, 24, 35, 39
Bass, Jack, 12, 175
Baxter, Tom, 54
Beatty, Mike. 139
Beck, Joe, 129
Bell, Bob, 38, 45, 61
Bennecke, Jen, 95-98, 111
Bennecke, Paul, 96, 104-109. 112, 115,
    122, 124, 126-129, 136-137, 140,
    161, 170-172
Bentley, Jimmy, 38-39
Bethune, Marion, 18
Binford, Michael, 54
Bishop, Sanford, 57
Black Belt, 34, 108
Black, Earl and Merle, 10, 43-45, 59, 176,
    200-201, 204
Blackburn, Ben, 37, 38, 39
Blitch, Peg, 147
Blodgett, Foster, 16
Bolton, Arthur, 48, 60
Bowen, Jim, 36
Bowen, Rooney, 79, 81, 145-147, 174
Bowers, D. Talmadge, 22
Bowers, Mike, 60, 66, 780, 99. 109, 137
Bridges, Ben, 68
Brooks, Tyrone, 56, 86
Broun, Paul, 79
Broun, Paul, Jr., 200
Brown v. Board of Education, 7, 34, 121
Brown, Jeff, 162
Brown, Robert, 87
Buchanan, James, 2
Bulloch, Charles, III, 13, 47, 51, 57, 70, 72,
    83, 86, 176, 203
Bullock, Rufus B., 16-20, 27
Burkhalter, Mark, 68, 151, 156, 162, 166,
    168, 172, 177-179, 185, 194
Busbee, George, 43, 44
Bush, George H. W., 12, 46, 57, 58

Bush, George W., 85, 93, 108, 132, 137, 139, 175, 199
Byrd, Garland, 35
Byrd, Harry, 7
Byrne, Bill, 104, 110-113, 116, 133

C

Cagle, Casey, 69, 83, 183, 192-194
Calhoun, John C., 24
Callaway, Howard W. "Bo," 29, 35, 36, 41, 53, 61, 70
Campbell, Phil, 38-39
Canty, Henrietta, 72
Capitol Clique, 38
Carmichael, James V, 22
Carter, Jimmy, 11, 39, 43, 44
Carville, James, 53
Casas, David, 202
Chambliss, Julianne, 127
Chambliss, Saxby, 58, 93, 102, 109, 127, 132, 139-140, 150, 182, 187, 199
Channell, Mickey, 184
Chapin, Ed, III, 35
Cheeks, Don, 79-80, 144-147, 174
Childress, Trey, 95, 111, 115, 120, 122, 137
Christmas, Barbara, 138
Civil Rights Act, 8, 11, 19, 34
Civil Rights Bill of 1874, 18
Clay, Chuck, 48, 83
Cleland, Max, 45, 64-65, 102, 108-109, 131, 133, 139-140, 150
Cleveland, Grover, 5
Clinton, Bill, 12, 58, 108
Cole, Don, 109, 138
Coleman, Terry, 46, 49, 81, 92, 152-157, 164, 169, 173, 177, 180, 184, 187
Coles, Michael, 72-73
College Republicans, 95, 103-106, 111
Colquitt, Alfred, 19
Conley, Benjamin, 16, 17, 19
Connell, Jack, 90, 154
Contract with America, 12, 59
Cook, Morgan Perry, 76, 83, 86, 88, 90, 101, 124, 127-128, 141-142, 147, 153, 163, 168, 189
Cook, Rodney, 23, 36, 37, 44
Cooper, Fred, 42, 85, 132, 137, 140
Cooper, Sharon, 149
Coverdell Leadership Institute, 69

Coverdell, Nancy, 47
Coverdell, Paul, 30, 40-42, 47, 57-58, 61, 69, 72-73, 84, 107-109
Cox, Cathy, 72, 160, 164, 182
Cox, Kathy, 138, 149, 183

D

Darden, Buddy, 59
Dark Years, 40, 44
Davis, Fred, 109-110, 113
Davis, Guy, 45, 183
Davis, James C., 24, 37
Davis, John W., 25
Day, Burke, 149
Deal, Nathan, 59, 175
Dean, Nathan, 147-148
Dewey, Thomas E., 6, 23
Dickey, Derrick, 104-106, 111
Dix, Scott, 163
Dixiecrat Party, 6
Dobbs, John Wesley, 24
Dole, Bob, 108
Douthat, Ross, 9
DuPont, Pete, 12

E

Eaton, Chuck, '83
Edge, Skin, 48
Egan, Mike, 23, 36, 37
Ehrhart, Earl, 48, 68, 149
Eisenhower, Dwight D., 6, 23, 24, 25
Evans, Mike, 66, 68, 84, 149
Everett, Doug, 68, 139, 199
Everson, Melvin, 202

F

Farrow, Henry, P. 16. 70
Felton, Dorothy, 33, 41
Flaggers, 122, 150
Floyd, Johnny, 184
Flynt, Jack, 42
Foner, Eric, 3, 17
Foster, Roy G., 36
Fowler, Alpha, 38-39
Fowler, Wyche, 44, 46, 57, 58
Fremont, James C., 2

G

Gambrell, David, 43

GARVEE bonds, 119-120
Georgia Regional Transportation Authority, 119
Gillis, Hugh, 78, 81
Gillis, Leigh Ann Wood, 97, 104, 134
Gingrey, Phil, 175
Gingrich, Newt, 12, 41-45, 54-55, 57, 59, 78, 83-85
Glenn, Dylan, 202
Golden, Tim, 78-80, 87, 91, 147
Goldwater, Barry, 6, 8-9, 26, 34-35, 40, 60, 150
GOPAC, 12
Gordon, General John B., 16
Gordy, Perry, 36
Gore, Al, 108
Gould, Lewis, 4, 5, 11
Grand Old Party, 4
Grant, Ulysses S., 5, 18, 20
Gray v. Sanders, 26
Great Reversal, 201
Griffin, Marvin, 25

H

Hall, Randy, 141
Handel, Karen, 161, 183, 192
Harbin, Ben, 69
Harp, Seth, 174
Harris, Joe Frank, 45, 53, 57, 183
Harrison, Carl, 48
Hatcher, Charles, 80
Hayes, Garrett Michael, 96
Hayes, Rutherford B., 4, 20
Heard, Paul, 48
Heath, Bill, 140-141, 193
Hicks, Mike, 45
Hill, Jack, 32, 61, 75-80, 82, 143-148, 174, 181, 190
Hitt, Greg, 201
Holland, Chad, 105
Holmes, Bob, 49, 56, 60, 63, 82, 118, 123, 130, 154-155, 165, 174
Home Rule, 4
Homestead exemptions, 126
Hooks, George, 35, 50, 73, 81, 89, 125, 148, 190-191
Houston Fertilizer and Grain Co., 113
Howard, Pierre, 31, 53, 60, 70-73, 80-81
Huckaby, Hank, 127

Humphrey, Hubert H., 9, 34, 38, 39

I

Irvin, Bob, 40-42, 50, 58, 65-66, 68, 84, 86, 90-91, 149, 174
Irvin, Tommy, 72, 183
Isakson, Johnny, 33, 40, 46, 48, 53-54, 63-64, 69, 77-78, 84-85, 101, 108, 151, 174-175, 187
Israel, George, 51
Ivey, E. Ralph, 25

J

Jackson, Bill, 166-167, 180
Jackson, Maynard, 24, 38
Jacobs, Mike, 185,
Jacoby Development, Inc., 121
Jenkins, Charles, 15
Johnson, Andrew, 3, 15
Johnson, Don, 59
Johnson, Eric, 63, 77-80, 82-83, 87-91, 101, 133-134, 141-142, 144-145, 147, 159, 161, 174, 186, 191, 198
Johnson, James, 15
Johnson, Lyndon B., 6, 9, 34, 35
Jones, Bobby, 23
Jones, G. Paul, 36, 37
Jones, Herb, 38
Joshua Hill, 17, 18

K

Kahn, Bobby, 86, 88-89, 91, 134
Kansas-Nebraska Act, 1
Keen, Jerry, 68, 133, 162, 172, 178-179, 194-195
Kennedy, John F., 6. 7. 24
Kiker, Benjamin and Charles, 21
King Roy, 113-115
King, Martin Luther, Jr., 8, 24
Kingston, Jack, 48, 57, 69, 175
Klein, Marty, 95, 105, 111
Knight, Alton and David, 98

L

Land, Clay, 83
Larios v. Cox, 160, 164
Lawrence, Tom, 49
Layfield, Don, 41
Lee, Dan, 142-145, 147. 174

Legislative Black Caucus, 56, 86, 165
Levison, Jarvin, 23, 25, 37
Lewis, John, 54, 55
Lewis, Julius Curtis, 36, 51
Lincoln, Abraham, 2, 24, 34
Linder, John, 41, 57, 175
Lindsey, Edward, 184
Long, Jefferson Franklin, 18
Longstreet, General James, 20
Lovett, Billy, 64
Lublin, David, 10, 50, 51, 76, 180

M

Madden, Eddie, 80
Maddox, Lester, 25, 36, 37, 39
Magelund, Corinna, 111
Marcus, Justice Stanley, 160
Markham, William, 16
Marshall, Jim, 201
Martin, Jim, 183, 199
Martin, Joe, 72
Mason, Wayne, 120
Massey, Lewis, 65, 71, 74
Mattingly, Mack, 37, 41-42, 44-45, 60, 84-
    85, 99, 109, 130, 132, 137
Max-Black Plan, 56-57, 86, 96
McCain, John, 199
McDonald, Lauren "Bubba," 199
McIntyre, Dan III, 25
McKinley, William, 20
McKinney, Cynthia, 56, 57
McLagan, Dan, 96-97, 99, 104, 110, 113-
    114, 119-120, 127, 129, 132,
    136-137, 147, 172, 176
Meade, General George, 16
Miller, Homer Virgil Milton, 17, 18
Miller, Zell, 44-45, 53-54, 60-63, 65, 70,
    80, 84-85, 108-109, 121, 175, 181,
    195, 202
Millner, Guy, 31, 46-47, 60-65, 70-73,
    108-109, 126, 135-136, 151
Missouri Compromise, 1
MMV Alliance, 171
Morgan, Jay, 43, 47, 54, 64, 176
Mueller, Anne, 149
Mull, Francis, Reid, 21
Murphy, Tom, xiii, 46, 49, 55, 89, 92, 140-
    141, 154, 181

N

Newbill, Sally, 48
Nigut, Bill, 114
Nixon, Richard M., 6, 7, 9, 10, 23, 24, 43
Norcross, Jonathan, 19
Northern Arc, 120
Norwood, Charlie, 59, 101, 175
Nunn, Sam, 43, 45, 63-64, 76

O

O'Callaghan, Jimmy, 25, 35
O'Kelley, Justice Bill. 160
O'Neal, Larry, 133, 163
Obama, Barack, 199, 201, 204
Oliver, Jack, 132
ORVIS, 47, 48, 65
Oxendine, John, 60, 71-72, 138, 183

P

Pannell, Justice Charles, 160
Parrish, Butch, 169, 177, 184
Patton, Earl, 38, 46
Paul, Rusty, 34, 59, 63, 65, 67-69. 78, 99,
    102, 115, 134, 137, 139, 148
Penn, Mark, 175
Perdue, Erwin, 77, 79-80, 153
Perdue, Mary, 78, 103, 127
Perdue, Sonny
    introduction, xiii-xiv, 31-32
    changing parties,73-82
    as Republican senator, 83-85
    2001 reapportionmment, 89, 91
    camapign planning, 101-104
    campaign organization, 105-111
    primary campaign, 111-116
    general election, 93, 100, 117-152, 191
    speaker's race, 153-157, 188
    as governor, 159-164, 166, 168-169, 187
    2004 elections, 172-173, 175
    2006 election, 181-183, 185-188, 202
    New Georgia, 197-198
Perdue, Tom, 57
Pettys, Dick, 39, 55, 58, 63, 80, 87, 115,
    118, 123, 134, 137, 140, 162
Phillips, Tim, 137-138
Pickett, Roscoe Hayes, Jr., 21, 35
Pickett, Roscoe Hayes, Sr., 21
Pickett, Will Hays, 21
Pierce, Franklin, 1

Pilcher, Crawford, 38, 39
Pinholster, Garland, 65, 66, 84, 149
Poitevint, Alec, 43, 50, 54-55, 78, 85, 99,
    101-104, 116, 127, 134, 137, 140,
    149
Pomerantz, Gary, 24
Populist Party, 4, 20
Poythress, David, 71
Price, Tom, 69, 82-83, 88, 91, 99, 101,
    133, 141-145, 159. 175
Prince, Jack, 35

R
Ralston, David, 21
Ray, Jack, 38, 39
Reagan, Ronald, 10, 11, 12, 44, 45, 59, 149
Reapportionment of 1991-1992, 54-57,
    184
Reapportionment 2001, 82, 85-92, 124-
    125,
    140-141, 149
Redistricting, 54-57, 74, 145, 164-170,
    174,
    181-182, 186
Reed, Ralph, 133-134, 160, 183
Republican Governors Association, 131-132
Republican National Committee, 47, 104,
    131-132
Republican Syndicate, 20
Reynolds v. Sims, 26
Rials, Scott, 83-84, 95, 99, 103-105, 115,
    129, 137-138, 155, 161, 171
Rice, Tom, 162
Richardson, Glenn
    election to House, 67, 69
    2001 reapportionment, 90
    Perdue campaign, 133
    as minority leader, 160-164, 167-171
    2004 elections, 171-172, 175
    as speaker, 178-179, 186, 194-195
Roberts, Jay, 187
Roe v.Wade, 10
Rogers, Joe, 85
Roosevelt, Theodore, 5, 20
Rove, Karl, 133, 137, 140
Royal, Richard, 184
Russell, Richard B., 43

S
Salam, Reihan, 9
Sales Tax Holiday, 126
Sanders, Carl, 25, 39
Savage, John, 23, 41, 43, 44
Schaefer, Nancy, 60, 70
Schrenko, Linda, 60, 71, 104, 110-113,
    116, 133
Scott, Austin, 69
Scott, C. A., 24, 28
Sentencing Reform Act of 1994, 62
Seymour, Horatio, 18
Shadgett, Olive Hall, 19b
Shafer, David, 65
Shapard, Virginia, 42
Shaw, Bob, 23
Simon, Tony, 105, 161
Skipper, Jimmy, 90, 177
Smith, Earl, 51
Smith, Ed, 25
Smith, James M., 19
Smith, Julie, 111
Smith, Tommy, 89-90, 173
Smith, Vance, 68
Smith, Willou, 65
Smyre, Calvin, 56, 177
Snodgrass, Robert, 23
Somers, Harry, 23
Spier, Angela, 139
Stancil, Cristal, 127
Stancil, Steve, 48-49, 59, 65-66, 84, 139,
    149
Starr, Terrell, 87
State flag, 61, 121-123, 150, 152
State Road and Tollway Authority, 119, 121
States Right Party, 6
Steed, Robert, 205
Steele, Michael, 202
Stephens, Bill, 72, 82, 91, 98, 127, 133,
    192
Stephens, Ron, 68
Strategic Perceptions, 130
Strickland, Frank, 44, 55, 69, 87, 89, 160,
    165
Sturrock, David, 54, 64
Sucker votes, 66
Suit, Hal, 39
Swearingen, Carl, 127
Swindall, Pat, 45

T

Taft, Robert, 36
Talmadge, Eugene, 22
Talmadge, Herman, 7, 22, 38, 44
Tanenblatt, Eric, 85, 132, 140
Tarlton, Willie, 202
Taylor, Andrew, 176
Taylor, Mark, 72, 82, 139, 143, 147, 149,
        159, 177, 182, 187
Terry, Alfred H. 18
Thompson, Fletcher, 36, 37, 38, 39, 41, 43
Thompson, M. E. 22
Thompson, Ronnie, 38, 43. 51
Thrower, Randolph, 23, 24
Thurmond, Michael, 30, 49, 56-57, 72, 75,
        86, 116, 123, 127, 181, 183-184, 204
Thurmond, Strom, 6
Tilden, Samuel J., 4
Towery, Matt, 54, 92
Towns, Hunter, 163, 165-166, 184, 189
Townsend, Kiliaen, 23, 36
Tribble, Joe, 36, 38
Troutman, Frank 36, 37
Truman, Harry, 6, 7
Turner, Loyce, 80
Tuttle, Judge Elbert, 23
Tysinger, Jim, 40

V

Victory 02 Committee, 132
Viguerie, Richard, 176
Voting Rights Act, 13, 54, 57

W

Walker, Charles, 74-75, 77, 79, 81, 87,
        140-141, 143-144, 174
Walker, Jay, 105, 161, 170-172
Walker, Larry, 46, 79, 81, 90, 92, 125, 153-
        157, 166, 169, 181, 188, 205
Wall, Vinson, 148
Wallace, George, 9, 39
Waters, Charles E (Dink), 25
Watson, John, 60, 67-68, 70, 99, 102, 110-
        114, 116, 124, 128, 131, 133, 137,
        152, 155-156, 173, 176, 178
    Webb. Lillian, 51
Weiner, Susan, 51
Weltner, Charles L., 25, 37
Wesberry v. Sanders, 26

Westen, Drew, 205
Westmoreland, Lynn, 68, 84, 89, 149, 156,
        161-163, 168, 171, 175
Whig Party, 1, 2, 17
Whiteley, Richard, 18
Williams, Roger, 68
Williams, Tommie, 72, 133, 191
Willkie, Wendell, 6
Wise, Stan, 183
Worley, David, 54

Y

Yates, Clayton, 24
Young Republicans, 47
Young, Andrew, 53
Young, Chris, 76, 78, 81-82, 95, 97, 99,
        104, 111, 117, 127, 137, 155, 169